The Spirit of the Berlin Republic

INTERNATIONAL POLITICAL CURRENTS
A Friedrich-Ebert-Stiftung Series

General Editor: Dieter Dettke

Vol. 1: Toward a Global Civil Society
 Edited by Michael Walzer

Vol. 2: Universities in the Twenty-First Century
 Edited by Steven Muller

Vol. 3: Multiculturalism in Transit: A German-American Exchange
 Edited by Klaus J. Milich and Jeffrey M. Peck

Vol. 4: The Challenge of Globalization for Germany's Social
 Democracy: A Policy Agenda for the Twenty-First Century
 Edited by Dieter Dettke

Vol. 5: The Spirit of the Berlin Republic
 Edited by Dieter Dettke

The Spirit of the Berlin Republic

Edited by
Dieter Dettke

Berghahn Books
NEW YORK • OXFORD

Published in 2003 by

Berghahn Books

www.berghahnbooks.com

© 2003 Dieter Dettke

Library of Congress Cataloging-in-Publication Data

Spirit of the Berlin Republic / edited by Dieter Dettke.
     p. cm. – (International political currents ; v. 5)
     Includes bibliographical references and index.
     ISBN 1-57181-343-8 (alk. paper)
     1. Germany—Politics and government—1990– 2. Germany—Foreign
relations—1990– 3. Germany—Economic policy—1990– I. Dettke,
Dieter, 1941– II. International political currents ; vol. 5.

DD290.29.S65 2003
943.087'9–dc21

                                      2003043792

British Library Cataloguing in Publication Data
A CIP catalogue record for this book is available from
the British Library.

Printed in the United States on acid-free paper

Contents

Foreword

Gerhard Schröder

The relocation of the Bundestag and the federal government from Bonn to Berlin in the summer of 1999 was the logical fulfillment of the instruction in our constitution to achieve "the unity and freedom of Germany in free self-determination." Fifty years after the establishment of two German states, the move to the joint capital overcame that aspect of Germany's division, too.

The term "Berlin Republic," which quickly made the rounds, particularly among artists and intellectuals, was meant to describe a new beginning, but certainly not a "new republic." Basically, the completion of German unity and the move to Berlin were nothing other than the conclusion of that historic process which the historian Heinrich August Winkler called the "long road to the West." This did not merely mean firm integration in the European Union and the Atlantic Alliance, but also close cultural links with the West, a clear orientation toward shared values of freedom, justice, democracy, and human rights.

Above all, the Berlin Republic would not draw a final line under Germany's past. Just as it was clear, in the words of Willy Brandt, that not even a nation's greatest guilt can be atoned for by a timeless division, it was and is clear that the united Germany and a government ruling from Berlin must face up to the historic responsibility of Germany and the Germans.

And so it is no coincidence that one of the first laws passed in the Berlin Republic was the one on the long-overdue compensation payments to be made to forced laborers under the Hitler regime.

This new beginning did not mark a break in the democratic traditions of the old Federal Republic. It is telling that another new term emerged at the same time as that of the "Berlin Republic": namely, the "Bonn Republic," a forty-year success story that laid the foundations for our democracy and created important preconditions for our country's reunification.

The political promise of the Berlin Republic was that it would combine the democratic culture of the West, which had evolved and proven itself—not least in some difficult times—over fifty years with the desire for freedom and the civil courage of the citizens of the former German Democratic Republic (GDR), whose courageous protests had brought about the peaceful revolution of 1989. A sense of community and the solidarity of an alert civil society have since carried new weight in Germany. No one who experienced the solidarity and the keen readiness to help of Germans from both East and West following the flood disaster in the summer of 2002 can help but feel proud of this sense of togetherness and of the Berlin Republic's willingness to shoulder responsibility.

Some things have changed in terms of foreign policy as well. The weight of the larger, united Germany has become greater on the international stage. Germany today is a mature, sovereign nation willing to take on increased responsibility. Whenever necessary for the preservation of peace and human rights, we are also prepared to make a military contribution—as our partners rightly expect us to do.

The need for solidarity with our friends and partners became clearer than ever in the wake of the terrorist attacks in the United States on September 11. Terrorism knows no borders, and no one state alone can any longer guarantee the freedom and security of its citizens.

We are also under an obligation arising from our natural solidarity with our friends and partners in the United States and Europe, without whose help and commitment we would not have been able to overcome our division and lack of freedom.

Freedom and security are indispensable prerequisites for a peaceful civil society. In this spirit, the Berlin-based federal government pursues a policy that shoulders responsibility and promotes civil and democratic societies across the world. Continuing along this path will remain the major challenge for the Berlin Republic.

Last but not least, the Berlin Republic is also an expression of a certain cultural shift. The divided capital was for many decades a focal point for new lifestyles, for unusual and sometimes startling developments in art, literature, music, and fashion. This "other" exciting Berlin also makes its mark on the capital. Close interaction with artists and intellectuals is therefore one of the characteristic features of our policy in the Berlin Republic.

The Spirit of the Berlin Republic is the first representation of the many aspects of this Republic, in many ways still in its test phase. It is a comprehensive and challenging project. I congratulate the editor and the authors on their successful and impressive portrait of the Federal Republic of Germany since 1990, and I very much hope that this important publication will find many interested readers.

Acknowledgments

This volume could not have been published without the extraordinary commitment of the staff of the Washington Office of the Friedrich-Ebert-Stiftung. In particular, Ursula Soyez has worked with me on this project from its initial conception. She conducted the initial research, kept in touch with the authors, and was instrumental in moving this book project forward to ensure its completion.

Dr. Jeremiah Riemer provided most of the necessary translations. His great skills ensured that nothing was lost in the process and the distinct cultural context of the original German texts is accurately conveyed in the English language.

I am particularly grateful to Heidi Whitesell, who first and foremost used her skills as an accomplished editor for a final inspection of the manuscript, valuable linguistic improvements to the texts, and for the index. She also translated several contributions to this book.

As always, Marion Berghahn and Berghahn Books gave us full support and encouragement, and never failed to move forward the publication of this fifth volume of International Political Currents, a Friedrich-Ebert-Stiftung series.

Most importantly, I want to thank each and every contributor to this volume for taking the time and making such a great effort to contribute original texts to this volume. It is their cooperation that enabled us to capture "the spirit of the Berlin Republic" and to offer a comprehensive portrayal of Germany after unification and its evolving role in the world.

Introduction

Dieter Dettke

Even if history is not going to adopt the "Berlin Republic" as the most appropriate concept marking the difference between the Federal Republic of Germany before unification and the new Germany that emerged after East and West Germany grew together again,[1] it is useful to explore in a more systematic way the degree to which the new Germany after unification is different both in the perception of the German people and the outside world. The old Federal Republic of Germany, founded in 1949 after World War II, was popularly also known as the Bonn Republic,[2] particularly when West Germany was able to establish itself as a major European power. As long as the German question remained open, the term "Bonn Republic" would only make sense with two separate German states living permanently next to each other, an impression the Federal Republic tried everything possible not to create.

In all likelihood, the term "Berlin Republic" will withstand the tides of history and establish itself as the most obvious, concise, and compelling concept capturing the spirit and meaning of the new

1. Former Chancellor Willy Brandt used this eloquent formula to express the essence of unification, "Jetzt wächst zusammen, was zusammen gehört," on 10 November 1989 upon the fall of the Berlin Wall.

2. Fritz René Allemann, a Swiss journalist and author of *Bonn ist Nicht Weimar* (Cologne, 1956), one of the best books on the old Federal Republic of Germany, used the term *Bonner Staat* (and not *Bonner Republik*). Allemann wrote the book in the mid-1950s and tried to capture the emergence of the two German states as a result of the Cold War. See particularly the last chapter: "Bonn ist nicht Weimar," 411–40.

Germany after the fall of the Wall.[3] A cultural pattern of localizing historical landmarks exists in Germany. After Germany's defeat in World War I, the fathers of the constitution of the first German democracy met in Weimar and not in Berlin to draft the new constitution. Officially still called the German Reich, Germany's first democracy became known for all non-official purposes as the Weimar Republic almost unanimously among writers, journalists, and historians. Although Berlin remained the capital of Germany after World War I, the term "Weimar Republic"—at first used derogatively by enemies of democracy in Germany—captures much more profoundly the departure of the new German democracy from the old German empire.

Bonn was chosen as the capital of the old Federal Republic of Germany primarily to underscore its provisional status as capital. The term "Bonn Republic," therefore, also captures the transitional identity that the old Federal Republic tried consistently to project in order to remind the outside world of the goal of German unity as stipulated in the preamble of the Basic Law—Germany's constitution.

Given the political and economic weight of the old Federal Republic of Germany in the new Germany and the almost complete takeover of what used to be the German Democratic Republic (GDR)—Deutsche Demokratische Republic (DDR), as East Germany preferred to call itself—an overwhelming continuity prevails between the political system and the institutions of the old and new Federal Republic of Germany. In fact, the new Germany continues to use the term "Federal Republic of Germany" as its official name. After all, from a legal perspective it was the GDR that joined the Federal Republic of Germany by way of accession according to Article 23 of the Basic Law. This strong pillar of continuity should not be seen as an obstacle to change, but rather to the new Germany's adjustment to a different world of politics as well as economics. Globalization is a fact of life and the new Germany, much more than the old one, must be ready to face the challenge of a growing global economy and additional global responsibility.

Unity has now been achieved and for the first time in history Germany has found its final territorial identity by uniting East and West Germany and excluding any territorial claims beyond the territory

---

3. One of the best accounts of unification remains *Germany Unified and Europe Transformed: A Study in Statecraft*, by Philip Zelikow and Condoleezza Rice (Cambridge, Mass., September 1995).

of the former GDR and the old Federal Republic of Germany. The German question as a territorial issue is now definitely a thing of the past and the mission of the Berlin Republic will be to resolve all remaining German questions. Germany has never had a better chance to achieve this mission. With the enlargement of NATO and the EU to include all of Germany's neighbors, Europe can now reach out again to where its cultural boundaries once were. In this context, NATO and EU enlargement represent a cultural and political return of the nations of Central and Eastern Europe to Europe.

The Spirit of the Berlin Republic is also a contribution to the search for the new Germany's identity. A thorough debate about Germany's new *mission civilisatrice* was never part of the political discourse after unification. An ersatz debate took place in the German Bundestag over the choice of Berlin as Germany's capital, but it generated little insight into the future of the Berlin Republic. Germans seem to know much better what the Berlin Republic does *not* want to be than what it wants to be. There is a solid consensus that the Berlin Republic does *not* intend to rebuild in any shape or form the old idea of a German empire. It is inconceivable that the Berlin Republic will ever be a fourth German Reich. The Berlin Republic will always be committed to the rejection of any totalitarian or authoritarian system, be it fascist or communist.

It is true that the return of the capital to Berlin is also an attempt to provide a measure of historical continuity. Although difficult to define in the case of Germany, continuity can certainly not be identified with negative symbols of German history, either of older Prussian origin or the more immediate authoritarian past. The departure of the new Germany from the Third Reich is profound, total, and absolute. It could not be more radical. Germany's new identity, its spirit and its *Weltanschauung,* or view of the world, and its *Selbstverständnis,* or understanding of itself are in complete opposition to Hitler's Third Reich.

Normalization with regard to Germany's Prussian past is clearly more complex. The fact that the German Bundestag seat is now the old Reichstag built during the Kaiserreich definitively incorporates Prussian history into the Berlin Republic. Prussia's militarism and the excessive influence of the military in Prussian society stand out as a dangerous development and a negative experience in German history. There is no real danger, however, that any Prussian model could ever return. This specter has outlived its usefulness. Not all Prussian traditions are negative: the tradition of a "clean" administration and, more importantly, Prussia's tolerance of foreigners and willingness to accept multiethnic realities, resulting from enlightenment, form a positive example.

The strongest positive foundation to build on also for the future of the Berlin Republic is West Germany's more than forty years experience with liberal democracy. The transition to democracy after World War II was swift, compelling, and finite. Not only has the democratic foundation of Germany been permanent in legal terms ever since, after the fall of the Wall and the unprecedented contribution of the East German opposition to a peaceful democratic revolution in the former GDR, it is also firmly anchored in the hearts and minds of the German people.

The Berlin Republic will be a post-national state, open to integration particularly in Europe; it will at the same time be a conscious partner of the international community and its institutions, for example, of the EU, NATO, the UN, and the World Trade Organization (WTO). German patriotism therefore must always be dedicated to the preservation of a democratic and pluralistic system at home and an international order based on multilateralism. The arrival of the Berlin Republic is a great opportunity for Germany to embark on a path toward a new modernity based on universal values, liberal democracy, and tolerance. The "German way" will by definition not be a German Sonderweg, but rather a paradigm of connectedness and integration. The Berlin Republic is in essence committed to a European Germany, not a German Europe.[4]

The devastating experience of World War II led to a profound change in Germany's foreign policy. The post–World War II consensus created a powerful impulse to reject the use of force and very often even the legitimacy of armed forces. In light of more recent developments, however, the Berlin Republic will have to rethink Germany's civilian power paradigm. A foreign and security policy based on the non-use of military force can achieve little if confronted with aggression and brutality. The civilian power paradigm saw its shortcomings in Bosnia, Kosovo, and the war against international terrorism in Afghanistan. Together with its EU and NATO partners, Germany participated in military actions beyond German borders. The culture of reticence is not a negative tradition, but it needs to be adjusted to a more complex world with more uncertain boundaries between war and peace. International terrorism is an example of this new uncertainty.

---

4. For a discussion of this issue, see Michael Mertes, "Ein 'deutsches Europa.' Nachruf auf ein Schreckgespenst," *Internationale Politik* 57, no. 9 (2002): 19–24.

Adjustment cannot simply mean the automaticity of warfare if the EU, NATO, or the UN legitimizes military action. Shouldering more international responsibility will be unavoidable to some degree, and Germany will have to make the necessary changes in order to meet the new requirements for the use of military force. But there are also clear physical limitations binding Germany's international military engagements. Any kind of supremacy in Europe or beyond Europe's borders is not and will not be on the agenda of the Berlin Republic: to be a good neighbor is.

Part I

THE IDENTITY OF THE BERLIN REPUBLIC

1. Historical Foundation of the Berlin Republic

Bernd Faulenbach

The aesthetic of the Berlin Republic—symbolized both by the Reichstag building with its new dome, designed by British architect Norman Foster, and by the new Chancellor's office, by German architect Axel Schultes—clearly differs from the aesthetic of the Bonn Republic, which was characterized by a certain degree of understatement. In German journalistic circles, it has recently become common to speak of a "Berlin Republic." The journalist Johannes Gross has attempted to explain the concept,[1] and some of the Bundestag's younger members of the Social Democratic Party (SPD) now publish a journal with the same name, in which they pose questions relating to German unification; from their perspective, apparently, a new phase in the country's political development has begun.[2]

The "Berlin Republic" is, nevertheless, a contested concept. Those who criticize it are especially keen to point out that nothing essential about the political and social order has changed simply because the capital has been switched from Bonn to Berlin. From the perspective of constitutional law, today's united Germany still bears the title "Federal Republic of Germany," which would appear to underscore the new Federal Republic's continuity with the old one that was confined to West Germany.

1. Johannes Gross, *Begründung der Berliner Republik: Deutschland am Ende des 20. Jahrhunderts*, 2nd ed. (Stuttgart, 1995).

2. The journal *Berliner Republik* is in its fifth year as of 2003. It is published by Hans-Peter Bartels et al.

The question of the "Berlin Republic" is unmistakably linked to a more general question: What does German unification mean for the Germans, for the self-image of German democracy, and for the German role in the world? Here the issues at hand are:

- On what historical foundations is the Berlin Republic based?
- Against the backdrop of German history, to what extent should the Berlin Republic be seen as the resumption of earlier lines of development in German history; to what extent should it be viewed as a newfangled political construct; and (especially) should the Berlin Republic be construed as a political order that has overcome or that continues the tradition of the Bonn Republic, i.e., the "old" Federal Republic?
- What events have shaped the historical and political self-image of the Berlin Republic?

In a short essay like this, needless to say, the answers to these questions can only be sketched in broad outlines.

Unified Germany and Europe after the End of the East-West Conflict

The upheaval of 1989/90 is one of the watersheds in twentieth-century European history: Europe's (and, by 1991, also the Soviet Union's) communist systems dissolved, and the division of Germany into two states with opposing ideologies and societies was overcome. With regard to Germany and Europe, these were some of the consequences of that upheaval:

- Unified Germany is Europe's second-largest state in terms of population, and its strongest by virtue of economic power. It is therefore larger than the other major Western European countries—France, Great Britain, and Italy.
- Germany is back in its traditional position at the center of Europe. On the one hand, it is strongly attached to Western Europe; on the other hand, it now borders on Eastern Europe.

In 1989/90 former Chancellor Willy Brandt advocated talking about Germany's "unification" rather than its "reunification." He wanted to make it clear, first of all, that decades of separation were going to make it hard for Germans simply to reconnect on what had once been common ground and, secondly, that Germans had never really lived together before within this particular territorial framework, so that Germany would have to find its role anew. To be sure, Willy Brandt only got so far with this proposal, yet his reflections were (and are) worth pondering. The special fact worth emphasizing is that a united Germany, unlike the organized states that preceded it from the nineteenth century onward (the German Federation, Wilhelminian Empire, Weimar Republic, and Third Reich), has no outstanding territorial disputes with its neighbors and lives in peace with them, which is all the more astonishing when one considers how Germany has more neighbors than any other European country.

From all this, it should already be apparent that today's united Germany differs from traditional nation-states. It is part of the European Union, onto which it has devolved essential sovereign rights. At the same time—within the political elite and among the majority of the population—it is largely undisputed that Germany is going to remain a member of NATO, which does not exclude the possibility of Germany joining with other European states in an attempt to create a European security policy identity, within the NATO framework, expressing European self-confidence vis-à-vis the United States as well.

In any event, a unified Germany is prepared to shoulder a greater measure of international responsibility than was exercised by the old Federal Republic—as demonstrated by Germany's participation in NATO deployments in Bosnia, Kosovo, Macedonia, and Afghanistan. To be sure, in light of twentieth-century history, with its two world wars in which Germany tried to assert hegemony in Europe, German policy really has to see to it that Germany cooperates closely with other European countries and the international community of nations when it deals with conflicts. A united Germany will not be returning to the traditional polices of the classic nation-state.

Not least of all, one consequence of the East-West conflict's demise is Germany's changed relationship with the nations of Eastern Europe, most of whom are determined (some more, some less) to join the European Union. The Berlin Republic supports their efforts, especially those of Poland, Hungary, the Czech Republic, and Slovenia. Yet, as the EU's largest net contributor, and as a country bordering on Eastern Europe, Germany has to be particularly mindful that the problems associated with EU expansion (such as expansion's consequences for eastern Germany's labor market) are taken into consideration.

Unified Germany, which has recently been displaying a certain self-confidence in making its appearance on the European stage, assuredly plays an important role in Europe; yet it is not a "Fourth Reich," as some German and international observers feared in 1989/90. This actor is not simply replaying Bismarck's empire.

The Constitutional Order of the Berlin Republic and German History

The constitution of the Berlin Republic—apart from some minor modifications (for example, the provision calling for reunification was rendered moot and stricken from the constitution, while environmental protection was introduced as a fundamental goal of public policy)—is the same as the one debated and passed by the Parliamentary Council in 1949 and then ratified by the parliaments of the various Länder. In 1948/49 the Western Allies participated in the process of developing the Basic Law (as the constitution was then called, in order to emphasize its provisional nature) to the extent that they demanded (in the London Documents) the establishment of a federal state founded on the Western zones. The constitution, compiled after preliminary work done by a committee of experts at Herrenchiemsee and then discussed with characteristic German thoroughness, tried to accomplish two things:

- to avoid the shortcomings of the failed Weimar Republic's constitutional system by opting for a consistently representative system (i.e., by giving up on any plebiscitary components), for a strong chancellor and for a president as head of state who would be equipped with limited powers and not directly elected by the people, for the fundamental principles of what came to be known as *streitbare Demokratie* (a militant democracy that does not hand the opponents of democracy the means with which to undermine democracy)—to this extent, the constitution of the Bonn and now Berlin Republic is also the anti-constitution of the first (Weimar) Republic;
- above all, to create a counter-constitution in opposition to the Third Reich, which is why certain basic rights, i.e., human and civil rights, were placed at the beginning of the constitution and elevated to the status of currently valid law, and which is also why a carefully constructed system of checks and balances on power was erected.

Deliberations on the constitution, moreover, took place in a climate that contrasted starkly with developments in the Soviet Occupation Zone, so that the constitution matched the anti-totalitarian consensus of the postwar era's major democratic parties. During the deliberations on the constitution there was, to be sure, an occasional clash with the Allies about how to divide powers between the central government and the Länder, which usually resulted in the Germans getting their way. The outcome was a federal order that has withstood the test of time for several decades. This federal order picked up on an older German tradition, yet Germany's constitution simultaneously moved a bit closer to its American counterpart while distinguishing itself ever since from the French constitution, which has remained characteristically centralist to this day. In light of Germany's vital federal structure, which guarantees important rights (including participation in numerous federal matters) to the Länder, even the transfer of the government and parliament from Bonn to Berlin, approved in 1991 and completed by 1999, has not led to any new kind of centralism. Berlin is, to be sure, attracting a variety of institutions to the old-new capital. Yet, this does not mean that the old Federal Republic's polycentric structure is being undermined, especially since the largest federal states such as North Rhine-Westphalia and Bavaria, regardless of whatever political party might be in power at any given time, pursue policies that are independent of Berlin on a number of matters.

Although the Basic Law was regarded as provisional in 1948/49, it was drawn up carefully, especially since this Federal-Republic-in-the-making was regarded as the core of a future, larger Germany. In years to come, to be sure, the Basic Law would be supplemented with several new provisions—such as the creation of a military defense and state-of-emergency legislation—yet it has withstood the test of time and, unlike the Weimar constitution, is recognized today by all the country's major political and social forces.

In 1989/90, when a peaceful revolution toppled the communist Socialist Unity (SED) regime and the process leading to unification began, the Basic Law was not a matter of debate as far as the West Germans were concerned; but East Germans wanted, most of all, to live just like the West Germans and therefore pushed for rapid unification, as the Volkskammer (East German parliament) election of March 1990 revealed. Unification took place when the German Democratic Republic (GDR) joined the Federal Republic of Germany (FRG), which meant reviving the dormant federal structure of Länder in the GDR. To put it differently: with the kind of (re-)unification that took place in October 1990, on the basis of the Unification Treaty, the political order of the Federal Republic was transferred to the GDR. All in all, the transfer in the 1990s of governmental and administrative institutions took place quickly and efficiently. Yet, a variety of social problems emerged in the course of unification.

The enlarged Federal Republic of Germany is a democratic, pluralistic constitutional state with a federal structure, parliamentary system, and developed social-welfare system. The Berlin Republic continues a German welfare-state tradition that goes back to the nineteenth century, yet the current government is trying to accommodate this tradition to the changed circumstances of a globalized economy. The kind of "Rhenish capitalism" (or "social-market economy") that took hold in postwar Germany and Europe is going to be defended, to be sure, but it will also be modernized in light of the realization that Germany cannot cut itself loose from transnational economic trends. In this regard the two major parties, the Christian Democratic Union/Christian Social Union (CDU/CSU) and the Social Democratic Party (SPD), are not so far apart, although the current government led by the Social Democrats under Chancellor Gerhard Schröder has had more success than the preceding government of Helmut Kohl in pressing ahead with modernization based on a society-wide consensus (including the trade unions).

On the Historical Dimension of the Party System

Looking at political parties and the party system provides important information about the historical character of political culture in Germany. The party system of the old Federal Republic has largely been carried over into the party system of today's unified Germany: it is a multiparty system with two large popular parties and two smaller parties, to which unification has added a third—East German—party. One major popular party is the CDU (with its Bavarian version, the CSU), founded after World War II as a bourgeois, bidenominational catch-all party, with a working-class wing that has been getting weaker since the 1960s, and as a repository for the old Catholic Center Party along with some conservative, but also some liberal, forces. For most of the time during the old Federal Republic this was the dominant party, initially controlled by

Konrad Adenauer, who was federal chancellor from 1949 to 1963. His name is associated with the policy of Western integration, just as Chancellor Helmut Kohl (in office from 1982 to 1998) is linked to the unification of the two German states.

The second major popular party, the SPD, is the oldest German party, with roots going back to the revolution of 1848; it represented a democratic labor movement that fundamentally opposed the political and social order of the Wilhelminian Empire, then helped shape the basic character of the Weimar Republic in 1918/19, but was soon forced into opposition again and ultimately became just about the only party defending the Republic. In 1933 Hitler and the Nazis banned the SPD, its representatives were persecuted, and a great number of them went into the resistance. After 1945 the SPD helped set up the Federal Republic of Germany, while in the Soviet Occupation Zone (later the GDR) it was forcibly merged with the Communist Party (KPD) to form the SED, a move resisted by a number of Social Democrats who were therefore also persecuted by the Communists. With the Godesberger Program of 1959, the party transformed itself into a modern left-of-center party open to all social strata. Under Willy Brandt, the mayor of Berlin at the height of the East-West confrontation (1957–1966), it provided the Federal Republic with the chancellor of a Social-Liberal coalition (under Brandt from 1969 to 1974) whose Ostpolitik substantially advanced East-West détente; Brandt was followed as chancellor by another Social Democrat, Helmut Schmidt (1974–1982), who earned a reputation above all as a world economist promoting closer cooperation among the major industrial powers. Gerhard Schröder, SPD chancellor since 1998, whose policy of *Neue Mitte*, or New Center, represents a new phase in Social Democratic politics, has continued the tradition of his Social Democratic predecessors in a coalition with the Greens.

The smaller parties are the Free Democratic Party (FDP), the Greens, and the Party of Democratic Socialism (PDS). In the postwar FDP—unlike what happened under the Wilhelminian Empire and Weimar Republic—national liberals and left-liberals have teamed up in a single party; it is now a party that has helped to govern the old Federal Republic and a united Germany longer than any other. The Greens started out in the 1970s as the party of environmental protection; following unification, the party teamed up with Alliance '90, which had emerged from the civil rights movement in the GDR; since 1998 the Greens/Alliance '90 have joined with the Social Democrats to form a coalition government in which the Green politician Joschka Fischer has served as foreign minister. Initially presenting itself as an alternative party—an anti-party—the Greens have now become a "normal" party.

Rather insignificant on a nationwide scale, so far, has been the PDS (Party of Democratic Socialism), which emerged out of the SED, the official governing party of the GDR. Since 1990, in two federal elections, the PDS has barely made it into the Bundestag, where it initially pursued a course of fundamental opposition to the system and was ostracized by the other parties. Over the last few years there has been a certain weakening of this confrontational stance, yet the PDS—owing to its opposition to NATO and similar positions—has to be ruled out of any federal coalition for the foreseeable future. Since a piece of the old GDR lives on inside this party, the PDS remains a political factor in the new Länder, where the party routinely gets about 15–20 percent of the vote, which lends the party system a different look there than it has in the Länder making up the old Federal Republic. By virtue of its presence in Berlin, Brandenburg, Mecklenburg-Western Pomerania, and Saxony-Anhalt, the PDS has either forced the governments of these eastern Länder into Grand Coalitions (CDU-SPD) or into coalitions or toleration pacts between the SPD and PDS. In its own unique fashion, the PDS combines a leftist-socialist party program with resentment against the West; it represents a party leadership that has tried accommodating itself to new circumstances with a membership that overwhelmingly consists of old SED cadres more or less nostalgic for the GDR.

On the whole, it is clear that continuities in the party system have predominated across the epochal threshold of 1989/90, although certain changes have resulted from the GDR's accession to the Federal Republic. The party system in the new federal Länder departs from that of the old Länder, in which about four-fifths of the population lives, not only to the extent that the PDS is relatively strong in the East (whereas in the West, despite the relative popularity of Gregor Gysi, its best-known politician, it hardly has any supporters), but also because the Free Democrats and Greens are quite weak in the former GDR. The large popular parties are dominant both in the East and in the West; yet in the East they have comparatively few members, quite apart from the fact that voter fluctuation in the East (even with respect to the popular parties) is higher than in the West.

Political Culture as an Expression of Historical Experiences

The peaceful revolution in the autumn of 1989 that overthrew the SED system and the ensuing unification have not yet led to a unified German political culture. This much is evident from the way the party system looks today: forty years of divergent history in the two German states is bound to continue to keep them separate in a way.[3] To be sure, the West's political institutions, including its administrative organization and educational system, were extended to the former GDR. Yet today there are still a number of important differences, not just in income (which is lower in the East) and unemployment (which is higher there), but also in Germans' consciousness about their different experiences and modes of behavior in the East and West.

In certain ways, the orientations and attitudes of East and West Germans diverge; sometimes the differences are large, at other times small, depending on the generational cohort.[4] The differences are discernible in the way democratic institutions are assessed, in how much willingness there is to participate in politics and society (less in the East, so far, than in the West), in dealings with foreigners (xenophobic acts tend to be more frequent in the East than in the West), in relation to values and standards (as in attitudes toward freedom and equality), and even in such questions as how to assess German participation in military actions in the Balkans (in the East, there was a more negative assessment of the Bundeswehr's participation than in the West.)

In interpreting all these differences, one should not forget that the West was able to develop a democratic political culture under comparatively favorable circumstances during a decades-long process, while people in the East had to live under a communist dictatorship lasting from the end of the Nazi dictatorship through 1989. Nor should the asymmetry of the unification process be overlooked: there was little that changed for the West Germans, while the East Germans had to adjust to a completely different set of societal and cultural circumstances than they were accustomed to, so that a

---

3. On this point, cf. Gerhard A. Ritter, *Über Deutschland: Die Bundesrepublik in der deutschen Geschichte* (Munich, 1998).

4. Cf. Martin Greiffenhagen, *Politische Legitimität in Deutschland* (Gütersloh, 1977); *Wirklich ein Volk? Die politischen Orientierungen von Ost- und Westdeutschen im Vergleich*, ed. Jürgen Falter, Oskar W. Gabriel, and Hans Rattinger (Opladen, 2000); Bernd Faulenbach, Annette Leo, and Klaus Weberskirch, *Zweierlei Vergangenheit: Lebensgeschichte und Geschichtsbewußtsein von Arbeitnehmern in West- und Ostdeutschland* (Essen, 2000).

number of them felt (and still feel) overwhelmed. It is against this backdrop that a feeling of being at a disadvantage vis-à-vis the West Germans has become widespread throughout the East, a notion conducive to a certain nostalgia about the GDR in which that regime's repression is more or less filtered out.

Presumably it will take several more decades before this East-West divide in political culture is closed. Whether Germany might then—as some contemporaries were saying in 1990—become more "Eastern" and more "Protestant" than the old Federal Republic seems doubtful. There is some evidence indicating that, in addition to the North-South tension that had defined the old Federal Republic, an older East-West tension will reemerge, though in a way that will allow this conflict between the GDR and the Federal Republic to be transcended in the Hegelian sense. In any event (this much we may surmise), there will be no return to the kind of internal divisiveness so characteristic of German society and political culture since the nineteenth century.

On the Historical-Political Image of the Berlin Republic

Germany's unification in 1989/90 has reopened the question of the German self-image and evoked a discussion that is partly tied to the discussion that took place in the Federal Republic during the 1980s about national consciousness versus constitutional patriotism.[5] Part of the discussion about the German self-image following unification was the capital city debate, in which Bonn was frequently seen as a symbol for being oriented toward the West and overcoming nationalism (or the nation-state), while Berlin was viewed as a symbol of reunification, of reversion to the nation-state, and of leaning toward all-European ideas. At that time it was not unusual for the concept "Berlin Republic" to be tied to fears that the course of German history might steer back toward the kind of the German Sonderweg that had once led to the "German catastrophe," fears that have more or less proven to be groundless. Against the backdrop of German history, the following four points may be viewed as characteristic of the Berlin Republic's (admittedly still fluctuating) historical-political self-image:

---

5. Cf. Bernd Faulenbach, *Erfahrungen des 20. Jahrhunderts und politische Orientierung heute* (Essen, 1996), 67ff.

1. The new Federal Republic may be conceived as a new type of nation-state, contrasting starkly with the older German nation-state tradition. This Federal Republic is not an autonomous state that is sovereign in every respect; rather, it is integrated into the European Union's network of states and usually conducts its foreign policy in cooperation with the other countries of the EU (which does not rule out the possibility that on occasion—as in 1991/92 with respect to Yugoslavia—individual countries in the European Union might act in ways revealing the lingering after effects of older patterns and orientations).

   United Germany is also a new type of nation-state to the extent that the governing coalition of Social Democrats and Greens has now modified German citizenship law by combining *ius sanguinis*, the blood-based principle of citizenship traditionally dominant in Central and Eastern Europe, with the territorial principle of *ius solis*, a reform that initially met with fierce resistance from the CDU. Yet even this party started to revise its previous position on immigration law, so that a consensus between the major parties on these questions seemed possible.

2. The Federal Republic of Germany sees itself as a Western country. Since the middle third of the nineteenth century, Germans had believed that they could chart a course along the way between East and West, an idea that lost all foundation in political realism with the historical catastrophe that culminated in Nazi Germany. The Federal Republic became part of the Western world, the GDR part of the Communist domain aligned with the Soviet Union.

   At its outset the Federal Republic was allied with the West in terms of power politics, above all; in a lengthy process it developed a Western political culture, albeit one in which rules laid down by the state have played (and continue to play) a bigger role than in the Anglo-Saxon countries. In the process of Westernization, the lure of Western, and especially American, everyday culture was important, as was the educated strata's communication with Western democracies and the political elites' orientation toward the West; in the postwar period, Adenauer and the CDU were champions of Western integration. But German Social Democracy, too, was traditionally oriented toward Western politics and culture: Carlo Schmid, Fritz Erler, Willy Brandt, and Helmut Schmidt were representatives of this Western orientation.

Also contributing toward the acceptance of a Western civil society, finally, were movements such as the student movement at the end of the 1960s, which, although pursuing a complete overhaul of society, ultimately ended up helping to overcome traditional patterns of behavior and to strengthen civil society.

The social philosopher Jürgen Habermas has characterized the move toward the West as the real political achievement of West Germany's postwar generation.[6] Indeed, traditional German political philosophies really did increasingly fade into the background, and a broad-based kind of political thinking emerged that is ultimately indebted to the philosophy of the Enlightenment.

With respect to the present, however, one must note that reservations about the West and about Western political thought still play a role among intellectuals socialized in the GDR. To this extent, the "long road to the West," which the historian Heinrich August Winkler has designated as characteristic of German history in the nineteenth and twentieth century, still has some distance to be covered.[7]

3. In a variety of ways, German historical consciousness today refers back to the Third Reich, and especially to the Holocaust, which functions almost as a kind of negative point of reference. In comparison, earlier, in the immediate postwar period, it was the experiences of the war and of Germans' own suffering that overshadowed their historical-political consciousness. As of the 1960s it became the genocide against the Jews, perceived as an incomparable event that began occupying the center of German historical-cultural consciousness. Since then, each generation has been preoccupied with the Third Reich, and especially with the murder of Europe's Jews. A multifaceted culture of remembering, manifested in innumerable memorials sites recalling the Nazi period, is characteristic of today's Germany. The Holocaust Memorial designed by the American architect Peter Eisenman, which will be built on an enormous space near the Brandenburg Gate in Berlin, also demonstrates a determination not to forget Nazi crimes.

---

6. Jürgen Habermas, "Geschichtsbewußtsein und posttraditionale Identität. Die Westorientierung der Bundesrepublik," in idem, *Eine Art Schadensabwicklung: Kleine Politische Schriften VI* (Frankfurt am Main, 1987), 159–79.

7. Heinrich August Winkler, *Der lange Weg nach Westen*, vol. 2 (Munich, 2000).

The GDR was also oriented in opposition to the Third Reich; it defined itself as an antifascist state claiming to pursue a more uncompromising confrontation with the legacy of the Nazi period than the old Federal Republic. In reality, though, this kind of antifascism, even when it was informed by certain authentic experiences of the Communists' antifascist struggle, mostly served to legitimate the SED system. It was characterized, above all, by an almost complete omission of the genocide against the Jews and other groups victimized by Nazi policy; at the center of the official GDR recollection of the Nazi past stood the sacrificial, though ultimately victorious, struggle of the German Communists and the Soviet Union against Nazi Germany. In the meantime, this aspect of East Germany's narrow historical perspective has been largely overcome, as may be seen by what has been done with the major concentration camp memorials at Buchenwald, Sachsenhausen, and Ravensbrück.

Some observers, such as the writer Martin Walser, believe that the German public is too exclusively fixated on the Nazi period; in his view there is such a thing as a specifically German "obsession with history" or "pride in sinning."[8] This critique has been passionately rejected by others, such as the late Ignaz Bubis, former chair of the Central Council of Jews in Germany. Presumably, this discussion has not yet come to an end. In any event, the Nazi period's relevance is something that gets debated over and over again, although earlier postwar efforts at dealing with the past have also been turned into a history topic, which may be seen as a sign of how the Nazi period has become historicized.

4. The experience of the communist past does not play a role comparable to the Nazi past in contemporary German consciousness. This has something to do with the fact that only a part of the German population experienced communism. Still, it needs to be said that, recently, the SED dictatorship and communist injustice have been quite thoroughly scrutinized, with postwar Germany's confrontation with the Nazi period—including the mistakes made during this earlier confrontation (errors that one hopes can be avoided in scrutinizing the more recent dictatorship)—serving as a kind of

---

8. Cf. Aleida Assmann and Ute Frevert, *Geschichtsvergessenheit – Geschichtsversessenheit. Vom Umgang mit deutschen Vergangenheiten nach 1945* (Stuttgart, 1999), esp. 53ff.

model. The process of scrutinizing the communist era was difficult partly because the SED system lasted for more than forty years, so that the regime encompassed several generations and extensively penetrated East German society—Jürgen Kocka speaks of a *durchherrschte Gesellschaft* (thoroughly ruled society).[9] In this kind of society it was hardly possible for most people to find jobs beyond the reach of the SED—apart from the (not entirely hazard-free) clerical sphere—so that people's lives were woven into the system, which inevitably encumbers today's critical confrontation with that past. Psychologically, the scrutinizing process was and remains impeded by the fact that it has largely been restricted to the eastern part of Germany, and this asymmetric character has prompted strong defensive reactions from many East Germans. Against this backdrop, the validity of making comparisons between the Nazi system and the SED system has been fiercely disputed. Nonetheless it must be said: the joint experience of dictatorship under the Nazis and the SED now constitutes an anti-totalitarian consensus that extends across the different political parties.

And yet the upheaval of 1989/90, the dissolution of the GDR, and German unification have not resulted in invalidating or, as it were, revising the watershed of 1945 in German historical consciousness. The experience of the Third Reich and the sweeping catastrophe in which it ended are also formative for the Berlin Republic.[10] Some commentators—such as Karl-Heinz Bohrer—even think that the fixation on the Nazi period has made the rest of German history disappear from the collective consciousness.

Germany today can certainly draw on positive as well as negative traditions. The positive legacy includes the liberal democratic movement and the revolution of 1848, the tradition of the German labor movement, the resistance against National Socialism, the uprising of 17 June 1953, in the GDR and the peaceful revolution there in 1989, and (not least of all) the old Federal Republic's success story. These episodes also play a role in contemporary consciousness, a role that might assume greater significance in the long run.

---

9. Jürgen Kocka, "Eine durchherrschte Gesellschaft," in *Sozialgeschichte der DDR*, ed. Hartmut Kaelble, Jürgen Kocka, and Hartmut Zwahr (Stuttgart, 1994), 547–53.
    10. Cf. Jürgen Habermas, *Die Normalität einer Berliner Republik* (Frankfurt am Main, 1995), 165ff.

Conclusion

Democracy has become matter of course in German society today. The Berlin Republic is a comparatively normal, functioning democratic state with institutions that completely continue (and a political culture that largely continues), in a manner of speaking, the existence of the old Federal Republic. To be sure, the process of integrating the Länder and the society of the former GDR has not yet been concluded; this will take more time. On the positive side, however, we may note that for the first time in German history since the nineteenth century, the opposition between democracy and the nation has been overcome, and for the first time, too, Germans live within secure borders at peace with all of their many neighbors. After unification the old path of the German Sonderweg was not resumed. "The new Germany ..., even after reunification, is a civic republic."[11]

After the upheaval of 1989/90, the German-American historian Fritz Stern spoke about the Germans getting a "second chance."[12] Whatever incalculabilities might still exist, it does look as if the Germans, given their history, are not going to squander their chance this time around. The Berlin Republic is not a political order in which the Federal Republic has been overcome, nor is it a state that has simply resumed traditions demolished by the catastrophe of the Third Reich and Germany's division. The only thing the modernized Reichstag building has in common with the old Reichstag is the building's outer frame; and the new Chancellor's office building has nothing in common with the old Reich Chancellory building that went under with the demise of the Third Reich. And, not far from all these government office buildings, the memorial to Europe's murdered Jews will be built. The Berlin Republic is founded on the democratic success story of the old Federal Republic and the peaceful revolution of autumn 1989 in the GDR, and its ideational foundation may be found, not least of all, in Germany's confrontation with its Nazi past.

11. Kurt Sontheimer, *So war Deutschland nie: Anmerkungen zur politischen Kultur der Bundesrepublik* (Munich, 1999), 9.

12. Fritz Stern, "Die zweite Chance? Deutschland am Anfang und Ende des Jahrhunderts," in idem, *Verspielte Größe. Essays zur deutschen Geschichte* (Munich, 1996), 11–36.

2. The Political Philosophy of the Berlin Republic

Richard Herzinger

In the fall and winter of 1989 when the communist dictatorships of the Eastern bloc fell, highly unusual flags surfaced on the streets of Eastern European capital cities. The demonstrators had cut out the communist coat of arms from the national flags with the respective country's colors. Where once hammer and sickle or hammer and circle hung resplendently, there now yawned a gaping hole.

It would have been a good sign if the newly formed democracies of Eastern Europe had held on to this symbolism. Even more: The hole could have been incorporated as an emblem also into the national flags of the Western democracies. This points to the paradoxical nature of modern pluralistic societies: they lack the center of meaning that creates a binding identity in all societal orders heretofore known. It is, however, precisely the presence of this empty place that ensures its cohesion.

The Berlin Republic, anticipated in part with euphoric and in part with worried expectance, is experiencing this today above all: open societies must make do without a substantial middle, without a clearly definable ethnic, moral, cultural, or religious core identity. German society, whose social and political model of consensus has long lent it a homogeneity unusual for Western countries, is now also learning, under intensified pressure, that the only dependable normative basis of a free order is the regulated, discursive, and nonviolently conducted conflict. Whether in the questions of naturalization and immigration or in the dispute about the equality of marriage and same-sex life partnerships, the attempt to deduce societal rules from unquestionably self-styled traditions and conventions is doomed to failure. Whoever is or may become a German can be determined neither by skin color nor place of birth, neither by religion nor by certain cultural traditions. Ethical standards presupposed as societal and cultural facts prove, one after the other, to be negotiable— as the object of temporary agreements that must be met in the midst of the scuffle between the many voices of interests and motives. Thus, the debate over the question about which long-term relationships may be granted the legal status of a family shows how distanced the increasingly individualized reality of life has become from the notion that the actual, meaningful purpose of a marriage is procreation and the reproduction of the societal order. The debates about progress in genetic research and biotechnology make it starkly clear that not even the definition of when a human life begins and from which moment it enjoys the full protection of human rights is concretely established; also clear is that the characteristics of human existence are not conclusively tied to a certain kind of reproduction or a certain constitution of the organism.

The trust in the omnipresent state and its ability to find a single, authoritative solution for all problems of coexistence in a society is dwindling. The wrangling over the results of the American presidential election in fall 2000 shook in a spectacular fashion even the certainty that democratic elections give authentic expression to the will of the majority. In fact, democratic legitimacy also lacks a substantial core: it exists much more in the agreement on certain formal procedures that establish the results of the question of the will of the people. Not just "the people" in toto, but also the principle of the majority is a made-up construction: the more diffuse and less manageable the societal whole becomes, the more important are the agreed-upon procedural rules than the sole objectifiable authority of societal opinion. The rules gain objectivity precisely through the fact that their genesis is comprehensible and they are thereby changeable. All attempts to give new hold to the society through the restoration of a non-negotiable moral canon must be fought: only morals that can be called into question are genuine, actually workable and reliable morals.

The price for the constant expansion of the free room for plural moral concepts and lifestyles through the retreat of a decreed state is progressively to legalize all areas of life. It thereby becomes clear, however, that no substantial truth speaks even from the law. It regards much more the ongoing interpretation of the respective appropriate relationship of rule and exception. The controversial verdict of the U.S. Supreme Court, which in the end decided the U.S. presidential election, was obviously not free of political interests. However, this does not indicate any specific deficit of American democracy. No pure, untarnished justice is to be found even at the level of the highest legal authority of a state under the rule of law. Nonetheless, the defeated party bowed in the end to the verdict of the Supreme Court. If even the law can offer no objective justice, but rather is influenced by the societal balance of power, in a free society the possibility still exists to again change this balance of power in a non-violent manner. Democratic legality, as shown by the American lesson, is based in the final analysis on subjective decisions—on words of authority that interrupt the endless discussion process about the way a civil society sees itself and the direction that it should take. Yet this interruption lasts only for an ideal moment in which the constellation of words of authority is newly configured. Then the endless debate sets in again. After the game is before the game; no word of authority can ever remain the final word.

Precisely because this argument can never come to an end, it offers everyone—disregarding extremists and sectarians, who establish themselves in fiercely shielded alternative worlds—the greatest incentive to participate in it. Every position, however, has the opportunity at some point to replace the respective prevailing paradigms with its own model. Yet the conclusive clarification, the ultimate solution to the conflict is never achieved. The last and final answer to the question of who is right and who is wrong remains structurally out of the game.

Thus, in the lively, permanent conflict the democratic public circles its own center—the place where it supposes the source of truth to be. All parties to the conflict strive to capture this magical center and to hoist there the flag of their own persuasion. However, the more that subjective truths collide on the way there, the more complex become the questions they must answer. In that the opposing truths collide with one another and mutually and argumentatively challenge each other, they mutually force themselves into an ever-increasing differentiation. Public debates tend to broaden beyond all bounds—instead of leading to consensual solutions, they multiply the open questions, which give rise to new discussions. If need be, topics discussed fully to exhaustion are set aside for awhile and give in to a temporary amnesia—although only, upon opportunity, in order to be taken up again even more intensely. The arguments' flow of energy that surges toward the center is thus diverted into an endless loop. Yet no path leads to the original goal because where one imagines the center of power by which the political-moral unity of the society is powered there is nothing. Can a society that is no longer held together by a core consistency of irrefutable truths or by any preconceived moral order endure over the long run? Does it not have to either fizzle out into an unsurpassable ultra pragmatism or drown in a sea of purposeless, uncontrollable communication? Does it not have to in the end plunge even into chaos and violence, to disintegrate into its individual parts in the struggle of all against all? The fear of the empty middle is great.

The End of the Great Standardizations: The Radical Breakup of 1989

With the end of communism in Europe the attempt ended to orient entire societies toward a single state-regulated central ideology. The failure of this project was as complete as the claim of its Marxist-Leninist creators to subject all previous history to one infallible pattern of explanation. Only National Socialism left even more devastating civilizational damage behind. Both great totalitarianisms of the twentieth century were the most extreme outgrowth of the attempts to force the disintegrating powers of the modern age into a similarly focused unity. Yet for a long time even the democratic nations of the West were dominated by the obsessive notion that they are called upon to shape the world according to the image of their own ideals. Nationalism, imperialism, and colonialism were the results of a misled belief in progress that, from the putative superiority of one's own idea of civilization, deduced a claim to supremacy over and a duty to educate the rest of humanity.

In World War I Europe aimed the ideology of dominance's destructive logic against itself. The final renunciation of it was closely associated with the experience of the totalitarian break in civilization. Yet the rise of fascism and National Socialism on the one hand and communism on the other constituted a resultant effect of the devastating great war that undermined Europe's civilizational norms. The victory over National Socialism, in that it sharpened worldwide the consciousness of the inalienability of universal human rights, sped up the process of decolonialization, which for its part took place not without bloodied victims. During the course of decolonialization the romantic projections, which looked for the dawning of a revival and liberation of all of humanity in the Third World's uprising, were fundamentally disillusioned: in place of the colonial regime native dictatorships often stepped in that were even more cruel and murderous than their predecessors. When decolonialization came to an end in the 1970s, so began the fall of communism, which had built its identity to no small degree around the claim of being the protector and patron of the struggle for emancipation of all of the damned peoples on earth and of those deprived of their rights.

The liberal democracy emerged from the age of aggressive ideologies as the victor. Yet no shining historical vision and ultimate, world-satisfying philosophical explication remained that would not have been discredited by the excesses of inhumanity. Even the most honorable ideals themselves of good, truth, and beauty can, one now knew, serve to legitimize the most atrocious deeds. The peaceful revolutions of 1989/90 thus marked not just for Eastern Europe, but rather also for the Western democracies, a paradigmatic decisive point. The belief in a linear agreement of idea and reality, of correct thinking and acting was destroyed forever. The laws of humanity and progress can no longer rely on any metaphysical certainty or historical legitimacy. The way that an open society sees itself increasingly draws hope from the negative maxim of "Never Again."

Universal human rights have steadily gained in importance in the past decades as a guiding principle for the domestic and foreign actions of Western democracies. Ethical and moral standards are thus very much of great significance for the way open, liberal societies see themselves. Their pluralism is no moral relativism: moral standpoints must allow themselves, if they claim equal validity, to be measured according to their compatibility with absolute, valid fundamental values. Yet these fundamental values of free democracies are of another kind than the maxims of ideological world happiness or moral education of humankind, whatever kind they wish to be. One could say that it regards "negative" morals. They define the freedoms that dictatorships withhold from the society. They do not, however, describe a "positive" goal in the sense that they would show the citizens the way to the right, fulfilled life. The inalienable norms of the open society, which are laid down in constitutional civil rights and the declaration of human rights, spring precisely not from a positive consensus about the right life, but rather from the historical experience with destructive conflicts that get out of hand and that result from the confrontation of different, "more positive" world designs. In this respect, in terms of human rights and civil rights this regards a negative catalogue: the norms guarantee the individual and minorities protective rights in case of interference by the state and other superior collectives, and define their claims in terms of the whole. Civil rights of freedom do not prescribe what to do, but rather what painful historical experience establishes is not to be allowed: namely to impose upon others one's own political, religious, or worldly cultural convictions.

Developing the simultaneity of incompatibilities that characterizes modern, liberal societies requires a new picture of society: this must break from the image of a homogeneous community that moves together in unity in the same direction and thus for which only one unified perspective exists. What is required is a self-reflective, sober understanding of the modern age that regards contradictions and contrasts not as a dialectical transitional stage allowing itself to be lifted to a higher historical level, but rather that understands the nonhomogeneity and conflict, uncertainty, and insecurity about the soundness of its own existence as the normal condition of a free society.

The Shock of September 11 and the Dilemma of the Liberal Civilization

The terrorist attacks of September 11, 2001, have heightened dramatically the question of the fundamentals of the open society and plunged the Western democracies into their most difficult existential crises since the final hot phase of the Cold War. A new kind of totalitarianism has surfaced that has not reached the military and political potential of its predecessors, but that is more unpredictable and thus much more difficult to comprehend than those that came before. In the form of terrorist Islamic fundamentalism, an absolute enemy confronts Western society, radically negating its fundamental civilizational principles and declaring total war. This declaration of war places the self-awareness of open societies under a difficult endurance test—and yet, coming under a widely held belief that the era of ideologies had definitely ended, these were in no way prepared for the reemergence of such a deadly enemy.

In order effectively to assert oneself against this new existential threat, it is now not just a matter of mobilizing the necessary military and psychological resources in the middle of an internally satisfied pluralistic society oriented around balanced compromise. The still greater challenge lies in withstanding such a lengthy and hard-to-define "war against terror," without thereby harming or even destroying the open society's principles of freedom to the defense of which this war will, indubitably, lead.

Germany will be particularly affected by this new constellation. In rapid course German politics had to free itself after September 11 from its fundamental reservation about active participation in international military action—a reservation which, given German history, had made good sense for a long time. German soldiers are now not just stationed in Kosovo and Macedonia for peacekeeping purposes, but they are also in faraway Afghanistan; and special forces of the Bundeswehr are obviously engaged in active war duties there. Also engaged against terror are forces of the German marines, such as tracking tanks, which are stationed in Kuwait. The relative—and, following the hefty debates of the 1980s and 1990s—astounding equanimity with which the German society seems to accept this new situation cannot, despite itself, mislead on the lasting consequences this development will have for the country's foreign policy and for the internal state of the Berlin Republic. These are consequences that do not at all seem to have entered in their full capacity into public consciousness.

Thus, Germany's evolving responsibility, in the end to be increasingly enforced by the UN, will require a drastic increase in military equipment for world freedom. This means that the role of the Federal Republic—as part of the European Union—in the Atlantic Alliance needs to be redefined. The Germans are suddenly confronted with the fact that their integration into NATO is hardly taken for granted, but rather that its basis will increasingly become an object of an urgently necessary new definition. The German integration into the West, which until now presented quite a comfortable position in the shadow of a superior protective force, now needs a new determination as regards content. It also becomes clear that its internalization by the German society has progressed much further than one had assumed. An inner reserve in parts of the German public against too deeply integrating into the West (above all among the East Germans, who for decades had lacked experience with the advantages of the Pax Americana) becomes clear and breathes life into hefty anti-American rhetoric.

In order to avoid all misunderstanding: The politics of the U.S. government following September 11, 2001, in some regards give reason for necessary, even sharp criticism. Measures such as the creation of military tribunals or the internment of suspicious foreigners widen the government's authority above the law in an unsettling manner and limit the rights of freedom. Moreover, it is not just the right, but rather the obligation of Europeans and other allies of the United States to hold up the United States' course of war against their own standards and definition of political interests. Yet the manner in which the German public meets American politics with mistrust, if not with a rash general suspicion, from time to time generates doubts as to whether critics are really on the mark.

Since U.S. President George W. Bush spoke of an "axis of evil" and intimated that he was contemplating military action against Iraq, the fear in the German public of possible war-driven actions on the part of the United States overrides the concern about further terrorist actions on the Islamic side. Yes, here and there one gains the impression that the reality of this threat has already completely disappeared from the German consciousness, and one sees the American warnings about Islam and rogue states in the end as a pretext by the U.S. administration to implement its plans for world dominance or its oil interests in the Arab region disregarding international law. Not only the liberal left and the right-wing conservative intellectuals, but rather also journalists and even a few leading fundamentally pro-American politicians react with anti-American clichés that should have been overcome a long time ago. For example, Günter Grass declaring that for the United States obviously a few thousand "whites" murdered in the World Trade Center disaster count more than the innumerable victims in the Third World who suffer under war and hunger shows an alarming ignorance about the reality of American society. The victims in the World Trade Center disaster were, of course, in no way only white and were not just Americans, but citizens of numerous nations with the most varied skin color. Just as ignorant is the frequently heard suspicion that the perpetrators of the anthrax attacks have long been known but have not been arrested because it might involve Americans and not Arabs. The "itinerant booksellers" of such rumors—educated people, among which are also authors of leading German quality newspapers—obviously do not know, or do not wish to know, how many Arabs live and work in the United States, and how many Americans of Arab descent there are—also in the professional area of chemistry and physics to which one suspects the perpetrator of the anthrax attacks belongs.

Such alleged anti-racist and clichéd thinking projected against America thus makes it unintentionally apparent that the growing eagerness of anti-American criticism is actually a symptom of regression. Taking refuge in the familiar attack on America allows one to distance oneself from the difficult discussion about the complexity of the situation that Europe and Germany now face. When one assumes now that the United States remains the white-dominated society of the 1950s and has long since ceased to be the model of a multiethnic, transnational nation, one suggests that there is, for oneself, the option of a retreat into the harmonious autarky of a homogeneous national society. The fact that advocates of such subliminal nationalism at the same time indirectly claim to possess a higher humanistic morality different from the Americans does not always make it easier to recognize it as such. However, it allows the creators of this mechanism to have a good, stable conscience that immunizes itself successfully against every self-critical reflection.

These kinds of regressive tendencies have completely direct tangible effects on German domestic politics. Following September 11 there was no lack in commentators, who, with a triumphant undertone proclaimed the end of the (American) leisure society and demanded an identity debate, deliberation on the self and on the religious and cultural inheritance of the Christian West. The shock of the terror exploded in the middle of the debate about the long overdue immigration law—a debate that resulted from the late, reluctant acknowledgement also by the conservative parties that Germany has long since become a modern land of immigrants. Now, however, the passing of this law was first of all postponed, and then scaled down to a law on the limitation of immigration. Only hesitantly and with full reservation will the political class accept immigration as the central problem of a modernization of German society. Not just the Christian Democrats/Christian Social Union (CDU/CSU), but also the Social Democratic Party (SPD) create the false impression that an immigration law would slow down the wave of immigration. Just looking at the hundreds of thousands of foreigners already living in Germany shows how limited the possibilities for the regulation of immigration also in the case of such a polished legislation would be. "Integration" is the magic word that the right and the left together overexhaust in the debate about citizenship and immigration. Conservatives believe that a foreigner must first assimilate to inauspicious German customs before he can assume German citizenship or claim a right to an enduring right to be present. But also the left's ideal of integration follows in its own way the obsession that the coexistence of the old-established and the newly arrived must find a harmonious togetherness. If one were only to welcome the newcomers heartily, they would for their own part be more peaceful and friendly to the native citizens.

Yet neither natives nor foreigners build homogeneous groups that can be bound together in familiar togetherness. The lines of conflict in an open society run in all directions. All sides must practice the capability to endure contrasts and confusing contradictions. The goal of integration, however, creates the confusing expectation that one can get over such ruptures at some point and that one day a new identical societal whole will develop.

Germany is not a classical land of immigration like the United States, or so sounds the resounding voice of German politics repeatedly. "American" conditions are on the whole dreadful for the societal planners on both the left and the right. Nevertheless, all want to be as productive and economically successful as the United States. What constitutes the inner strength, however, that makes America so uniquely capable to transform potential fracturing cultural forces into productivity and self-assuredness? From the local standpoint it is the almost inconceivable pragmatism in connection with contradictions and conflicts. Or more precisely: the readiness to perceive an element of commonality in extreme differences. The cause is to be sought in the individualistic-universalistic American picture of humanity. In order to be recognized today as a good American, it no longer plays a critical role which cultural or religious traditions one celebrates. This is fundamentally viewed as a private matter. It is the same also whether one seeks one's own well-being in isolation or in togetherness. It is critical that one attaches oneself to the American belief in the self-reliant effort toward individual success as the actual meaning of existence. The belief that this effort toward happiness is inborn to every person, regardless of whether it stems from a distant cultural circle, establishes the advance of trust that is fundamentally shown to immigrants. Paradoxically, it is precisely the renunciation society's image as a homogeneous unity that secures the American society its extraordinary strong feeling of togetherness and its exemplary capability for renewal.

The lamentable debates on the meaning of a German *Leitkultur* or about the pride in being a German show, in contrast, how far behind the consciousness in this country still lags from the reality of an increasingly mobile global society. We have irreversibly entered an epoch of "transnationalization": nation-states will, of course, in the foreseeable future continue to exist as a framework for order and identity. However, national citizen loyalty is increasingly expanded, and a cosmopolitan confusion of differing feelings of belonging overlays it. Neither the principle of lineage nor of territory can suffice in the long run for the definition of a national cohesion. Should, for example, the grandchildren of German-Turks, whose children have moved to a third country, be given a Turkish passport and in addition yet a third—that of their country of birth? Multinationality opens up the dynamic of ever more complex relationships of belonging that makes an increasingly international regulation necessary. The criteria of residence will become even more indistinct in the age of globalization. There will be ever more people who have more than only one life and work focus, whose life concentration lies in different phases in differing world regions.

Already today there is no longer a way back to any kind of clearly outlined form of national society. Moreover, the bigoted demand that a suitable immigration law must above all be a law on the limitation of immigration overlooks the notion that immigration only functions if it is not seen as a threat one has to limit as much as possible. Rather, immigration functions only if one affirms it as an enrichment that cannot be foregone; at least it is accepted as an inevitable challenge. It does not suffice to invite highly specialized experts to fill in holes in certain new technology branches until enough local specialists have emerged to take their place—thus to some extent to practice a guest worker principle at a higher level. For internationally sought-after specialists that country is attractive which offers them unlimited working and development possibilities and in which a corresponding cosmopolitan cultural climate exists. So that immigrants can establish their usefulness, they must first of all be given the opportunity to prove themselves in a freely competitive society. In order to achieve productive results from immigration policies, one needs immigrants from the most different social strata and levels of qualification—meaning something like a societal biotop from which in the course of one or two generations new elites may emerge.

Regression into the "Middle"

Yet the democratic parties are lacking the courage to prepare their voters for such impending, defining changes in the entire structure of German society. The federal election of 2002 once again revolved around the great rhetorical dispute about the ominous "middle": Gerhard Schröder possessed it steadfastly; Edmund Stoiber and Angela Merkel wanted to win it back. The ritual incantation of the healing "middle" should uphold the fiction that there remains something like an intact constant factor of a kind of core German society in which social and cultural agreements are automatic.

If both big political parties fight so eagerly for the predominance over the legendary middle, this clearly means: they are fighting over who is in the best position to guard, build on, and thereby to still make the existing social-welfare state consensus model splendently effective. In light of this system-determined compulsion for an unconditional consensus, the differences between the SPD's and the CDU/CSU's fundamental programmatic declarations tend toward meaninglessness. Their recurring pattern is the promise to be able to do the one thing without having to sacrifice the other. The advantages of international economic and scientific-technical progress could be used, so goes the constant message, without the familiar societal structure having to be touched. "Innovation and justice" are "no alternative," declared SPD General Secretary Franz Müntefering in a recently published position paper on the "Politics of the Middle in Germany," but rather they are "simultaneously necessary and simultaneously possible and successful only together." "Individualization and cohesiveness" belong just as inseparably together as "consensus and leadership" or "subsidiarity and the state."

The principle of the rhetorical harmonization of contradicting societal demands from which in the end a soothing "same as usual but always a little better" notion must evolve has long since become a powerful brake on reform. Thus, the new immigration law is rededicated into a law on the limitation of immigration because the political parties are afraid of a constituency alarmed by a fear of foreigners in regards to high unemployment. And in fact: the productive economic effects of generous immigration can take place only if they meet a flexible, flourishing labor market that generates work instead of preventing it. Both consensus parties do not risk approaching the necessary reforms in this sector because the deregulation of the bureaucratic redistribution apparatus in this country is reflexively considered equal to a total social deforestation. The self-induced stagnation on the labor market is then again presented as an argument for erecting dams against the invasion of foreign workers—thus, as if in terms of the economy it is a matter of a zero-sum game that still consists only of distributing the scarce commodity of work carefully under state supervision. In the meantime, society is expanding into the realm of a shadow economy that does not even receive mention in politics. The constant and devoted rhetoric of totality held forth on the "middle" plays over the fact that there are ever-growing sectors in the society that are no longer included in the traditional societal politics. These sectors can no longer follow the multifarious ways of social and cultural self-organization into which potential future new societal structures and moral standards are developing.

In order to exit the spiral tied to avoiding reform, a new societal image is necessary that accurately reflects the changes in an increasingly diverse, individualistic society. This must break from the image of a homogeneous togetherness that moves continuously in a single direction and for which there are only unified solutions embracing all particularities. The coming years will show whether the Berlin Republic in this sense moves in the direction of a modern, open society or proceeds backwards due to stagnation.

3. On "Westalgia": Why West German Mentalities and Habits Persist in the Berlin Republic

Tobias Dürr

Much has been expected of the new generations that came of age in Germany during the years following the revolution of 1989. Observers both at home and abroad assumed that these young Germans would outfit the united Germany with the institutions, attitudes, and habits that the country now needed in order to remain an internationally dynamic force, an economic powerhouse behind the European Union, and a self-confident strategic partner of the United States. The new Berlin Republic, it was widely assumed, would differ greatly from the Bonn Republic of the Cold War years. Expectations were high—so high that even some well-meaning observers of the German scene have since turned extremely skeptical. "In Germany ... a ferocious blandness has set in. Public life has the congealed quality of a Bavarian Kartoffelsuppe left cooling on the stove overnight," Joe Klein noted after a trip across Germany in the summer of 2002.[1] "Germany, like Japan, is trapped in a paralyzing network of political obstacles and economic arrangements," John B. Judis wrote following a similar visit.[2] Word of "the sick man of Europe" has been making the rounds.

The author wishes to thank Jedediah Purdy for his helpful comments on this essay.

1. See, for example, Joe Klein, "How Germany Was Suffocated," *The Guardian*, 19 June 2002.

2. John B. Judis, "Domestic Threat: Can Europe Survive German Nationalism?" *The New Republic*, 24 June 2002.

In fact, when it comes to a readiness for tackling new jobs with new energy, the new generation is not up to much. But it is not enough simply to note this fact and then lament it. If anything is to be done about changing these deplorable circumstances, their underlying conditions need to be more accurately illuminated. This essay takes a look at the intellectual, social, and cultural sources of the "German malaise." I arrive at the paradoxical conclusion, to put it briefly, that a deep-seated West German consciousness about the success of the West German societal model prior to 1989 is what is responsible for blocking timely changes in politics, economics, and society for Germany as a whole.

Tomorrow Is a Different Country? Not Quite

In the early 1980s, a riddle circulated around West German high school yards that captured the character of the Bonn Republic at that time: "What is the mission of the German Army? The answer: "When war breaks out, it has to detain the enemy at the border until the military arrives." The military, of course, was the American Army.

A central feature of the Bonn Republic up until 1989 was the unreality of any war in which the Federal Republic might actively participate. Back then nobody in the Federal Republic of Germany could or would deploy its army "out of area." Where the Bonn Republic was located geographically—on the frontline of the global conflict between liberal democracy and communism—the only likely war was a final conflagration with nuclear weapons. These, however, were in others' hands. The weapons, to be sure, were stored on the territory of the Bonn Republic, but the Bonn Republic itself did not possess any weapons of this type. Germans represented a passive position, and all they could do was protest against the NATO defense strategy—as hundreds of thousands did in the 1980s. The impossibility of exercising German power shaped the country's self-image and the political consciousness of those generations, born after 1945, who had never experienced anything but the West German constellation.

All that changed dramatically since the European revolutions of 1989 and Germany's reunification in 1990. This became increasingly obvious in the course of the 1990s, with the various Balkan wars culminating (for Germany) in the deployment of four Bundeswehr Tornado jetfighters during the Kosovo conflict of 1999. Just how dramatic the transformation of Germany's role in Europe and the world turned out to be became completely clear after September 11, when Chancellor Gerhard Schröder responded positively to the American invitation to participate in the "war against terror" in Afghanistan and elsewhere. By now it should have become quite clear to every last ex-West German that the citizens of the old Bonn Republic no longer live in the same state they inhabited through 1989/90. *Tomorrow is a Different Country* is the title of a clear-sighted book analyzing the political upheaval in South Africa after 1990.[3] For West Germans, too, the present and the future after 1990 constitute another country.

The Past Is Not Dead—It Is Not Even Past

For all that change, as William Faulkner remarked, "The past is not dead, it is not even past." Faulkner was referring to the persistence of traditional attitudes and mentalities in the American South long after the Civil War. In her autobiographical novel *Kindheitsmuster* (available in English both as *A Model Childhood* and *Patterns of Childhood*), the writer Christa Wolf translated this sentence into German, addressing it to the aftereffects of National Socialism: "Das Vergangene ist nicht tot; es ist nicht einmal vergangen."[4] This sentence, too, applies to the Berlin Republic and its prehistory. From the standpoint of foreign and security policy, the Bonn Republic may now look like another country, but culturally and intellectually it is by no means a thing of the past. It is precisely this precarious simultaneity that constitutes today's Berlin Republic.

Where the question of upheaval or status quo is concerned, there is something to be said for the seemingly trivial finding that each society has its own rhythm, its own tempo whereby it processes and copes with new experiences and changes in its surroundings. It drags around its past and collective experiences even when almost everything about it seems to have changed. And the more confused things seem to be, the more fervently the West Germans cling to what they possess. Why is this so?

The notion "No man is an island" remains true, no matter how individualized and fragmented, accelerated and borderless,

---

3. Allister Sparks, *Tomorrow is a Different Country: The Inside Story of South Africa's Road to Change* (Chicago, 1996).

4. Christa Wolf, *Kindheitsmuster* (Frankfurt am Main, 1977).

flexibilized and globalized German society may have become in the "runaway world."[5] Even this world remains populated by people living together in families, surrounded by friends and colleagues, groups and milieus, localities and regions. Much like the inhabitants of other Western countries, today's Germans witness the world's major events in real time on the TV screen every evening: the fall of the Wall, for example, the snipers' war in Sarajevo, the bomb attacks on Belgrade, the collapse of the World Trade Center towers, the war in Afghanistan, suicide bombings in Jerusalem, or the occupation of Palestinian territory by Israeli troops—but the next morning finds them again commuting to their jobs in Frankfurt or Munich, Hamburg or Hanover, to the nation's offices, factories, and shopping centers. Just as they will always be doing. And just as they would have been doing if there had been nothing to see on television the night before apart from talk shows and soccer matches. For most people—subjectively at least—life goes on largely uninfluenced by world events beyond their immediate horizon. Most people in West Germany still feel most at home in all the local settings, in family and friendship circles.

The German Search for "*Sicherheit*"

If one does not entirely disregard such aspects of the current scene as German society's propensity for stubbornness, its members' penchant for taking their own good time, and their tendency toward self-preoccupation, then the opposition of upheaval to status quo quickly dissolves. For when we take a closer look, we invariably encounter both dimensions, in a complex interaction with each other. The German habit of keeping things as they are even when changed circumstances demand a new approach can have ironic results: change is delayed for a few years, and then comes with more upheaval than would have been necessary, had the country acted more promptly. The trouble is that, since reform is only possible with political support, even obviously necessary and appropriate reforms are stalled by popular indifference or quiet hostility.

From a societal perspective, nothing changes overnight—at least not so long as new experiences are of no immediate concern to the

5. Anthony Giddens, *Runaway World: How Globalisation is Reshaping Our Lives* (London, 1999).

world people actually inhabit—their private well-being, lot, and livelihood. And because the West German Bonn Republic was undoubtedly a successful model in the years between 1949 and 1989/90, there is an almost irresistible temptation for the majority of West Germans to imagine the present and the future as an almost seamless sequel to a well-preserved past. During the 1970s people talked about "Model Germany" when referring to the Federal Republic. These were good times—why should anyone voluntarily say goodbye to all that?

"One has to accept people just the way they are. There are no other kinds."—this is something Konrad Adenauer, the Bonn Republic's first chancellor, already understood. Precisely because he knew this all too well, he was able to become a successful head of government. For better or for worse, Adenauer contributed to the consolidation of the West German can-do mentality more than any other postwar German politician. From the outset West Germany's political parties tried winning elections by using an all-embracing concept of "*Sicherheit*." This was no accident. The German term "Sicherheit" means "certainty," "security," and "safety" all wrapped into one. "Sicherheit with Ollenhauer" (referring to the former Social Democratic candidate for chancellor) is what the SPD promised in the election of 1953; "Sicherheit for Germany" was what the Social Democrats were promulgating even in 1980, at the frostiest moment in the Cold War; "Sicherheit in the midst of change" is the prospect Social Democracy has been offering again more recently. Germany's Christian Democrats, for their part, wanted their country to go "Sicher into the 1970s" in 1969 and "Sicher into the world of tomorrow" in 1998. And, not to be forgotten, it was the brilliantly crafted slogan "Mit Sicherheit Schill"—with "Schill" meaning both "to be sure" and "to be secure"—that brought the right-wing populist "Judge Merciless" Roland B. Schill 20 percent of the votes in the September 2001 elections to Hamburg's local parliamentary assembly.[6]

The Complacency of "Generation Golf"

How does a society like West Germany really change? Unqualified "Give-us-a-jolt" pep talks, like the ones former President Roman

---

6. On the Schill phenomenon, see, for example, Richard Miniter, "Cell Block," *The New Republic*, 24 December 2001.

Herzog used to make Germans get a move on, certainly do not lead anywhere. And West Germans are not impressed by politicians and business leaders making empty appeals for "new departures" and "renewal" without acknowledging the basic changes in attitudes and habits that would be necessary to give life to those fine-sounding phrases. It makes about as much sense (meaning hardly any) to induce some artificial definition of a brand-new "generation Berlin" simply by asserting its existence, as the sociologist professor Heinz Bude recently did.[7] Characteristically, not even the category "generation of the 89ers" managed to gain acceptance among West Germans.[8] Some kind of cleverly placed collective singular designation for this generation might yet prove to have a formative effect. But this can only work when a label picks up and captures a mood that can already be detected atmospherically.

It is, therefore, quite revealing that the existence of a "generation Golf" should have been asserted at the same time as the "generation Berlin." "Golf," of course, is the German name for the Volkswagen Rabbit, that practical little car that has sold better than any other automobile in Germany for the past several decades—truly the people's car.[9] This "generation Golf," which was discovered by Florian Illies, a young reporter for the *Frankfurter Allgemeine Zeitung*, is at cross-purposes with the "generation of the 89ers" precisely because the year 1989 plays absolutely no role in their hermetically sealed world. In Florian Illies's best-selling book, the defunct German Democratic Republic (GDR) is mentioned incidentally only twice—just as many times as Lake Starnberger (the exclusive excursion site near Munich), or the clothing brand Fruit of the Loom (regarded as fashionable in the 1980s), or the minor city of Heilbronn somewhere in southern Germany. The children's toy Playmobil crops up eleven times in Illies's bestseller. His book deals exclusively with growing up in the commercial world of West German merchandise during the 1980s.

Without a doubt, Florian Illies's approach is appallingly trivial. Yet at the same time it is clear that the author has taken some kind of significant phenomenon by the scruff of its neck with his book *Generation Golf*. Otherwise the book would not have become such a bestseller. It may be assumed that the author is, to some extent, treating his subject ironically or self-critically. But this is not how

7. Heinz Bude, *Generation Berlin* (Berlin, 2001).
8. Claus Leggewie, *Die 89er: Porträt einer Generation* (Hamburg, 1995).
9. Florian Illies, *Generation Golf: Eine Inspektion* (Berlin, 2000).

his public reads him. Instead, readers are taking Illies at his word: This is our West German world, all right; that's just how we are, a little feeble and maybe slow-moving, a bit mentally lazy perhaps, closed for business early, aging before our time—but it is really for the best that way. That young Herr Illies from the prestigious *Frankfurter Allgemeine* has certified and legitimated our condition with his book.

Seen in this light, the immense commercial success of *Generation Golf* is a symptom—the symptom of a mentality. It has to do with a tenacious West German mentality that is not terribly impressed by how much conditions have actually changed. Or to put it more pointedly: Just when it is obvious how dramatically conditions are changing, anxiety about the unknown grows along with nostalgia for what is done and gone. *Generation Golf* is a book about a type of nostalgia, or to put it more precisely: it is about a certain kind of "Westalgia," dimly afraid that the best times are already gone by.

How Success Has Bred Stagnation

What kind of a mentality is that? And where does it come from? "The mentality of ... sixty million Germans is a mentality spoiled by success," the highly respected historian Hans-Ulrich Wehler has written. "It results from economic progress since the currency reform, from a dense network of social security, from widespread acceptance of the political system and that system's basic efficiency. If the agenda should now turn, as it is inevitably likely to do, toward far-reaching changes, this success-oriented mentality will balk at these kinds of intrusions, since they can apparently be quite painful. Why should the [postwar German] success story (this self-confident conviction appears to be deep-seated) be interrupted and require any correction?"[10]

Wehler is right. And, to this extent, "generation Golf" is a cultural and sociological fact. Only in reality we are dealing less with a "Golf generation" than with an all-West German "Golf mentality" extending well beyond a few age groups. "Generation Golf" is the generationally specific expression of a general West German "Golf mentality"

10. Hans-Ulrich Wehler, "Bonn – Berlin – Weimar: Droht unserer Republik das Schicksal von Weimar?" in *Umbruch und Kontinuität: Essays zum 20. Jahrhundert*, ed. Hans-Ulrich Wehler (Munich, 2000).

that does not exist outside its historical context. "The German tribe likes to have things leisurely," is how the political scientist Wilhelm Hennis quite accurately described things a few years ago. "We have bad memories of all the turbulent, exciting times, the Thirty Years War, the atrocious wars of this century, the mobilization that accompanied these wars, all the unrest, the loss of all the certitudes and traditions…. We have experienced too many 'upheavals' to tempt us toward any more of them."[11]

It is precisely at this point that "generation Berlin" comes into play again. Its central shortcoming is that it does not represent any social or cultural reality for Germany as a whole. There is an idea of "generation Berlin," but no such generation to bring the idea to life. Instead, "generation Berlin" is a politically motivated ideal, a prophecy of the media that its propagators hoped would be self-fulfilling. The real lives people lead in the West German provinces are a different matter. Not that much is going to change in the mental or institutional state of the republic simply because a couple of intellectuals move to the capital in order to write commentaries, compose essays, edit periodicals, or publish books.

For institutions—and this, for good reason, is their essential purpose—are durable, steadfast, and weatherproof. And mentalities are tough, long-lived, skeptical, and resistant to change. As the success of *Generation Golf* so impressively demonstrates, mentalities are most likely to reflect back upon themselves when the conditions that produced them come under pressure. Changes—however desirable they may be—cannot be forced simply by issuing ex cathedra pronouncements when overpowering mentalities and experiences stand in their way.

Those who discovered and promulgated "generation Berlin" should have borne this in mind. Heinz Bude presented "generation Berlin" as a community of those who linked the dawn of the Berlin Republic with hopes for a pragmatic and undogmatic new beginning *ab ovo*, for some kind of new communicative networking, for fresh curiosity about anything and everything that lies ahead. In the meantime, Bude has become disillusioned. The revamping of the republic he envisioned failed to materialize. The Wall inside people's heads remains firmly in place. The old mentalities persevere.

11. Wilhelm Hennis, "Totenrede des Perikles auf ein blühendes Land: Ursachen der politischen Blockade," in *Auf dem Weg in den Parteienstaat: Aufsätze aus vier Jahrzehnten*, ed. Wilhelm Hennis (Stuttgart, 1998).

Mentality as a Filter for Reality

Bude's disillusionment is easy to understand. Only, one might have known that social upheavals are not made by acclamation. It never turns out that way—the history of the American South in the decades following the Civil War offers us the most persuasive case in point.[12] Not too long ago, the young new mayor of Berlin, Klaus Wowereit, talked incessantly about the need for an immediate *Mentalitätswechsel* (change of attitude). That was well intentioned. But mentalities are not simply "changed" on such short notice. Over time they may change, but they certainly cannot be suddenly "replaced" by attitudes more suitable to changed circumstances. Attractive rhetoric is one thing, sluggish reality quite another. "Progress is a snail," as Günter Grass wrote many years ago. The same applies to social change in general, for as Hans-Ulrich Wehler also stated: "All the concrete problems of social, tax, health, and defense policy require political majorities, and these in turn require insight into the necessity of reforms and ... a transformation of attitude [*Mentalitätsverände-rung*]." That, in turn, calls for a lot of patience, a lot of discussion, and very long endurance, since "experiences always have to go through the filter of mentality."[13]

The "filter of mentality" that new experiences have to pass through before change is possible—this is a most apt and illuminating image for a problem preoccupying all societies but currently giving Germany's Federal Republic more than its share of trouble. But does that also mean that the West German mentality has to remain as it is ad infinitum? Of course not. This complacent can-do mentality cannot and will not stay as it is for much longer, because its economic and social preconditions are crumbling.

This is hard to accept for those who have been successful for such a long time. In the meantime, therefore, we just experience a growing gap between mentality and reality. Germans of the old West have grown complacent and sluggish beyond their achievements. The leisurely West German tribe of the present—to use Wilhelm Hennis's formulation—seems to put up resistance against the realization that the resources that fed a can-do mentality for decades are finally drying up. One need not refer to the world's new-found fragility after September 11 or to the deployment of German troops in the Hindu Kush, in order to explain this. It had already

---

12. Cf. the classic study by W. J. Cash, *The Mind of the South* (New York, 1941).
13. Wehler, *Umbruch und Kontinuität*.

been clear for quite some time that we have been living in an age of accelerated transitions since 1989. One need only mention all those processes lumped together under the concept "globalization," with its attendant repercussions on the Federal Republic's model of economic and social welfare. Also noteworthy are all the problems of social integration under conditions of individualization and "flexibilization," of migration pressures and the demographic crisis. Similarly troubling is the blatant failure of the project ritually characterized as "domestic unity," of leavening (as it were) every last trace of a defunct GDR within the West German Republic. Nothing will remain as it was before—anyone who went around the country with eyes wide open could truly have appreciated this long before the attack on the World Trade Center.

From Success to Panic?

The only remaining questions are how, when, and by what means the contradiction between the accelerated pace of change and the tenacious West German mentality will dissolve. When will quantity turn into quality? Will that ever happen? What happens next? One should not underestimate the West German mentality's willingness, in the face of diffusely perceived threats, to withdraw further into itself. Florian Illies's latest book came out just a few days after September 11. Its title is *Anleitung zum Unschuldigsein* (Instructions for Innocence) and it preaches a world-weary, inner-directed, apolitical escapism. It may or may not just be a harmless sign that the book has been selling like hotcakes since then.

There are other, weightier examples of collective reality denial. Here one needs to take a closer look at all the important organizations traditionally associated with the old-style, consensus-oriented "Model Germany," with its lobbies, trade unions, and two major official churches. Especially revealing, owing to its location on the interface between society and the political system, is the party landscape. The representatives of the old, established postwar German parties still act as if they were the self-evident proprietors of a societal legitimacy that in fact has long been eroding. So, for example, the general secretary of the Christian Democratic Union (CDU) declared, on the eve of the election to the Berlin city parliament in October 2001, that he was "shocked" at the showing of the post-communist Party of Democratic Socialism (PDS). One may think whatever one likes of the PDS, but in the eastern half of Berlin they received four times as many votes as the Christian Democrats' "popular party" and only one percent less in Berlin as a whole. The CDU in Hamburg was recently thrilled to be providing that city with its first mayor from that party in forty-four years—although they had managed to get backing from only one-fourth of the voters and were dependent on the right-wing populist Roland B. Schill, whose electoral support was just barely behind the CDU's. There should not be even the slightest doubt about the ability of Germany's traditional parties and organizations to win back their status as deeply rooted representatives of society—someday. Yet that is exactly how they are behaving in the here and now, all evidence to the contrary. In the long run that attitude can only turn out badly.

Here the right-wing populist phenomenon of Schill proves so revealing. Schill was a harmless foretaste of what can happen if, on top of everything else, the tenacious West German mentality panics. The 20 percent of the vote Schill managed to get in Hamburg was the consequence of a cognitive process gone pathologically awry. Comparable events have also happened elsewhere. Those who vote for right-wing populist parties are quite accurately aware that reality is changing in some way they find threatening. Yet they react to this change in a spirit of stubborn denial. Seen this way, the current populist boom truly is the outcome of a growing, if diffusely refracted, perception that there are problems requiring attention.

Yet the new right-wing populism in the West German case is not an expression of new social situations or dispositions—on the contrary. It is, in many respects, a new expression of the old attitude, a change of that self-satisfied mentality in the direction of a resolute insistence that there must by all means be Sicherheit as in the past. This stubborn and "Westalgic" mentality, however (and this is the real novelty), threatens to become uncoupled from its time-honored representatives and guarantors; it is becoming an independent factor and calling off its allegiance to traditional political organizations. This paradoxical relationship between persistence and upheaval is precisely the kind of thing that might characterize the Berlin Republic in the future. It is no longer possible to speak of the status quo; that is a thing of the past. Just as little might we expect to experience an upheaval leading toward some new, stable sociopolitical formation with the prospect of lasting as many decades as the old order did. We do not know exactly what is going to happen. Only one thing appears certain: The future of the Berlin Republic will be different from what its euphoric proclaimers had imagined.

4. The Foreign Policy of the Berlin Republic

Hans-Ulrich Klose

German foreign policy today, after the end of the Cold War and reunification, has become not easier but more difficult. One of the reasons for this is that Europe and the world have greater expectations where German foreign policy is concerned. Many people say that, as a major player on the world stage, we should assume greater responsibility politically, economically, and militarily and be prepared to shoulder greater burdens.

As we too are aware, German politics continue to be regarded with special interest, at times even mistrust, precisely because in the eyes of the world the country has grown bigger and more powerful and because the world has experienced German power. Sometimes one has the impression that its partners and allies regard Germany with greater suspicion than others who are further away from us and who were not directly involved in the aberrations of German history.

This should not really come as a surprise. More surprising is the speed with which Germany—defeated, destroyed, and divided after World War II—changed from foe to partner, each part in its own sphere, the West Germans on the more fortunate side. The explanation lies in the enmity that developed between the erstwhile wartime allies, the West and East, during the Cold War. There was a new enemy, and this made the Americans in particular see things from a new angle. It was not that suddenly people loved us—the West Germans were just as unloved in the West as the East Germans were in the East—but both were needed. The East Germans were needed to shore up Soviet domination over Central and Eastern Europe, the West Germans to defend Western Europe against Stalin's Soviet

Union, something which seemed virtually unfeasible without the Germans. This (and Konrad Adenauer's astute politics) made Germany a partner. Since, moreover, the West German model of democracy and the social-market economy became a success story, the West Germans became America's (the dominant Western power) success story and—as compared to those under communist rule— the good Germans.

Things are different today. The Cold War is over. The Germans— today this means West and East Germans together—have one thing in common: a burdensome history, a history of which Germans are reminded more frequently and in a less friendly way today than during all the years of the East-West confrontation. Against the backdrop of the political landscape of the time, such reminders did not formerly seem appropriate, but today they do.

This is unquestionably the case where the United States is concerned. The only remaining superpower, whose overriding foreign policy goal is to remain exactly that, still regards Germany as a partner, but as one among others, a partner who, in the absence of an enemy, is no longer quite so urgently needed as before. The United States also regards Germany, both in its own right and as a member of the European Union, as a competitor, not (yet) militarily but politically and economically; and it is the economic part that is, from the American point of view, particularly important. To simplify, one might say: the common enemy is gone and, as a partner, Germany is (a) no longer as interesting and easy to deal with for America, and (b) also not quite as important as before. The partnership has lost some of its coherence.

This makes it all the more important for us Germans to be sure we know where we stand. Where are we? Where are we going? What do we want? There is astonishingly little discussion in Germany about these questions, but not because we are unsure of where we stand and hence are unpredictable. Quite the reverse: what distinguishes the foreign policy players of the reunified Germany is that, despite the odd dispute over individual issues, they have been and, even thirteen years after unity, still are in agreement on the fundamental decisions and guiding principles on which German foreign policy is founded.

In essence, there are five main elements.

1. We, the Germans in the Federal Republic of Germany, belong to Western Europe. We are committed to the Western European model of an enlightened, pluralistic democracy. The

expression of and guarantee for our integration in Western Europe is the special German-French relationship, a relationship that we must nurture and foster. Former Federal German Chancellor Helmut Schmidt recently referred again to the "symbiosis with France," quietly questioning whether German politicians still perceive the relationship in this light. He need not worry: we do indeed regard the relationship in this way, even if the behavior of those involved on the German and French sides is not always characterized by amiability alone.

2. The Federal Republic of Germany has given up sovereign rights to join international Atlantic and European systems of cooperation and security: the European Union—formerly the European Economic Community (EEC) and the European Community (EC)—and NATO. In doing so it has regained its sovereignty. Even in changed times the Germans remain committed to a foreign policy based on membership in these two alliances and on partnership (which does not rule out adjustments, made in a spirit of partnership, to accommodate altered circumstances).

3. During the Cold War, (West) Germany successfully embarked, after years of confrontational politics, on a new policy of détente with the East (agreed on with the Western Alliance), aimed at developing a regulated form of cooperation with its eastern neighbors—at that time its opponents. This led to both German states joining the UN and also guaranteed the success of the Helsinki process. This process—originally conceived in Moscow—did not seal the division of Europe, but culminated instead in the overcoming of this division, the reunification of Germany, and the disintegration of the Soviet empire. Today reunified Germany is a respected member of the UN and an important player in the Organization for Security and Cooperation in Europe (OSCE), the successor to the Commission on Security and Cooperation in Europe (CSCE). Membership in both international organizations is axiomatic to German foreign policy.

4. Within the UN and the Western alliance, reunified Germany has taken on international (co)responsibilities and has participated in a military operation for the first time since World War II, deploying troops to serve in the Kosovo conflict. German involvement was and is crucial to the success of this operation (signed on to the German side by a red-green government!)

and for the ongoing management of conflict resolution in the region.

5 The Federal Republic of Germany recognizes its historical obligation to do all in its power to help overcome the division of Europe. It wants to see the European Union expand and is prepared to bear its share of the costs entailed. It gives its backing to the candidate countries who wish to become members of NATO.

It is important and right that we should be clear in our own minds that these fundamental decisions and guiding principles underlying Germany foreign policy continue to be valid, so that we ourselves, as well as our partners, are certain of where we belong and what our aims are.

Europe is our focal point. The Federal Republic of Germany, the most populous and economically most powerful country of the European Union, wants to play an appropriate, but not a dominant role in Europe. It is appropriate for Germany to look after its interests. It is in the German interest to do this in a way that is accepted by its partners; in a political union that is not a hegemony, each country, whether large or small, can assert its own interests only in concert with its partners, not in opposition to them. We are well advised, therefore, to retain the cooperative style of our foreign and security policy.

We also want to hold on to the concept of an integrated European Union, which, on the basis of a European constitution, progressively develops into an independent subject under international law; this is desirable not only to ensure greater effectiveness but also for political reasons. German potential should be incorporated on a permanent basis into European structures to make Europe strong and secure. This political will—not the desire to escape Germany's own history—is the basis of German policy on Europe. Our partners understand this very well, but it is a policy that is not fully accepted. France and Great Britain, and in truth most of the member states of the European Union, acknowledge the need to reflect on European "finality," but think more in categories of national sovereignty and intergovernmental cooperation. This also applies quite explicitly to most of the candidate countries in Central and Eastern Europe, which won or regained their sovereignty only a few years ago and which are therefore very reluctant to cede sovereign powers to Brussels beyond the current *acquis*.

All this is pushing German policy on Europe in a pragmatic direction, with two tasks being paramount:

1. The EU must make itself ready for enlargement so that, progressively, it can absorb the candidate countries into the Union. We Germans have a national interest in this: first because after the accession of the countries of Central and Eastern Europe, Germany, for the first time in its history, would no longer be a frontier country but would be surrounded on all sides by partners. We should actively work toward such a constellation, not primarily on economic grounds but for political reasons. Former Chancellor Helmut Kohl used to say, quite rightly, that European policy is peace policy, that by enlarging and deepening the EU, as we are doing, we are establishing a stable European order of peace that resonates beyond Europe.

   There is another important aspect to consider here. Enlarging the EU to take in the states of Central and Eastern Europe is not simply a matter of extending EU law or seeking territorial expansion. It is also about making amends for historical wrongs. The division of Europe was not something that was wanted by the states concerned. It was forced on them by Stalin, and the West bowed to this pressure. Seen in this light, therefore, it is a matter of helping Central and Eastern European countries to return to Europe, of reuniting the continent that was divided so arbitrarily. We Germans bear a particular responsibility in this respect since the war that emanated from Germany paved the way for the division. Overcoming this division should therefore be no less important to us than overcoming the partition of Germany.

2. The EU must shape its structures in such a way that it can continue to function and act effectively with twenty, twenty-five, or twenty-seven members. The primary need is to strengthen the Commission and the rules and regulations for expanding the catalogue of majority decisions. Those who feel this is not enough because they had hoped for more should draw comfort from the realization that the EU is at least moving in the right direction and is already perceived as an international player, not only economically but also politically. It may not yet draw level with the United States, but it is in the process of becoming a partner of equal weight and with equal rights.

In the United States, this development is regarded in part positively and also with concern: positively because the European potpourri has always met with unease and incomprehension in America; positively also because America has always expressly welcomed greater military contributions from the Europeans; and with concern because there is a suspicion in America that Europe's attempts to gain greater foreign policy responsibility and military independence are in reality an attempt by the Europeans to defy American power and question America's leading role in NATO. The European Security and Defense Identity (ESDI) in particular is occasionally regarded in America as a first step toward Europe decoupling itself from America.

Because this is so, it makes sense to repeat the three main reasons that have prompted the Europeans to develop an independent European security and defense policy:

1. The constant urgings on the part of the United States that the Europeans should do more have not gone unheard. The Europeans know they must do more; they also know they must engage in closer military cooperation to achieve better results. As is known, Europe spends about two-thirds of the amount on defense that the United States spends. However, the benefit derived is only around 25 percent of that achieved by the Americans. Since the financial resources at the disposal of the Europeans are limited, it is, and always has been, obvious that the cost-benefit ratio needs to be improved through better cooperation. If this happens and, moreover, defense spending rises over the medium and long term, the military capability of the Europeans will improve and the gap between American and European potentials narrow, strengthening rather than weakening NATO as a whole.

2. It is not uncommon to meet representatives and senators in the U.S. Congress who make it clear to their European colleagues, often very outspokenly, that the Americans will no longer be prepared in future to intervene in European conflicts and that the Europeans will have to deal with such problems themselves. That may not, and probably does not, represent the feeling of the majority in Congress, but these voices exist, and there will be more. Since the change of government in Washington, there is increasing speculation that this is also the position of the new administration (intervention only if vital American interests are at stake). Who can

therefore blame the Europeans for reflecting on such issues and developments and preparing for the eventuality, albeit not very probable, that the Americans lose interest in Europe?

3. The European Union is not an alliance, and the European security and defense policy is not in the first instance about defense but about the so-called "Petersberg Tasks" (rescue and humanitarian tasks, peacekeeping, and crisis management, including peacemaking). European security and defense policy is also of particular interest to the future members of the EU who have no chance of becoming members of NATO in the foreseeable future. It would be desirable for all member countries of the European Union to be or become members of NATO as well; but it is well known that others think differently about this and would, for good reasons, decide against it. If a negative decision had been reached (i.e., against allowing the Baltic states to join NATO), there would be, alongside membership of the European Union and a partnership for peace, a second military component for these states, the psychological effect of which should not be underestimated.

There is another issue that needs to be addressed here: America's dominant role in NATO is based on hard facts. In terms of military capabilities there is currently a considerable class difference between America and Europe which it will not be possible to even out in the near future. It would be desirable from both the European and American perspectives to even the balance, but if this happens at all, it will only be achievable in the long term. This may be regrettable, but history teaches us that alliances only work when there is or was clear leadership. And it is also still true that the American presence and leadership have helped, and not harmed the Europeans over the past fifty years. We Germans in particular will never forget the wholly positive contribution made by the United States to the reunification of our country. German policy therefore is clear on this point, too: we want to strengthen, not weaken NATO, and we want the United States to remain a power in Europe. And we are certain that our European partners—including France—see things the same way. For the countries of Central and Eastern Europe seeking accession in particular, the American presence offers a double guarantee: security to the east (Russia) and security to the west (Germany).

German foreign policy is—as can be seen time and again—heavily influenced by experience and history. As a consequence of this experience German foreign policy is consciously rooted in the principle of cooperation. This means that as a partner, we may sometimes be difficult but, at the same time, we are reliable and predictable. Nothing will change in this respect in the future German foreign policy is based on continuity and consensus.

Of course, German foreign policy is not confined to the multilateral European and Atlantic dimension. Germany has interests in Eastern Europe and is seeking cooperation with Russia. A European security architecture without Russia would be difficult, many think impossible. It is not yet quite clear whether America shares this (German/European) perception, because opinions on Russia's policy in Europe and toward the West evidently differ on either side of the Atlantic—ample reason to step up the transatlantic dialogue. Cooperation with China, as well as with India and Japan, is high on our list of foreign policy priorities. Particularly where China is concerned, the Europeans and Americans do not always see eye to eye. Here again we need to talk. Europe, and Germany, need to take greater pains to explain to the political community in Washington why we endorse multilateral policy, more international dialogue, and the strengthening of the UN and the OSCE. Precisely because we Europeans take issue with the American inclination for unilateral action, we should talk to our partners about it. The onus here is particularly on us Germans, who years ago, before the end of the Cold War even, were offered a "partnership in leadership" by George Bush senior, the father of the present American president. There is no talk of that in America any longer. Yet Germany's voice still carries weight in America. It would carry even more weight if we exploited all our political opportunities, and that is not happening at present. The tasks facing us in our own country and in Europe are too great and onerous (but also full of opportunity). That creates the impression, which is sometimes voiced aloud, that we Germans are too focused on ourselves and are therefore not mature enough for world politics. That may be so, although we should not make ourselves smaller than we are. It is true, though, that we can only continue to exert influence in the long term if we see ourselves as an EU power and appear on the world stage as a European player.

Hans Arnold summed up the situation as follows: "Germany will be able to satisfy its interests not by seeking an ominous new normality but only by accepting the reality of a European Germany."[1] In the Bonn Republic, that was the German stance and perception. It remains unchanged in the Berlin Republic.

1. *Neue Gesellschaft Frankfurter Hefte* 7/B (2001).

5. The Berlin Republic in a Global Age

Daniel Hamilton

Hans-Ulrich Klose notes in this volume the deep continuities binding the emerging policy profile of the Berlin Republic to the highly
successful approaches of the Bonn Republic—its commitments to
Westbindung, European integration, multilateralism, overcoming
the division of Europe, and accepting responsibility for German
history. These continuities are strong, and the policy foundation
laid by the Bonn Republic remains critical. But it is critical in relation to a very different setting.

The Bonn Republic was a product of the Cold War and a response
to two world wars. It was a divided, semi-sovereign front-line state
dependent on its allies for its security and eventual reunification. It
advanced its national interests in the language of economics and
multilateralism. Redemption from historical tragedy was to be found
in "Europe." Its overriding foreign policy principles: do not get out
in front; do not go it alone. It had a habit of thinking like a light-
weight long after it had become a heavyweight. A related perception
was that military power was a declining asset. The future belonged
to civilian powers; most crises, it seemed, could be resolved through
nonmilitary means. It had a correspondingly narrow view of its
alliance obligations. Nuclear weapons were renounced. Independent military capabilities were forsworn in exchange for strong security guarantees and deep integration into NATO and European
structures. The sole task of German defense was defense of German
territory. NATO was there to protect Germany. It was deemed unlikely that Germany would be called on to protect others. Outside
the NATO area it was less a player than a payer. Checkbook diplomacy bailed the Bonn Republic out of many a jam. Overlaying all of

these elements was a consistent refrain of reassurance by the German political class to non-Germans about their bearings and adherence to Western values and structures

The Berlin Republic, in contrast, is the first liberal, democratic, market-oriented, united Germany in history, surrounded for the first time by democratic allies. EU and NATO enlargement is transforming it from Europe's eastern edge to its heartland, the crossroads and central power of a continent in tremendous flux. It bears virtually no resemblance to Wilhelminian, Weimar, or Nazi Germany, not to mention the German Democratic Republic (GDR). It has maintained the constitutional structures and many of the basic habits of the Bonn Republic. But it finds itself in a profoundly different situation. The Berlin Republic no longer has the antagonistic Soviet superpower or the blood feud across the Wall that defined much of the Bonn Republic's foreign and domestic policies. It has abandoned what probably was the very symbol of the Bonn Republic, the deutsche mark, in favor of the euro. It is an international heavyweight whose abstinence from the world stage can be as important as its action. It faces greater pressure to send soldiers, doctors, diplomats, police officers and aid workers, not just checks, to deal with world trouble spots. It is less reticent internationally, more pressured economically, more diverse demographically, and more open yet less settled politically than was the Bonn Republic.

In short, while large parts of the German political class are inclined to stick to the tried-and-true approaches that proved successful during the Bonn Republic, the ground is shifting. This transition has come relatively slowly, in large part because German leaders continue to be extremely cautious in dealing with their enhanced weight, and because German opinion shapers and the German public at large have been preoccupied with domestic issues—particularly knitting the two parts of their country together again and with the headaches associated with their sputtering economy. Yet despite these strong inertial currents, new influences during the 1990s—the effects of globalization, the pressures generated by the EU's pending enlargement, and recurrent Balkan tragedies—were forcing German decision makers to reconsider some basic policy premises. By the beginning of the new century, it was becoming clearer that on a host of economic, foreign, and defense policy issues, many of the Bonn Republic's methods were proving inadequate to the Berlin Republic's challenges.

Then came September 11, which proved to be less cause than catalyst for the red-green coalition to press more urgently for new departures in German foreign policy. Chancellor Gerhard Schröder not only called for a "new conception of German foreign policy," he risked his government on it by deploying German troops to Afghanistan. Standing before the Bundestag on October 11, 2001, Schröder declared Germany's "unlimited solidarity" with the United States, advocated an "irrevocable" change in Germany's foreign policy, and committed German forces to defend freedom, human rights, and the restoration of stability and security far beyond the European continent.[1] As Karl Kaiser has suggested, Schröder's actions may herald the third great reorientation of German foreign policy in the past fifty years, beginning with Konrad Adenauer's *Westbindung*, followed by Willy Brandt's Ostpolitik, and now the global agenda facing the Berlin Republic of Gerhard Schröder and Foreign Minister Joschka Fischer.[2] In fact, of all of America's European allies, Germany is the one most likely to be transformed by the events of September 11 and their aftermath. The new era has sharpened the choices facing German decision makers, who are finding it harder to hide behind their history, their economy, or the multilateralism of reluctant power.

The yearning for continuity remains strong in Germany, however, and there is tremendous ambivalence about a more activist effort. Schröder's decision to opt out of the debate on Iraq highlights the public's deep ambivalence, and underscores that the transition is likely to take some time. During this period German foreign policy is likely to resemble something of a meandering medieval dance, lurching two steps forward and then one step back. Observers should not be surprised to see German leaders asserting themselves forcefully on some issues and abandoning the field on others, donning their green eyeshades at times and succumbing to high-flying bursts of moralistic rhetoric on other occasions. And yet the trend line is clear. With each passing year since unification, the consequences of German diffidence have become increasingly visible. Domestic support for a more self-confident German foreign policy is growing, gradually and hesitantly.

1. Schröder's speech is available at www.spdfraktion.de.
2. See Karl Kaiser's contribution for a study group project the author coordinated for the American Institute for Contemporary German Studies, "German Perspectives on the New Strategic Landscape after September 11," November 2001, available online at www.aicgs.org. Hanns Maull argues similarly in "Internationaler Terrorismus: Die deutsche Außenpolitik auf dem Prüfstand," *Internationale Politik* 56, no. 12 (2001): 1–10.

The second major factor accelerating Germany's foreign policy transition is the administration of U.S. President George W. Bush. The Bush administration's unilateral and unidimensional approach has forced German leaders to reflect deeply about their most fundamental foreign policy priorities, and to consider very seriously how far they are prepared to go to advance them—even at the risk of alienating a Republican administration. Under the Bonn Republic, close alignment with the United States on any particular issue usually enhanced Germany's weight on a range of other issues, and often relieved German leaders of making tough choices. This is no longer the case. On issue after issue, Germans are finding the need to consider tradeoffs between key German interests and fealty to a U.S. administration with which they often profoundly disagree.

These cross-cutting forces were all on display in the red-green coalition's approach to Iraq. At home, Schröder's decision to opt out of the debate on Iraq was perhaps the most visible example to date that domestic politics in the Berlin Republic are different—and East German votes matter. Down in the polls, but with an opportunity to secure significant Social Democratic gains in the east, particularly after having demonstrated forceful leadership in dealing with tragic summer floods that ravaged that part of Germany, Schröder gambled that an *"Ohne Uns"* stance could milk enough anti-war sentiment in the east to eke out the one to two percentage points he needed to win reelection. It demonstrated that an opportunistic German chancellor was not only prepared to thumb his nose at an American president, he was willing to tolerate and even encourage those who conflated policy criticism of the Bush administration with criticisms of American society more broadly. Of course, Schröder was able to tap into deep German skepticism of the Bush administration's own conflation of the campaign against terrorism—which has been strongly supported by Germans—with its aggressive campaign against Saddam Hussein and the "axis of evil," which has been strongly opposed by Germans. But Schröder's surprising reference to *"der deutsche Weg"* (the German path), a special German way of acting in international affairs, was a demonstration that unilateral rhetoric sells even in oh-so-multilateral Germany.[3] On a central issue of the day, Schröder broke a

3. Schröder's references were particularly surprising since he has gone out of his way in the past to distance himself from such phrases: "… special paths do not lead to a European future, they really and literally lead astray." Gerhard Schröder, "Die Grundkoordinaten deutscher Außenpolitik sind unverändert: Frieden und

fundamental tenet of the Bonn Republic's foreign policy: no singularization. He broke ranks with his key European allies as well as with the Bush administration, undercut any prospect for EU or NATO solidarity, and even questioned German support for the United Nations. Schröder blunted criticism by joining immediately with the Netherlands to assume joint command of the International Security Assistance Force (ISAF) based in Kabul and to draw NATO planning capabilities into the process—underscoring that Germany was prepared to play its part on the international stage, but would be more selective in its engagement, based on its own perceptions of German interests.

Seen in this way, Schröder's Iraq decision cannot be dismissed simply as a temporary interlude, driven solely by domestic political necessity. That interpretation is premised on the notion that the Berlin Republic is simply the Bonn Republic writ large, and ignores the new setting in which unified Germany finds itself. It is also implausible to reduce Schröder's decision to a new triumph of German pacifism, because that ignores German military efforts in Afghanistan, the Balkans, and the Horn of Africa, or active German efforts in the global campaign against terrorism. The cross-cutting forces driving decisions in the Berlin Republic are simply more complex than such monocausal interpretations allow.

In sum, events since September 11 have posed urgent new challenges to German foreign and defense policies and offered Chancellor Schröder a public justification to accelerate and strengthen new policy directions, many of which were already discernible on September 10. These new accents are evolving unevenly. They are subject to considerable and often conflicting domestic pressures. But they share a common theme, and that is a new readiness to use Germany's greater *Gestaltungsmacht*—shaping power—more assertively to advance both German interests and German perceptions of broader Western interests. These efforts are evident in various areas, but for the sake of illustration, I shall highlight three: Germany's role in Europe, its evolving strategic culture, and its response to globalization.

Sicherheit und stabiles Umfeld für Wohlstand festigen." Rede bei der 37. Kommandeurstagung der Bundeswehr in Hamburg, 29 November 1999, in *Bulletin* 83 (1999): 886; "The time of the German 'special path' and its disastrous consequences is irreversibly over …" Gerhard Schröder, "Verläßlichkeit in den internationalen Beziehungen. Rede von Bundeskanzler Gerhard Schröder zur offiziellen Eröffnung des Sitzes der Deutschen Gesellschaft für Auswärtige Politik am 2. September 1999 in Berlin," *Bulletin* 55 (1999): 575.

The Fulcrum of Europe

Throughout the unification process, former Foreign Minister Hans Dietrich Genscher sought to allay concerns about a dominant "Deutschland." "Our aim," he said, "as Thomas Mann wrote as early as 1952, is to create not a German Europe but a European Germany." Events since then indicate that the reality is likely to be a little of both: a more European Germany in the heart of a more German Europe. The German public and German elites remain committed to European integration. But in a larger and looser Europe they have less confidence that there are always European solutions to German problems, and more confidence in framing European approaches in ways that more explicitly advance German interests. The economic costs of unification and global competitiveness challenges have led them to be wary about the economic costs of "Europe." They are less inhibited about using Germany's position to retool old institutions and shape new ones. They are less hesitant about building new coalitions to supplement the Franco-German axis, which remains crucial but no longer exclusive.

There is also a more forthright style. Soon after taking office, Chancellor Schröder said he was convinced that Germany's European neighbors "want a self-confident Germany as a partner, because it is more calculable than a German partner with an inferiority complex. It is just as natural that Germany stands up for its interests as France or Great Britain."

The Nice Summit in December 2000, which focused on the distribution of power in a larger European Union, underscored the changes under way. Not only did Paris and Berlin fail to agree on their traditional eve-of-summit joint letter attempting to shape the outcome; in the end a stunned French Prime Minister Jacques Chirac was presented with an Anglo-German document setting forth the final compromises. While France retained parity of votes in the Council of Ministers, Germany agreed only after securing its other objectives, including greater representation in the European Parliament. France's antics failed to win the confidence of its partners, whereas Germany's consensus-building approach reassured smaller partners.

Chancellor Schröder is far more comfortable than were his predecessors with the idea that the Franco-German tandem need not be the sine qua non for German initiative and leadership. At Nice he served notice that Germany would speak with a bigger voice and, in the process, would include other players as well. Germany's new self-confident approach worried Paris, and in Schröder's first term the Franco-German motor failed to ignite.

Aware that their partnership had languished, both Schröder and French President Chirac moved quickly after the French and German elections in 2002 to reengage. This resulted in important compromises on the size of EU agricultural subsidies following the next wave of EU enlargement in 2004, a flurry of joint proposals for the European Convention on the future shape of the European Union, and joint efforts to push for early 2005 as the likely date for opening the EU's accession talks with Turkey. On the surface, these new initiatives suggest renewed commitment to each other, as well as the end of Tony Blair's flirtation with a more European Great Britain. A strong Franco-German tandem is good for Europe. But if one looks deeper, one may wonder whether real differences are being bridged or simply papered over. In the new, larger Europe, other inner-European permutations are conceivable, and the ability to strike new coalitions rests more with Germany than with France.

In short, the Franco-German partnership remains crucial for Europe and crucial for both partners. But in the new Europe, Germany, not France, is increasingly at the center of inner-European bargaining. The nation that once embodied Europe's division is once again *das Land in der Mitte*—both geopolitical pivot and central catalyst to the continent's economic and political integration.

Still Reticent after All These Years?

Germany's "culture of reticence" is still powerful, but there have been key changes to the defense consensus that prevailed during the Bonn Republic.

First, Germany has changed from frontline, divided state to unified democracy surrounded by democratic allies. The former border crossing between East and West Berlin, Checkpoint Charlie, is a museum. The Soviet threat has disintegrated, and Russia is now a partner in such common causes as fighting terrorism. Russia's potential for internal chaos and its inability to protect its nuclear material or know-how are more of a threat than its intention for aggression. The risks of European turmoil have shifted toward southeastern Europe and Europe's southern periphery. Security challenges have arisen there in large measure due to weak state structures and the challenges posed by the transition from communism. Addressing these challenges means employing better conflict prevention and conflict management capabilities at considerable distances.

Events have also challenged comfortable assumptions. The Gulf War shattered the belief in the notion that all conflicts could be resolved through peaceful or "civilian" means. The Balkan conflicts destroyed the notion that war had been banned from the European continent. And the attacks of September 11 and their aftermath underscored that the German homeland remains directly threatened, but that these threats are of a new kind.

The greatest potential threat Germany faces today remains nuclear missiles launched from a prominent nation. But that threat has receded. Germany's more likely threats are biological weapons in the mail or a spray can, chemical weapons in a ventilation system or a subway, or nuclear or radiological weapons in the back of a truck or the hold of a ship, delivered by a group—or a person— with no return address. The threat of terrorism and the threat of weapons of mass destruction are now joined. Together, they are our worst nightmare. And events near the Khyber Pass between Pakistan and Afghanistan may now be more central to German security than those near the Fulda Gap in Germany.

These new threats require serious adjustments in German force posture and capabilities. The continuing legacy of the Bonn Republic and its focus on a land war in Europe means that the German armed forces remain the least deployable and projectable of NATO's leading powers. The shift toward more mobile, projectable forces poses greater challenges to Germany than to any of the major European allies. Reforms have been sluggish and uneven. The Bundeswehr is being reduced and reoriented to new missions outside of Germany, but a considerable gap remains between the Bundeswehr's capabilities and the threats it faces.

Germany's forthright response to September 11 means that German support for collective military action in out-of-area operations may no longer be a question of whether but when, where, and how. Germany is clearly shifting from being an importer to an exporter of security. This has also had an important domestic impact in the sense that the German public strongly believes the German military, in the words of one senior official, "is finally on the right side." That means growing public support for the notion that the Bundeswehr's mission is not just to defend German soil but also to defend others and to contribute to crisis management outside the NATO area.

As a result, the red-green coalition has pushed Germany's global military role further than any of its predecessors. More than 10,000

German troops are engaged in Afghanistan, the Balkans, and the Horn of Africa. In fact, Germany is second only to the United States in the number of troops deployed on such missions abroad. Berlin's willingness to assume joint command with the Netherlands of ISAF in Afghanistan was coupled with its insistence that NATO play an integral role. This is a significant departure from the Bonn Republic, when most politicians questioned both the constitutionality of sending German troops abroad and the notion that NATO should ever go "out of area."

Unfortunately, the defense budget has failed to keep pace with these new commitments. As a consequence, German forces are stretched to the max, but are ill-equipped and ill-prepared for their new missions. This high operations tempo is likely to increase once the European Security and Defense Policy (ESDP) and the NATO Response Force are activated. It will take time before the serious deficiencies in military capabilities that characterize Germany's possible role beyond NATO's borders will be overcome. If defense spending is not soon aligned with defense commitments, something is likely to snap.

In this context I must disagree with Klose's interpretation of American motives and perceptions regarding European security and defense policy. "There is a suspicion in America," writes Klose, "that Europe's attempts to gain greater foreign policy responsibility and military independence are in reality an attempt by the Europeans to defy American power and question America's leading role in NATO." I believe this to be a misreading of American views. Seen from this side of the Atlantic, the danger is not that the Europeans succeed, it is that European capabilities fail to keep pace with European rhetoric, which could lead them into some ill-considered adventures from which their American partner would have to bail them out. European Commissioner Christopher Patten is more on target:

> The United States does not so much fear the success of a European Security and Defense Policy as the possibility that we will fail to deliver. For our American friends, who have long pressed us to do more, the worst of worlds would be one in which our rhetoric excited expectations that we failed to match. That would encourage the unilateralists in Washington. So it is in everyone's advantage to ensure that our common policy works.[4]

4. Speech by Christopher Patten, Member of the European Commission at Berlin, 16 December 1999, "The Future of the European Security and Defense Policy (ESDP) and the role of the European Commission," *Internationale Politik Transatlantic Edition* 1 (2000).

The 2002 NATO-EU agreements on ESDP and NATO's proposed Response Force are both important signals that Washington is encouraging European force transformation.

The Berlin Republic is weighty enough today so that Germany's ability to transform its military has become an important bellwether of overall European will and commitment to military transformation. Smaller allies are happy to hide behind Germany, asking why they should engage in difficult and controversial reforms if Europe's central power does not. If Germany can help forge a new European consensus to enhance European defense cohesion based on greater capability to project force, it will be easier for Americans to deal with Europe as a global partner. If the Bundeswehr does not keep pace on reform, neither NATO nor the EU will meet their respective goals. Without faster and further transformation of European forces, our militaries will lose the ability to fight together. This would only reinforce Europe's relatively weak capacity to project power, exacerbate the very American unilateralism Europeans find so unsettling, and decouple the mission of the U.S. military in Germany from that of the Bundeswehr.

On September 11 a line was crossed for which even European experience with Baader Meinhof in Germany, Basques in Spain, or the Irish Republican Army in Ireland does not prepare us. Those terrorist groups typically executed limited attacks so as not to undermine political and financial support for their causes. Today's terrorists have no such qualms. Their capacity to kill is limited only by the power of their weapons. Their goal is not to win minds; it is to destroy societies. They have brutalized us into an age of catastrophic terrorism, and America and Europe are equally threatened. Al-Qaeda not only used Germany as a planning base, it plotted major operations for Germany, France, and Italy. One of the terrorists who crashed into the World Trade Center once flew a precise flight plan over unprotected nuclear installations and key political and economic institutions along the Rhine and the Ruhr rivers.

In the face of nuclear terrorism, non-nuclear Germany is defenseless on its own. Only through NATO and the nuclear link to the United States does Germany have access to any element of deterrence. NATO thus remains existential for Germany, but in this new world classical deterrence no longer applies. For thirty years two superpowers preserved stability despite their animosity because they felt equally at risk, they shared the view that the prospect of suicide would deter anyone from actually using weapons of mass destruction, and they were willing to negotiate certain rules of the road together and with other nations. Today, all three premises have vanished. Other nuclear powers have emerged—and the rules of their road are unclear. Terrorists are not deterred by suicide, and they are not at the negotiating table. They have nothing to protect and nothing to lose. In short, Cold War deterrence will not work as it once did, and in some cases it will not work at all.

A new agenda is calling that includes deterrence but that also must include more serious attention to defenses, active efforts at prevention, and an integrated approach to "homeland security," as it is being called in the United States. This is a fully integrated effort at domestic readiness that puts as much emphasis on law enforcement, public health, and hospital preparedness as on disaster scene rescue capabilities. Such an effort is necessary regardless of whether terrorists ever brew nerve agents or master the microbe, since industrial chemicals are pervasive in modern society and pathogens can jump continents overnight.

The U.S. response to the dangers of today is likely to be a grand national project on the order of the Apollo project that sent a man to the moon. What is the German response? Are authorities in Germany and Europe prepared to cope with a cyber attack on air traffic control systems in Frankfurt as scores of commercial aircraft are trying to land in morning rain and fog? How about an aircraft taking off from Paris and crashing into the Deutsche Bank tower in Frankfurt? In Europe there is a need for integrated response plans that can rush capabilities from one country to another, and deal with any kind of outbreak of human and agricultural disease. EU efforts since September 11, such as a common EU arrest warrant, while useful, remain limited. And it is an open question whether Germany and its EU partners are prepared to make the tough choices required by European Commission President Romano Prodi's call for the creation of an integrated European force to combat terrorism and organized crime.

"Strategic Multilateralism" in an Era of Globalization

Military change is but one element of the Berlin Republic's shift from being an importer to an exporter of stability—crisis prevention, development assistance, and other attributes of policy are also involved. The events of September 11 have widened Germany's horizons beyond Europe. The Bonn Republic very much focused on Europe as almost the exclusive frame for German foreign policy. "Europe is our focal point," Klose confirms. This European agenda will, of course, remain central to the Berlin Republic's foreign policy. But increasingly a new agenda is imposing itself.

That agenda is globalization, and it poses considerable challenges for the Berlin Republic and for transatlantic partnership. The September 11 attacks brutally clarified an emerging reality: the daily agenda of transatlantic relations today is less about what Americans do for Europeans in Europe and more about what Europeans and Americans are prepared to do together in the wider world, to meet a range of challenges no single nation can meet alone. The greatest security threats to the United States and Europe today stem from problems that defy borders: terrorism and the proliferation of weapons of mass destruction or environmental degradation and pandemics such as HIV/AIDS. The threats stem from challenges that have previously been marginal but increasingly contentious in the transatlantic security dialogue: "out-of-area" peacekeeping; post-conflict reconstruction and rehabilitation; rogue states, failed states, and states hijacked by groups or networks. And they come from places that, for the most part, the transatlantic agenda has largely ignored: Africa, the Caucasus, South and Central Asia.

When Europe and America agree, our partnership drives progress on almost every world-scale issue. When we disagree, we are the global brake. Are we prepared to devise transatlantic answers to global challenges? Will Americans have either the patience or the inclination to assemble—and be part of—multilateral coalitions in response to globalization's challenges? Will Europeans have either the capacity or the will to generate the coherence of action that will be required? Or are we more likely to drift toward some ill-defined division of labor that would pull Europeans and Americans in different ways?

These are open questions that will test leadership on both sides of the Atlantic. Foreign Minister Fischer has urged the EU to turn "from a western European Union into a Union for the whole of Europe capable of global action." But many Germans and their European neighbors still argue that the challenge of a global partnership is too much too soon for a Europe overwhelmed by its agenda at home. Others will argue that the best way to enhance European cohesiveness and influence is not through closer Atlantic partnership but through greater European independence.

Both of these arguments only feed American unilateralism. Americans are unlikely to change their ways unless their European partners do as well. The danger is that each side points to the other to justify why it is not they but others who have to change. The real imbalance in the transatlantic partnership is not that there is too much America, it is that there is too little Europe.

German foreign policy leaders understand this, and have begun more energetically to shape multilateral efforts in ways they would have been unwilling or unable to do during the days of the Bonn Republic. Berlin is committed to multilateralism, but the nature of its multilateralist engagement is changing. In the past, multilateralism allowed Bonn to compensate for its partial sovereignty. At times German officials used it to assert their interests; at other times they used it to avoid decisions. They used multilateralist structures to hedge bets or maximize options within a broad framework; they could do little to alter the framework itself. Today's officials are also reflexively multilateralist. They know that solo German adventures have reaped disaster and cooperation and integration have brought extraordinary success. But they are less reticent in employing the Berlin Republic's *Gestaltungsmacht*. The commitment to multilateralism is viewed increasingly less through its old function—as a comfortable and convenient framework in which to embed German power and manage Germany's rehabilitation—and more as a means for Germany to project stability beyond Europe onto the global stage.[5]

In private conversations German officials have begun to use the term "strategic multilateralism" to describe their more assertive approach. They argue that greatness is measured today not so much by raw power as by the capacity for influence, that it is more important to convince than to threaten, more important to bind than to rule, and more important to win partners than to confront opponents.

In this globalizing world, senior German officials are trying to take these principles and project them onto a broader stage. This means protecting and expanding the zone of democratic peace, bolstering and where possible integrating new democracies into this democratic community, and promoting global governance where possible by rule of law. Outside the zone of democratic peace it means supporting nation building, treating failed states, engaging rather than isolating rogue states, and being prepared, if necessary, to use force in the service of international order.

5. Rainer Baumann documents the changing argumentation for multilateralism in his article "The Transformation of German Multilateralism: Changes in the Foreign Policy Discourse since Unification," *German Politics and Society* 20, no. 4 (winter 2002).

"Strategic multilateralism" means being less troubled about asserting national interests and advancing German influence within multilateral frameworks. It also has meant a nuanced change in the use of the word "responsibility." During the Bonn Republic, the term was used to convey responsibility for Germany's history, for overcoming the division of Europe, or for broad themes such as peace and freedom. Now, as Rainer Baumann has documented, the call for greater responsibility and the reference to Germany's global responsibility based on its greater "weight" is dominant. "Taking over responsibility" now usually denotes greater German political influence or more German military capacities and the willingness to use them.... Responsibility and power are no longer seen as opposite poles. In fact, "assuming responsibility" has become a synonym of "exerting influence" or of "participating in military operations"; thus, its meaning has become pretty close to "using power."[6]

Berlin has an opportunity to put "strategic multilateralism" into practice through Germany's tenure on the UN Security Council that began January 2003. This also gives Germany a major vote on any decision to confront Iraq, and the government quickly began a nuanced effort to bring the country back in line with its allies' views.

Conclusion: Can Germany Go Global?

In ways perhaps not yet fully understood, the events of September 11 have become a defining moment for German foreign policy. Led by Chancellor Schröder and Foreign Minister Fischer, German foreign policy elites are advancing a more activist but uneven agenda. The tremendous social and economic challenges resulting from unification delayed a good deal of these adjustments. But changes are now discernible. The Berlin Republic is emerging slowly from the Bonn Republic's cocoon. While mindful of history and genuinely proud of the achievements of the Bonn Republic, German leaders are increasingly willing to see their country as an active shaper of events in Europe and beyond.

6. See Bauman, *German Politics and Society*, and also Rainer Baumann and Gunther Hellmann, "Germany and the Use of Military Force: 'Total War,' the 'Culture of Restraint,' and the Quest for Normality," in *German Politics*, no. 1 (2001): 61–82; Gunther Hellmann, "Der 'deutsche Weg.' Eine außenpolitische Gratwanderung," in *Internationale Politik* 57, no. 9 (2002).

Schröder and Fischer have moved the country toward a fuller sense of its responsibilities while being careful neither to awaken excessive fears among Germany's neighbors nor to get too far in front of German public opinion. Changes have been gradual, step-by-step, cautious, and sensitive to the sensibilities of Germany's neighbors. They have been framed meticulously within the familiar language of European integration and international multilateralism—for which there remains domestic consensus across the entire political spectrum—while infusing those terms with new meaning. The question now is the degree to which the emergence of a more global German foreign policy might be limited by four other legacies of the Bonn Republic. First is the relatively weak educational and training opportunities available in Germany to prepare a new generation for globalization. There is a growing mismatch between how leaders and specialists are trained and organized to manage international affairs, and what skills will be required to meet twenty-first century challenges. The dense network of German specialists and experts on European issues contrasts sharply with rather thin resources on other world regions—not only Asia, Africa, or Latin America, but even the United States. As various studies have shown, despite widespread public perception that "Germans know America," serious scholars or experts in American Studies are relatively rare, especially those with a solid grasp of U.S. domestic policies or the influence of America's domestic setting on U.S. foreign policy. Concern about Germany's gaps in these areas has even led prominent German opinion leaders to issue the "Stuttgart Appeal" for greater international educational opportunities.

Second, a more activist agenda could also be frustrated by the distinctive domestic institutional arrangements established during the Bonn Republic, which are not well suited to the task of responding to or effecting quick or dramatic changes. Germany's dense institutional networks, corporatist business behavior, and consensual style of politics promote experimentation *within* institutions rather than broad changes *of* them. The need to harmonize European positions adds another buffering layer. Such a system tends to absorb incremental changes but to blunt demands for sweeping transformation.

For Americans accustomed to measuring change in more fundamental ways, it is sometimes hard to understand how Germans manage change. This is compounded by constant German reassurances that nothing is in fact changing. The German foreign policy establishment, ever mindful of history, is so adamant about reiterating the mantra of continuity every time the topic of German foreign policy comes up that it is hard to have an open discussion of the changes buffeting Germany and Europe. This is further exacerbated by use of the term "normalization." In his article, Hans-Ulrich Klose goes to great lengths to emphasize continuity, quoting the former German ambassador to the UN, Hans Arnold: "Germany will be able to satisfy its interests not by seeking an ominous new normality but only by accepting the reality of a European Germany." In the Bonn Republic that was the German stance and perception. It remains unchanged in the Berlin Republic. I agree that the term "normalcy" is not very helpful. Whose normality? Normal like France and Great Britain? Or normal like Switzerland? If you have to ask if you are normal, you already have the answer. Moreover, left-leaning political circles in Germany have equated "normalization" with "militarization," so that open discussion is skewed from the beginning. And yet German foreign policy is changing. Germany's political leaders are using familiar and reassuring terms from the Bonn Republic such as "multilateralism" and "responsibility" and infusing them with new meaning. As Baumann demonstrates, "this enables the speakers to place themselves in the valued and established tradition of German foreign policy while reinterpreting this tradition for their own purposes."[7]

Third, the sputtering German economy is a tremendous drag on the Berlin Republic's ability to step up to new responsibilities. If Germany proves unable to tackle its serious structural rigidities, then the economy that was the *Wunder* of the Bonn Republic may turn out to be the Achilles Heel of the Berlin Republic, not only robbing united Germany of its potential but dragging a good deal of Europe down with it.

Finally, the German strategic community is small, and serious strategic debate is notable by its relative absence. Only a handful of German parliamentarians see their political future in foreign or defense policy. The contrast with Germany's global business elites is striking. Germany must address the relative lack of experienced German civil servants with global experience who are prepared to assume the most senior slots in international organizations. Germany remains underrepresented in such bodies.

September 11 did not herald a completely new world. But it may have destroyed under a million tons of steel and glass the

7. Baumann, *German Politics and Society.*

complacency with which Americans and Europeans were confronting the world of September 10. Seen in this way, the campaign against terrorism is about far more than hunting down terrorists. It is about the obligation we have to recast our partnership to confront new challenges no longer bound by the Cold War or the problems of the European continent alone. This new world is transforming Germany's choices and its challenges. The Berlin Republic is starting to take on these challenges; changes are palpable. But it is an open question whether those changes can keep pace with a world in fast-forward.

6. Germany's Role in a Global Economy

Ditmar Staffelt

Intensifying competition on commodities and services markets, falling transaction costs, and disappearing market segmentation are all evidence that globalization is the characteristic feature of the world economy today. Globalization means greater efficiency and, consequently, higher prosperity. What are its effects? Does increasing integration of the international economy restrain a country's ability to influence its own economic development? Is the political community deprived of its role, and do powerful corporate groups decide on a country's economic wealth? What impact have the dramatic changes of past decades had: the collapse of the communist regimes in the East and the EU's willingness to accept the accession of many of these countries; the new economy and the associated technological progress; new challenges caused by demographic changes in many European countries and Japan? The better a country's competitive position is, the larger the potential is for resolving these issues vital to the future. A simple correlation exists between a country's international competitive strength and a society's well-being that is becoming ever more important in the globalization age: the greater the economy's competitive capacity, the greater the possibility of benefiting from globally expanding trade and investment and hence of generating wealth. This chapter focuses on Germany's international competitiveness and the political foundation that must be laid to improve it.

Germany's Attractiveness as a Business Location

Germany is one of the world's economically most powerful industrial nations. In 2001, the country's real GDP was €1,980 billion, and its per-capita output €24,000. Traditionally, Germany has been second only to the United States as an export nation worldwide. In 2001 the trade surplus reached a record high of €87.1 billion. At nearly €200 billion, foreign investment in Germany in 2000 was nearly ten times greater than in 1998. Even if a major corporate takeover is not included in the calculation, the figures show an upward trend from 1999 to 2000. These simple data make it clear that Germany continues to be extremely attractive as a competitive location for economic activity. Even if lobbyists from one or the other camp attempt to paint a gloomy picture, it does not alter the facts. Thus, this analysis begins with a description of Germany's advantages as a competitive business location. The following are the most important features:

1. The educational level of Germany's labor force is very high by international standards. This advantage cannot be rated strongly enough, especially in view of the technological development that results in knowledge becoming an increasingly crucial factor in competition, and in the face of globalization that causes intensified competition for highly skilled manpower. The dual system of vocational training is internationally praised as a model worthy of imitation. It is therefore not surprising that only a few countries can boast even lower youth unemployment levels than are seen in the Federal Republic. Moreover, far-reaching advanced employee training programs enhance the country's international competitiveness. For the first time in quite a few years, since 2001 unemployment in Germany has remained below the EU average.

2. The rise in unit labor costs, which reflects a company's price competitiveness, is moderate in Germany. In the past few years, the country has recorded the smallest increase in unit labor costs in the EU. This is a result of a reasonable compensation policy and of productivity increases triggered by innovative enterprise activity. By international standards, the German wage system stands out for its moderate compensation policy and simultaneously a high degree of worker satisfaction. Only Switzerland, Austria, and Japan recorded less working hours lost due to strike activities.

3. Germany has an excellent supply and transport infrastructure and a reliable legal system. Due to its modern telecommunications infrastructure, it is a leader of the information age, particularly in Europe. Competition policy prevents unfair

competition, and intellectual property rights are suitably protected by international standards. Moreover, the country's economic structure features many strong growth development areas instead of a single, often excessively costly, core, as is the case in many other countries. Such institutional and political factors, and Germany's geographical position in the center of Europe, are frequently cited as decisive in terms of investment.

4. Despite some detractors, Germany has succeeded over the past few years in expanding its export activity and attracting direct investment, evidence of the German economy's excellent competitiveness. Exports can only be marketed if the goods and services offered are of better quality than those of other suppliers, and investments can only be attracted if investors anticipate higher returns than in other regions. With its 9 percent world market share, Germany is the world's second largest export nation; on a per-capita basis, the country sells a larger volume of goods and services on international markets than the United States. In 2001, its export volume grew 4.7 percent, while growth recorded in the Eurozone as a whole was only 2.5 percent, and the export volume of the United States and Japan even declined. Germany made further gains by recording the highest volume of direct investment by European standards. According to a recent survey, investors rank Germany third in Europe. Contrary to the general tendency, investment had grown from earlier.

These facts show that Germany's enormous attractiveness as a business location is by no means a thing of the past but rather of considerable immediate interest. Traditional advantages such as a high degree of social peace and solid infrastructure are accompanied by favorable conditions for foreign investors. In a recent comparative study on the international competitiveness of countries, the International Institute for Management Development of Lausanne, Switzerland, states that Germany, apart from the United States, is ahead of the other large industrial countries. This is particularly noteworthy because such extraordinary success was achieved despite the significant economic burdens associated with eastern Germany's adjustment from a centrally planned economy to a market economy. The financial assistance the West granted the East was considered necessary. Few other countries could cope with the effects of such a restructuring process that in Germany's case resulted from a major collapse in industry in its new federal states. The trend in construction has put additional constraints on the country. This sector is undergoing a painful adjustment process as a result of misdirected public assistance in the early 1990s that inflated the sector.

New Framework Conditions for External Economic Relations

The impact of external economic circumstances on economic developments is likely to increase further as globalization progresses. The most important change, already apparent, is the enlargement of the EU to the east, which offers enormous opportunities for Germany as the most important country bordering the acceding nations. Furthermore, Germany's reunification has led to an expansion of its political responsibility for world economic trends. This leads to the expectation, not only in the EU but also in other parts of the world, that Germany contribute increasingly to the multilateral debate. Globalization is, after all, strengthening the bonds between trading partners, and mainly with the United States. Despite the growing importance of external economic aspects, however, globalization does not mean that national economic policy is redundant. The ingenuity of policy makers will still be needed in the future.

With the integration of the neighboring Eastern states into the European Union the unique success story of Europe uniting politically and economically continues. The integration of the acceding countries into the EU makes it the world's largest internal market with a population of roughly 550 million. In the wake of the EU's enlargement to the East, Germany will become the major hub between East and West more than ever. Comprising approximately 40 percent of the EU's total trade with the acceding countries, Germany is already the most important trading partner for many countries, including the three largest transition ones: Poland, the Czech Republic, and Hungary. German investors also hold a leading international position as regards direct investment in the acceding countries. German exports to the acceding countries in 2001 amounted to more than €60 billion, and the volume has risen steadily, tripling since 1993. This figure alone shows the benefits to German industry of the EU's enlargement to the east. The border regions will gain particularly over the medium term. Increasing competition will without a doubt require adjustments. But the transition to a larger EU will by no means be abrupt. From an economic point of view, the enlargement of the Union to the East began in the mid-1990s with the association agreements that in many cases led to trade liberalization. Moreover, the political approach to the accession negotiations takes into account some more sensitive aspects. An arrangement has been found, for example, that provides for a flexible restriction of the right to the free movement of labor regarding manpower from the new member states. A seven-year transition period has been agreed upon. This is in the interest of planning certainty and helps to gain time for the necessary restructuring.

Even before the Union is enlarged the global importance of the European partners is great, evident by the EU's considerably politically important arguments in favor of a new World Trade Organization (WTO) round. For especially in the wake of the world economy's downward trend and the events of September 11, 2001, the situation of some of the developing countries has tended to deteriorate. In the face of globalization and in the interest of fighting international terrorism, however, equitable framework conditions for the developing countries are essential to their future economic development. Studies prepared by the World Bank demonstrate that a number of developing countries have been able to increase their share in world trade on a sustainable basis. This is true above all for those countries that have succeeded in attracting foreign direct investment and opening their markets. They are among the twenty-four newly industrializing and developing countries with a population of about three billion people that have benefited from globalization. Growing integration into international merchandise trade is the most promising way of bringing greater prosperity to other countries. That is why the new round of trade talks is geared to generating advantages above all for the developing countries, for instance through the advanced liberalization of agricultural trade and the opening of further markets for textiles in the industrial countries. This is extremely important to the developing countries because 70 percent of their exports consist of farm products and textiles.

Another major issue is the links between the German and U.S. economies. Slow growth in the world economy and the downward trend in the United States have also impacted Germany. The slower pace of the U.S. economy has slowed in particular owing to Germany's substantial exports of capital goods. The United States is one of Germany's most important trading partners. In 2001 imports from that country accounted for 8.3 percent of all imports, and exports amounted to 10.6 percent of all exports; in other words the amount included goods worth €67.3 billion. The close interdependence of the two countries' economies is also reflected in capital flows: the United States is by far Germany's most important foreign investor. Direct investment, mainly generated by subsidiaries of German companies in the United States and of American companies in Germany, is causing cyclical trends to be passed on more quickly and to a greater extent than in the past. Moreover, the new channels of influence include stock markets and the business atmosphere in general—for an economy with a strong international orientation, this is also an effect of globalization. A rapid recovery of the U.S. economy is thus also of great importance to Germany. This is, of course, true for the EU as a whole, but particularly for Germany because of the aforementioned factors.

The Political Course toward Greater Prosperity

A relapse into a protectionist policy would be destructive in view of the opportunities that globalization offers. For a policy aimed at erecting barriers between markets—at national isolation—cannot produce optimum results where a significant interdependence exists between different economic areas. As mentioned earlier this is particularly true of a country as economically liberal as Germany. There is no doubt that globalization also causes fear. Politically, such fears could reinforce support for the extreme right in Europe. The consequence could well be a dangerous xenophobia and a trend toward renationalization, which would jeopardize integration and its chances in Europe. All democrats are called upon to stave off such tendencies, point repeatedly to the positive potential that globalization offers, and of course stress that it is a question of the appropriate form of globalization. The freedom of markets is at stake, and this can hardly be separated from the freedom of the people and the joint responsibility for the development of the world as a whole. In the international context it is important, as envisaged in the recent world trade round, to integrate an even larger number of people into the world economy, thus making it possible for them to make use of the opportunity to boost prosperity. In a more internal context it is important to enhance partnership with other regions of the world, mainly within the framework of the EU. It is an important goal, therefore, to strengthen coherence within the EU by means of appropriate reforms and to prepare the EU for future challenges.

One would be well advised to start with changes at home because there they are not only immediately perceptible but could be exemplary and thus enhance credibility in the case of requests put to third parties. Germany's political concept is the sustainability strategy, referring not only to the ecological aspect but specifically to equally important economic and social sustainability. This is based on the awareness that for a policy to be lastingly successful and to increase a country's competitiveness, it must be geared toward long-term objectives. Important parameters have been set for this in the past few years.

The policy makers' achievements include, for instance, market liberalization in network economies. The reform of energy industry legislation and the liberalization of the postal and telecommunications sector have exposed large formerly monopolized markets to competition. In these sectors the state once more gave private initiative precedence over state powers. Growth and economic wealth are generated above all where functioning competition and favorable conditions for private entrepreneurship create an appropriate environment. Declining electricity prices not only relieve the strains on industry and small and midsize enterprises, thus fostering the competitive position of German industry; households also benefit. As a result of the abolishment of the Rebates Act and the Ordinance on Premiums, German enterprises in the electronics trade are on an equal footing with foreign competitors. Indeed, this step was in the interest of ensuring fair competition and new leeway for German industry. Moreover, it is a step toward the simplification of administrative procedures.

Ever shorter product cycles require a highly skilled and creative labor force and bold entrepreneurs not only to keep pace but also to assume a leading role in international competition. This is the only way of securing viable jobs in the long term. Innovation therefore is a core element of economic policy. Among the large European countries Germany has the highest density of innovative businesses. In automobile construction, mechanical engineering, and environmental technology Germany holds a leading position on world markets. From 1997 to 2001, about 92,000 additional jobs were created in industries with a high degree of investment in research and development. There are about 40,000 technology-oriented business startups in Germany every year. The German government supports this dynamic process through a variety of programs and provides venture capital, for example, for small technology enterprises. A comprehensive assistance program is available to potential startup entrepreneurs that comprises innovation-supporting structures in institutions of higher education, assistance in the phase preceding the startup, and financing aid for the project in question. Attention is given in particular to sectors involving special potential for the future, such as biotechnology and multimedia. The development of the telecommunications market is an example of the success of new technologies. Consumers and companies may choose from among 180 providers; the cost of long-distance calls has dropped 90 percent since the opening of the market. It does not come as a surprise, therefore, that the information and telecommunications sectors are recording rather dynamic developments: between 1991 and 2001 the number of suppliers of telecommunication services rose from about 150 to roughly 2,000. In the same period, the market expanded more than twofold reaching an overall volume of approximately €66 billion. Roughly 830,000 people are employed in the information and communications industries. Actively shaping the information society is a key objective of the German government, which is why it developed and implemented a program entitled "Innovation and Jobs in the Information Society of the 21st Century."

A forward-looking business location must also offer attractive tax laws. The volume of debts accumulated in the past means that the present generation is living at the expense of future generations. This is not in line with the sustainability concept. Almost every fourth euro of tax revenue has had to be spent on interest payments. There has been no room left for a creative economic policy, and growth prospects have been subject to intolerable constraints. Budget consolidation, therefore, was one of the red-green government's first major reform projects. Net government borrowing in the 2002 budget was down to roughly €21 billion, while it had been almost €29 billion in 1998. This means that for the third successive year it was lower than the level of the previous year. In addition, tax-related conditions for investments have substantially improved in Germany, and have been hailed by all experts—the Council of Economic Advisors, research institutions, the Organization for Economic Cooperation and Development (OECD), and the International Monetary Fund (IMF). The workforce, families, and companies are benefiting from substantial relief measures. In 2002 the volume of relief totaled €26.2 billion as compared to 1998; as of 2005 the volume of total relief agreed on thus far will be an annual €56 billion as compared to 1998. In the course of the corporate tax reform that also became effective in 2001, the corporate income tax rate was reduced to a uniform 25 percent. All of these figures show that Germany's competitiveness has again improved, one of the reasons being that the tax reforms have taken account of the social aspect in addition to the efficiency aspect. With its bold tax relief effort Germany holds a top rank by international standards and does justice to its role in contributing toward enhancing growth capacity. By taking such measures, policy makers promote Germany as a competitive business location without losing sight of the goal of sound public finance or neglecting necessary investments. Plans exist to eliminate the public sector deficit almost entirely by 2004. Germany explicitly recognizes the need for the European stability and growth pact. One of the aspects of the sustainability concept is that consolidation must not become an end in itself but must create leeway for government action such as tax relief and investment in forward-looking areas. Interest savings from Universal Mobile Telecommunication System (UMTS) proceeds, for example, are used to invest in the future. Priorities have been set mainly in the educational and research sectors, in rebuilding eastern Germany, in expanding transport infrastructure, and in family policy.

The Future of the German Economic Model

Germany's economic structure is characterized specifically by small and midsize business. This sector comprises 3.3 million enterprises providing more than 20 million jobs; it makes available just under 1.3 million training slots, and receives 46 percent of gross investment. Small business policy is thus an important buttress of economic policy. A broad-based initiative is helping to foster a culture of self-employment. It includes a school-based project entitled "Junior" in the framework of which students rehearse entrepreneurial behavior. The initiative also includes government support through counseling and training for self-employment, and a campaign aimed at assisting businesspeople in passing on their businesses to qualified leaderships. With a view to providing an important foundation for future self-employment to university students, the German government, together with partners from industry, established university chairs for startup studies. There are forty-two throughout the country. For example, he amended Meister-BAföG (Upgrading Training Assistance Act), which offers good prospects for startup entrepreneurs and paves the way for crafts workers seeking self-employment. The German government has committed itself to reducing administrative procedures. Excessive red tape often impedes individual initiative and leads potential startup entrepreneurs to shrink from their projects.

As the question of financing is frequently a crucial issue for small businesses, the government advocates taking account of the special borrowing features of small and midsize enterprises in the Basel II negotiations regarding the reform of capital adequacy. Export credit guarantees, such as Hermes guarantees from the German Export Credit Agency (ECA), are available for exports to risk-prone markets to provide cover against possible non-payment due to economic or political reasons. Further examples of an active small business policy are the specific promotion of information and communication technology through centers of expertise or the introduction of reinvestment reserves. The political community also considers itself to be a partner of industry in its external economic activities: projects such as the jointly established "ixpos" portal on the Internet or complementary political measures for projects implemented by German companies abroad are by no means directed exclusively at large-scale enterprises, but also at the small business sector. Professionally prepared information about foreign markets may be obtained from the Federal Office of Foreign Trade Information. Small and midsize enterprises are especially to benefit from federal government assistance in organizing events to exchange information and establish contacts with foreign companies; many small businesses welcome in particular financial aid that enables them to participate in fairs and exhibitions abroad. Contacts established today will pave the way for industry's success tomorrow. All in all it is no surprise that the promotion of external economic relations is an important element in German industry's successful export activities.

The term "German model," however, refers not only to the economic structure but also, above all, to social legislation as an essential element of the social-market economy system. In Germany, achievements in the social field have contributed to success in the economic field. And yet the welfare state, too, must be adapted to the requirements of our time. Sustained economic success will only be ensured if taxes and fees are kept from rising incalculably. Globalization also implies a competition of systems, favoring those that succeed in attracting sought-after production factors such as capital and highly skilled labor. An international competition now exists for these mobile factors that Germany cannot escape. It is important, especially in the face of the anticipated demographic changes, to take early precautions against the lack of skilled labor that is beginning to emerge. Competition of systems, of course, does not mean that the U.S. economic model alone would survive in global competition and the entire world economy would have to be tailored to this model. The social-market economy cannot be a matter for negotiation. Codetermination rights, free collective bargaining, and a social safety net for emergencies are vital elements for far-reaching social peace in Germany. This is not only reflected in cost savings and, as a result, constitutes an argument in favor of investing in Germany, but it also helps guarantee a high quality of life. In fact, social stability in Germany is not least a result of its social-market economy.

What Should Be Done in Future?

To maintain the present importance of Germany as a competitive business location and, furthermore, to approach the relevant reforms with determination, the country needs a broad social consensus, dedicated citizens, and enterprises as well as trade associations and unions that also keep an eye on the economy as a whole. And finally, Germany needs bold economic policy makers who fulfill their responsibilities at the regional, national, and global level. In fact, Germany has these necessary prerequisites.

In concluding, the reform projects on the national agenda should be briefly mentioned. For one thing, labor market reforms are required to eliminate the mismatch between job seekers and vacancies. Even though the German labor market is more flexible than is presumed, attempts are being made to enhance its capabilities, including improving the efficiency of job placement. In order to emphasize the principle of "assist and challenge" more strongly, Germany plans to pursue a labor market policy that triggers greater motivation. Various programs are to provide more freedom for individuals to take their own decisions and at the same time to demand that they take on responsibility on a larger scale. Some pilot projects are being implemented to test the merging of the unemployment support system and welfare benefits. Another pilot project is intended to support the low-wage sector where social security contributions of low-wage earners are subsidized. In 2003 and 2005 the next stages of the tax reform will become effective. Additional concrete plans for the near future relate to the reform of municipal taxes. The economic policy agenda also lists the further development of the healthcare system that, just as the pension system, is facing the problem of rising expenditure; due to the present system, healthcare also faces the problem of rising wage costs, which is linked to demographic changes and the costs of progress in medical science. The forward-looking and vitally important education sector must be continuously monitored: schools, universities, and advanced training institutions lay the foundation for the future of the economy. Education and training must be accorded a top rank at the international level; otherwise the ambitious goal of making the EU's internal market the most competitive and most dynamic knowledge-based economic area of the world will not be attained.

It would no doubt be the wrong approach to rest upon the success achieved so far. According to an old saying, you fall behind if you stop rowing. In the interest of being a competitive business location and at the same time in the interest of the people's prosperity, Germany's successful economic policy of previous years must be continued. Innovative policy aimed at keeping Germany competitive must be farsighted and, much more than in the past, take on international parameters. More than anything else, European integration and transatlantic partnership are the cornerstones of future economic wealth.

7. The Economic and Social Fabric of the Berlin Republic

Jochen Thies

Germany is a consensus society. Harmony is a part of the German soul and identity. There is an aversion to loud public arguments, including in parliament. One thinks of the famous verse in Friedrich Schiller's *Wilhelm Tell*: "Seid einig, einig, einig!" (Be united, be united, be united).

After the experience of a sharp class conflict in the Kaiserreich and after two world wars, the early days of the Federal Republic of Germany featured a kind of model society. This society was deeply influenced by Ludwig Erhardt (minister of economic affairs under Konrad Adenauer and later chancellor), by theoretical contributions from both the conservative and social democratic camps, and by the practical experience and help of the Americans and the British. Enormous economic growth rates over a period of twenty years, the rebuilding of the country, a well-trained and dedicated workforce, and the influx of millions of refugees and foreign workers all made it possible to adhere to this model until the early days of the first oil crisis. Then, for the first time in its postwar history, Germany was confronted with an unemployment problem and uncertainty. Unemployment figures have risen over the years and are now close to 10 percent nationwide, and up to 20 percent in the Eastern states; in certain places in the East, one-third of the population is not part of the workforce. The situation would be even more dramatic if many firms and public institutions had not granted hundreds of thousands of workers an early retirement. In most cases this deal is acceptable for the individual, because one is treated as if one had worked until the age of sixty-five. But the societal loss in terms of knowledge and money is big, and the real costs will surface only later. There is no other country in Western Europe where only one-fifth of the workforce continues on the job past the age of sixty. Eighty percent of the workforce leaves between the ages of fifty-five and sixty, some even earlier. Only a few civil servants, of which there are many in Germany, work up to the normal retirement age of sixty-five.

It is generally agreed that the battle against unemployment is one of Germany's key societal problems, if not its first priority. No political camp dare avoid the issue, and each must express the willpower and the highest hopes to attain full employment in the foreseeable future. Not just the East Germans, with their experiences under a command economy, but the majority of all Germans believes the state more than the market should play a major role in this battle. The consequences of global developments are not well understood. Only a few dare to say that the era of full employment in classical industries is over, and worse, that jobs are disappearing. This kind of debate about the future of employment is not really taking place. Since the days of Otto von Bismarck and the introduction of basic insurance, which reduced the class problem, the Germans have a kind of *Versorgungsmentalität*, or a mentality of state-sponsored care.

It is therefore not surprising that Germany is working hard to control the employment situation. Chancellor Gerhard Schröder knows the country will not accept a considerable rise in unemployment, and when he was elected he promised a great deal. Schröder is aware that any government would fall immediately if unemployment figures were to shoot up. During an election year, therefore, typically every public effort is made to create jobs. But the state no longer has the money to spend that it had in the 1970s, when deficit spending was the great hope for overcoming the energy crises. Other efforts, therefore, aim at cleaning up the statistics and reducing the number of those applying for social benefits. Given all the cuts in social spending during the past few years—all the statistical improvements—one can say that Germany as a consensus society endures. Even in difficult times, the country is ready to spend hundreds of billions of euros to help those who have lost their jobs. There is no real dispute over this matter between the Social Democratic Party (SPD) and the Christian Democratic Union/Christian Social Union (CDU/CSU), although from time to time the conservatives speak with a sharp tone. There are probably not too many countries in the world that treat their unemployed as well as

Germany. This explains, by the way, why Germany is more exposed to illegal immigration than most other countries in the European Union. One has also to admit, though, that the basic cost of living in Germany is higher than in many other countries and that the entry level into German society is high. The social fall, however, is steep for those who were once rich and successful. Also, divorces—one in three marriages ends in divorce—are contributing to poor living conditions, particularly for women with young children. On the other hand, an active black market for labor, similar to those in Italy and Mediterranean countries, provides the means to improve the living conditions of many unemployed. This is small comfort for academics or others whose skills are not in demand. The black market is particularly good for skilled laborers.

After two wars and two generations losing nearly everything, in relative terms Germany is rich for the first time. Of course, the country now has problems adjusting to a changed world. The famous Protestant work ethic is no longer valid. Unlike many generations before, Germans no longer define themselves through their job or paid labor. During the last twenty-five years, Germany has become in part a hedonistic society. Work is taken more seriously in France, Italy, or Spain, not to mention countries in Asia. Work hours have decreased from forty-eight hours a week in the early 1950s to thirty-five hours in many sectors today. The average German has between four and six weeks of paid vacation per year; many earn an additional month's salary. In a leisure society, work hours can become a *Nebensache*, or secondary matter. As a result, the famous, established German school and university systems have also suffered. By international standards, German universities offer only an average level of education. Many young academics are attracted to the United States and do not come back after completing their studies. Private schools and universities are an exception in Germany. There is no real competition between universities and their departments. The general expectation is that the state pays; it is easy to get public money for university studies. Many students seek real adventure by traveling far away or by having extravagant hobbies.

During the years following unification the West German economy profited from the new markets in the East and the introduction of the deutsche mark in the former East Germany even before unification took place. The events of these years prevented Germany from making the necessary adjustments to the rise of globalization. In addition, the long reign of Chancellor Helmut Kohl postponed for other reasons the recognition of the need to follow the path of reform, which countries such as the United Kingdom, France, the Netherlands, and even the Scandinavian countries— with their well-established welfare systems—were already taking.

It was therefore not an easy task for a coalition government of the Social Democrats and the Greens, who believe in a strong role of the state, to take over after a long period of conservative rule in Germany and to start real reforms. Within the first three years, the country's major problems were tackled, but when resistance grew in the rank and file of the labor unions, the Schröder government noticeably reduced the speed of reform. External pressure is not strong enough to convince the country to switch to a higher gear. The hard reality is that Germany is not doing enough to deregulate the labor market, currently the country's biggest problem.

Furthermore, the Germans still think in terms of the nineteenth century—the age of coal and iron. For many of them, the new world of the service industry, the third sector of an economy, is a strange one. Germans hate to serve. Many foreigners therefore work in restaurants or in the hotel and tourism industries. In deprived areas people wait for collective solutions, for example in the rustbelt of the Ruhr area. Not too many would dare to search further afield to find new jobs, as is typical for people in the United States. Mobility is not the Germans' strong suit; one reason for this is because many German homeowners have to pay off their homes for most of their lives—another legacy of the Bismarck era, when politicians and steel barons subsidized housing in order to quash revolutionary ideals among the working masses.

A typical example of German society's slow motion is Berlin—not East Germany. Eastern Germany has undergone the greatest change inside the country during the last ten or so years. Only one in ten people is working in his or her old job. Mobility is not a question. Hundreds of thousands work during the week in the West and come home only for the weekend. An endless chain of cars along German motorways on Friday nights moves East and returns to the West on Sunday night. Many young Eastern Germans go to the Western part of Germany because they find no apprenticeship or job at home.

The situation is different in Berlin. The old/new capital is still hurrying to gain more jobs in the third sector than are being lost in the industrial sector. For several years now the battle seems to have been won; but by German standards the speed of change was and still is a dramatic one. Until unification, West Berlin was also Germany's largest industrial city—thanks to federal subsidies that secured one-half of the city budget. When these subsidies suddenly stopped within a very short period of time in the early 1990s, 50 percent of 250,000 jobs in industry were lost. West Berliners lost more than any other population in the old Federal Republic. Their tax reductions and Berlin supplements disappeared overnight. Over the period of a year it meant a net loss of DM 10,000 for every West Berlin household, which may explain the mixed mood in the city between hope and skepticism. Today there are only two large companies in Berlin, the pharmaceutical company Schering and BMW, with its production of motorcycles. The rest of big industry has left as a consequence of first the war, then the Wall, and now unification. The belt around Berlin, in Brandenburg, is slowly developing and should soon reflect the growth of the capital. Berlin also needs a big international airport, probably the only prospect for the creation of many new jobs in the near future. It will take time to convince big publishing houses, private banks, or large law firms to come to Berlin, but the speed of change is increasing. The government's move from Bonn to Berlin in 1999 has had an impact. Berlin is now attracting young and bright people from all over Germany, and they are ready to accept risks. They work without contracts or on very short notice, which is a new phenomenon for Germany. A new kind of society that accepts risks is emerging from the ground up. One generation earlier it was believed natural to stay—as in Japan—in one job or profession for an entire lifetime.

Traditionally, the trade unions have been more concerned about the interests of the employed than the unemployed. A key issue for the unions remains maintaining the same salary system throughout a whole industry and across the country. Reality, however, is different. Many workers would accept lower wages in order to save their firm. And the difficult circumstances in Eastern Germany have led many firms to abandon the collective bargaining agreements in order to pay the salaries they are able to pay. Chancellor Schröder was able to start a program of the Volkswagen Corporation under the rubric "5,000 times 5,000" in his home state of Lower Saxony only with massive intervention. Under this program, 5,000 jobs would be created if the unions accepted a standard salary of (then) DM 5,000 and an extension of the general work hours, so that three shifts would be possible. The unions do not like the plan because Volkswagen's domestic salaries are even higher than the standard salaries in the northern German metal industry. In the end, however, the unions understood the company's needs.

As stated earlier, the kind of class conflicts present in the Kaiserreich and the Weimar Republic no longer exist; this is a competitive
advantage when comparing Germany with other European countries, for example, with Great Britain or France. Since the early days
of the Federal Republic, a consensus model has existed in Germany
between unions, workers, and factory owners. The rebuilding of
the country—referred to as *Stunde Null*, or the "zero hour"—brought
together the capitalist and the worker. And the proprietors who are
leaving office these days—the founding fathers of the postwar German economic miracle, who very often now do not find a successor—are aware of it. Many of them led a rather modest private life.
Many have refused to show how rich they really are. Probably nowhere in the Western world does such a silent understanding exist
between the two sides, the proprietor and the worker, as in Germany. The backbone of the German economy is not the big plant
but the small and midsize firm with up to 1,000 employees. Direct
contact between management and production is therefore possible. Owners very often have a technical understanding of or interest in the work. This understanding is reflected in the country's big
interest groups that meet with the chancellor on a regular basis.
German politicians and union leaders therefore are aware of wage
ceilings and their annual increase. The great advantage of this system is that strikes and labor-union conflicts are extremely rare,
which also explains why Germany is doing rather well on an international level, although work periods there are much shorter than
in many other countries, particularly in the United States and in
Asia. Union membership is decreasing, however, and individualism
is on the rise. This is also evident in the German political system
where the traditional identification with a particular party is fading.

The consensus within German society, and the country's relative
wealth, made it possible for industries that are no longer globally
competitive to be subsidized for decades: for example, the mining
and steel industries in the Ruhr and the Saar River valleys and the
shipyards along the coasts of the North Sea. Although this workforce of industries is no longer as important as it was in the 1950s,
it remains a symbol of the old days of the Social Democrats and
therefore receives subsidies that do not at all reflect the country's
new realities.

In a certain way, therefore, Germany experiences the impact of
globalization in shock waves. One of the most remarkable events was
the Mannesmann Company's unfriendly takeover by Vodafone. For
the first time, the country had to accept that takeovers can happen

from outside and not always from within its borders. For many years Germany observed the decline of famous manufacturers in neighboring countries and German firms set up production in these countries. Famous takeovers took place, such as the deal between BMW and the British car manufacturer Rover. Bertelsmann became one of the world's biggest media giants, penetrating the U.S. market. Now with the single European market and globalization, however, Germany is also exposed to such developments, and an open or hidden inclination to protect the home market is no longer possible. But there are, of course, exceptions. When the Holzmann group in Frankfurt—one of the country's biggest construction firms, operating worldwide—was at risk, just before Christmas 1999, Chancellor Schröder saved several thousand jobs through state guarantees. A small or midsize firm would never get this benefit. Schröder also knows, however, that such a deal cannot happen too often. More and more often rules of intervention come from Brussels; state ministries execute what is prescribed by EU law, and the role of the state in the economy is limited.

Germany therefore has to accept an unknown kind of inequality: the economic recovery of the country's East will take longer. Living conditions in Munich, Upper Bavaria, or Baden-Württemberg, in the booming parts of the country, are much different than in Mecklenburg-Western Pomerania or in Brandenburg, two of the five "new" Eastern Länder of united Germany. Here the outlook is so bad that villages are deserted; towns are losing one-fifth of their population in one decade, and young people are migrating to western Germany. The president of the German parliament, Wolfgang Thierse, is therefore probably right when he warns that the future of the East is at stake. The state must intervene. Otherwise, the imbalance between the country's West and East will grow.

Inequality also comes from another source: for the first time in modern German history a generation of heirs exists. There are many young people in the country who can afford to live on what they have received from their parents. On the one hand, this is a new experience. Yet one can argue that the German society is not prepared for this development. Many in the West and nearly all in the East have to live on what they earn on a monthly basis. Inheritances are so far not highly taxed. Germany's special problem is that because of the Nazi period and destruction of the prewar German society, nonmaterialistic goals are not sufficiently defined. The new generation of the very rich is not active enough in the public domain—neither in politics, nor in science, museums, endowments, or other fields. They just privatize. The media give the impression that every German who can afford it is building a residence in Mallorca, Spain. One can therefore only hope that Berlin is creating a general climate that is leading to a greater commitment of parts of society in public policy.

Moreover, the old German consensus society will break up because of the coming demographic developments. The population is getting much older within a short period of time, and therefore the gap will grow between older, very well-off parts of society and the young, who will certainly neither be in the position nor willing to pay for the pensions of the old. Germany in general is living on borrowed time. The labor market is, as said earlier, a closed shop. Too many are going into retirement too early; the pensions for the large number of civil servants are financed through the annual budgets of the Federal Republic and the Länder, and the financing of medical care will soon also spin out of control. The longer the government waits, the more costly will be the consequences. It will be therefore inevitable to reduce step by step what has been granted in better times in a generous welfare system. In other words: Pensions from public funds will decrease in the near future; medical care will be redefined in terms of what is necessary, and personal arrangements and provisions will be demanded.

Germans probably know this, and the individual understanding of a need for adjustment is much greater than politicians believe. But everybody is waiting for the other's effort. So far nobody in politics is really addressing the problems of a society that may decrease in population from a current 82 million to about 50 million within the next forty years—leaving aside immigration. Even if Germany were to develop into a country of immigration like the United States, however, this would not alter the general trend of a sharply shrinking population.

The outlook concerning the economic and social identity of the Berlin Republic offers many risks and opportunities. One of the first tests is the introduction of the new currency, the euro, that replaced the deutsche mark, the very symbol of German identity between 1949 and 2001. The silent majority of the country would have preferred to stay with the old currency. Now Europe must show whether it is able to replace some of the German identity through a new kind of growing common European identity and responsibility.

Germans must finally realize that they are living in a prosperous country with opportunities no other German generation has enjoyed before. The coming years will already show whether the Germans have learned a lesson from history: not only to define and to fore-see problems in the future but to adjust in time. The country usually waits with reforms until the last moment. Where are the new kind of Prussian reformers? A nice explanation may stem in part from the experience of a generation and a half that has lived without war and with the desire to live as long as possible on the sunny side of life. The stress of unification and the country's new international role will also play a role. A look at Germany's partners and neighbors, which in many cases are old and experienced democracies, should teach the Germans that the right mix between inclinations and obligations is the remedy to secure the future.

8. Cultural Federalism in Germany: The Core of the Political Culture of the Berlin Republic

Julian Nida-Rümelin

Federalism in Germany has a great tradition. It was not invented by the Basic Law. Federal elements can be traced back to 1919 (Weimar constitution), 1871 (Wilhelminian Empire's constitution), 1848 (constitution of the Paulskirche assembly in Frankfurt), through to 1863 (Perpetual Reichstag). This expresses a specific development within the German-speaking cultural space of Central Europe, where competition among peoples, princely families, regions, and local communities was always producing the kind of diversity and multi-polarity incompatible with a centralist, uniform nation-state.

Cultural federalism is at the core of the federalism in the Federal Republic of Germany. The jurisdictions over cultural policy assigned, *ex negativo*, to the Länder by Germany's Basic Law are essential for their identity and legitimization. Germany, to be sure, is not divided up into regions. Germany is not a union of independent Länder. Germany is certainly—for all its federal character—a nation-state. The country is culturally constituted in a way that matches the political constitution applicable to all German citizens. The nation-state's scope for common political action undoubtedly has a cultural dimension.

The common language that has become the constituent element of a German national culture since the late Middle Ages quite substantially determines this cultural dimension. Indeed, the German language forms cultural ties across national boundaries. The common space encompassing German-language literature and

German-speaking operas and theaters embraces several nation-states in Central Europe. Within this space, personal and substantive ties are close, although there is no claim to validate a common cultural policy corresponding to this network of cultural producers and productions.

There is no contradiction between how German culture, on the one hand, reaches beyond political boundaries (à la Herder) and how, on the other, a specifically cultural dimension of the German nation-state is recognized within given political boundaries and taken into account in the exercise of cultural policy by federal, state, and local governments. For centuries, the orientation of culture in Germany has been simultaneously national and regional. Bach is no Thuringian composer, Goethe no Hessian writer, Beuys no Rhenish artist, even if regional references show up in all of their works. These artists and what they have created form the cultural heritage of the entire nation, and not just of Bavarians, Saxons, or Mecklenburgers. It follows "logically" from the concept of a nation, Ernst Gottfried Mahrenholz, former vice president of the Federal Constitutional Court, has observed, that "the German nation, like any other, [has] a culture."

Since the government changed hands in 1998, even the political parties currently in opposition have come to recognize that the federal government's more sharply defined role in cultural policy is not a threat to cultural federalism. For example, the cultural policy spokesman for the Christian Democratic Union/Christian Social Union (CDU/CSU) Bundestag faction, Norbert Lammert, put it this way after an earlier Bundestag election: "I regard it as a colossal improvement, and one that is years overdue, for Germany as a *Kulturstaat* to stop hiding behind the Länder with respect to its self-image and operative responsibilities.... The federal government has an original responsibility for this cultural state." He linked this observation with a profession of his loyalty to cultural federalism: "I cannot see at all," he said, that the federal government "would thereby, in any fashion, be standing in the way ... of the need of the Länder to make cultural operations one of their political priorities." In the meantime, Angela Merkel, chairperson of the CDU, has confirmed this outlook.

If there is such a thing as a national culture, then the federal government has a share of joint responsibility for it, "by the [very] nature of the thing," as the Constitutional Court has asserted. Every level of government has the authority and responsibility for certain cultural matters. And one of the federal government's jobs is to champion the preservation of cultural diversity vis-à-vis European institutions. To be sure, I do not now see anything emerging from Brussels that might threaten federal structures and cultural pluralism in Germany and Europe. The European Union itself supports regional cultural structures and traditions; I need only recall the European Charter of Regional or Minority Languages from 1992. For me, there can be no doubt that the further development of the European Union, which is increasingly taking on the contours of a historic Europe now that the schism of the East-West conflict is over, should not try to orient itself after the United States, since the United States' linguistic and cultural standardization cannot be a proper model. Europe remains multilingual and multipolar, and multicultural diversity is what constitutes Europe's historic and cultural substance. Every attempt at standardizing has ended in a catastrophe: Nazi Germany was responsible for the last such attempt. There cannot be a European nation-state, lest Europe lose its soul.

An important condition for cultural federalism's continued good development is fruitful cooperation among federal, state, and local governments. In each isolated case, cooperation is not only compatible with a clear division of responsibilities; the one practically demands the other. Here, in my opinion, the federal government's priority for cultural policy ought to be maintaining the regulatory framework. The Bundestag, by virtue of the federal government's legislative authority, is a preeminent cultural policy actor. No one can reasonably deny that the design of the tax system (and here I am not just thinking about the taxation of foreign artists) significantly shapes such fields as copyright law, social insurance for artists, foundation law, price maintenance for books, and the framework conditions for cultural development in Germany. Part of the official role of the Federal Commissioner for Cultural and Media Affairs (quite independent of any formal executive responsibilities of the moment) is bringing his cultural policy expertise to bear upon the federal government's deliberations about all these subjects.

Currently, the office's budget amounts to about 10 percent of all government spending on cultural promotion. Even if cultural policy has acquired greater weight within the federal government, this does not threaten in any way the opportunities local and state governments have for shaping cultural policy. On the contrary: Even local governments and the Länder have an interest in the federal government taking its policies' cultural dimension as seriously as possible. The cultural policy of the Länder and municipalities can only stand to gain from a favorable legal framework for cultural development in Germany. One cannot expect there to be any substantial expansion of cultural promotion by the federal government, if only because of the consolidation course adopted by the Berlin city government. Where additional sponsorship has happened, this has never been concluded against the resistance of the relevant state or local government. This is how it ought to remain in the future as well.

The federal government is, to be sure, trying to reach systematic agreement with the Länder on joint responsibilities. Even a historical outgrowth needs to be scrutinized for its continued suitability. As mentioned earlier, cooperation and a clear division of responsibilities are not mutually exclusive.

Speaking before the Bundesrat in June 2001, North Rhine-Westphalia's then prime minister, Wolfgang Clement, stated that federalism allows for diversity without endangering unity. This is especially applicable to cultural federalism. Here, too, after more than fifty years, there cannot be any prohibition on thinking about up-to-date adjustments and modifications. I am very much in favor of precisely dividing up responsibility between the federal and state governments. We have taken a first step in Berlin, where, in agreement with the Berlin state government, we replaced the diffuse joint federal-state responsibility outlined in the Capital City Cultural Accord with exclusive federal sponsorship of four important institutions: Berlin's Jewish Museum, the Berlin Festival, the House of World Cultures, and the Gropius Building.

But there are also simply areas that have to be seen as joint responsibilities because, as the constitutional jurist Josef Isensee has said, our Basic Law promotes an "open, communicative, and cooperative observation of responsibilities." This applies, for example, to memorials of national importance. Here, local and state governments cannot be released from their share of joint national responsibility. Accordingly, our memorial concept envisions allowing federal sponsorship only up to half the total. And so, just as there is a consensus that future scientific research facilities should remain the joint responsibility of federal and state governments, I would also argue on behalf of continuing joint responsibility for cultural institutions and projects. Thus, it was the express wish of the Länder's cultural ministers that the National Foundation of the Federal Republic of Germany *not* become a purely federal institution, but instead be jointly supported by federal and state governments. This concept corresponds to the idea of joint responsibility and, to this extent, conforms to the logic of a cooperative cultural federalism committed to a balance between competition and joint responsibility.

Even the major project for promoting cultural infrastructure in the new Länder and for disposing of past damages is a nationally significant project in which the federal government cooperates with state and local governments in the new Länder. This joint project has been a great success, and in the budget negotiations for medium-range financial planning we have managed to double the allotment for the year 2002 from 15 million to 30 million euros. Here, too, continued cooperation in cultural policy has been sought.

"Whereby is Germany made great," as Johann Peter Eckermann records one of Goethe's thoughts from 1828, "if not by an admirable national culture that has penetrated evenly into all corners of the empire.… Suppose that, for centuries, we in Germany had only the two princely residential cities Vienna and Berlin, or even just one of them, then I would like to see how things might have stood with German culture?"

There are not just Vienna and Berlin, but also Munich and Dresden, Cologne and Weimar, Hamburg and Stuttgart, Frankfurt and Potsdam; there are Gotha, Eutin, Donaueschingen, and Bückeburg, to name just a few of the old residential capitals of some of the smaller principalities. Here and at many other places is where cultural life in Germany takes place. The diversity is fascinating, and we should do everything we can jointly to preserve and promote it. Without the engagement of local communities, Germany would become culturally impoverished. When we speak of cultural federalism, we must not forget its local foundation.

9. Berlin's Cultural Legacy and Prospects

Peter Glotz

What does it mean for the Germans to have decided on moving their capital from Bonn to Berlin, to return to the capital city of the Wilhelminian Empire, the Weimar Republic, and Hitler's Third Reich? Are the Germans reviving some Wilhelminian craving for the great man on horseback, or perhaps even the Nazis' barbarous politics of conquest? Or are they—conversely—capable of conjuring up again the Berlin of the early 1920s, the decade when (for a few years) the city held its own against Europe's great cultural metropolises? Will Berlin give rise to a new communication center for the elite in politics, business, science, and culture, from which a new lifestyle, a new self-confidence, a new sense of responsibility—in brief, a new spirit—might emerge?

I

To begin with, Berlin is a label that gets stamped on the Germans whether they like it or not. The reunification of Germany's two divided halves changed power relations in Europe. The decision for Berlin as capital city was the event that symbolized and emotionally charged this change. It was a risky decision: Germany's neighbors did not exactly have fond memories when they thought about Berlin. But this decision was irrevocable. That is why the Germans no longer live in a Bonn Republic but rather in a Berlin Republic. The whole world sees it this way. What does that mean, culturally speaking?

What it means cannot be deduced from what is happening in the capital. Germany is still a federal state. Günter Grass lives in Lübeck,

Martin Walser on Lake Constance, Hans Magnus Enzensberger and Alexander Kluge in Munich, Jürgen Habermas on Lake Starnberg; Cologne's and Munich's film studios are in better shape than Berlin's, and the universities at Heidelberg and Göttingen, not to mention Munich's Technical University, have many departments that are superior to those at Berlin's institutions of higher learning. By no stretch of the imagination does Berlin enjoy the kind of supremacy that Paris has in France or London in Great Britain. Many people say: Thank God! The intellectual condition of the Berlin Republic is by no means identical with the intellectual condition of Berlin as a city that remains quite provincial in many respects. Berlin is (currently) the patron saint lending its name to the Berlin Republic, not its intellectual breeding ground. To analyze the intellectual climate of the times in this Berlin Republic, therefore, one has to invoke developments from all over Germany. I shall endeavor to do this by looking at two cases: literature and universities.

II

Let us take a case almost at random: a novella written by an author named Thomas Lehr. The author was born in 1957 and seems to be living the typical life of a writer in Germany's highly subsidized literature business: he has written three novels and won a number of rather obscure literary prizes. Still and all, his novella *Frühling* (Spring) is now available in a second edition, which means the author must have sold somewhere between five and ten thousand copies of this book by now.

Now I shall do something that is frowned upon in Germany's literary business: I shall tell what the text is all about in a few brief sentences. The guild of German literary criticism (consisting of between fifteen and twenty people) would object: it means distorting the author's artistic concept. But an American public, of course, needs to know what is going on in a text like this.

The text, like much of European literature after James Joyce, is obscure. Reconstructing the story is no simple matter. Let's put it this way: it is made up of the thoughts and feelings that flash through the head of the main character, Christian Rauch, during the last thirty-nine seconds of his life. This protagonist has committed suicide with the aid of a cancer-stricken prostitute. He is the son of a concentration camp doctor. The text's key scene takes place when the protagonist is fourteen and comes home after fishing with his seventeen-year-old brother. Standing at the entrance to his house is one of his father's (that concentration camp doctor's) former victims. This visitor is reenacting the obligatory roll call required each day in the concentration camp. He takes off his clothes, carefully stacking them on the expensive car now owned by the doctor, who has built up a lucrative practice since the war. The doctor and his wife stand there petrified. Christian does not quite understand what's going on. But his older brother Robert figures it out. The concentration camp victim later kills himself, as does Christian's brother Robert. Christian survives them for another thirty years, living with a certain lady named Angelika and running a small business. He even has a son, Konstantin, who will work out wonderfully in the world. But Christian himself, at fifty, is at the end of his tether.

This story is developed in a highly complicated manner. The complication begins with the language; as a rule, the punctuation gets mangled. (Instead of "wie ich heisse, habe ich vergessen" [I have forgotten what I'm called], it says "ich heisse hab. Ich. Vergessen" [I'm called have. I. Forgotten].) There are some brilliant formulations, such as when the children drop the bare soles of their feet down into the "Astschatten-Muster der Wasserseide" (branch-shadow-patterns of the water-silk). There is also quite a bit of sour kitsch, for example in a miraculous military hospital modeled after Paradise, where revived, refreshed, redeemed naked bodies run around. A literary text like so many in Germany: hard to comprehend, unsuitable for the larger public, nearly impossible to translate, formally ambitious. The reader is not excited, entertained, or deeply moved; instead, he is required to decipher.

My intention is not to criticize Thomas Lehr as an author. He has apparently decided to become one of Germany's "serious" literati, meaning (more or less) to do without a sizeable readership. And so he will have to live off the proceeds of the Mara Cassens Prize awarded by the Hamburg Literary House or the Rheingau Literature Prize. He has every right to this kind of existence. I am interested in asking why hundreds of talented or—as in the case of Thomas Lehr—*highly* talented people rush headlong toward this corner of the literary stage. That this is the case can be seen by analyzing literary criticism in Germany—in this case, by looking at the reviews of Thomas Lehr's novella *Frühling*.

Here, too, I shall select a case at random: the review that appeared in the renowned national daily, the *Süddeutsche Zeitung*. The review was written by one Sybille Kramer and is entitled "The Heir to Guilt." We are dealing with a substantial, five-column critique (including a picture of the author), decidedly respectful, even panegyric. The review (like many such critiques) refuses, however, to perform any kind of service on behalf of the reader. It feels its way into the text, conducts an imaginary conversation with the author, but informs the writer about absolutely nothing.

Thus, the reader never learns that he will be confronted with a thoroughly shredded text, of the sort to which even the upscale readership of the *Süddeutsche Zeitung* is by no means accustomed. Not even the information provided on the book's dust jacket, that the last thirty-nine seconds of the protagonist are worked out in thirty-nine chapters, is plainly conveyed. Instead, the reader has this cryptic assertion bandied at him: "It is the step taken into the 39 seconds and chapters of his becoming one with a liquefied world without boundaries." Whoever has read the book will have a rough idea of what the reviewer means. Whoever has not read it will remain completely clueless about what is meant by this "becoming one with a liquefied world." And the last third of this review is, incidentally, not even devoted to the text in question, but rather to an earlier novel by the author; a habit Anglo-Saxon book review journals would hardly condone. A key sentence in the review states: "Cain and Abel are the sons of a German Adam who, as Hitler's concentration camp doctor, forfeited the firstness [Erstheit]* of German existence, the pre-genocidal condition." The firstness of German existence? Good luck to anyone who understands what this means.

Here I shall break off my analysis of this book review. It is just an arbitrary example of what goes on inside Germany's literary business. Of course there are exceptions; the most famous is Germany's best-known critic, Marcel Reich-Ranicki, who always has his eye on the reader and who understands that criticism should be seen as a service, not as a holy mass. As a rule, though, German literary criticism is not conceived as journalism, but rather as professional scholarly communication between literature departments. This would be justified if the professional communication were taking place in the appropriate professional journals. That is not the case by any means: this kind of specialized reviewing has become widespread in the major weekly newspapers and in the cultural feature pages of the national dailies, and it has even crossed over into the regional daily papers. In this fashion, somewhere between 150 and

---

*The obscure term "Erstheit" may be a translation of "firstness," used by the logician Charles Sanders Peirce and, apparently, in semiotic theory.—*Trans.*

300 authors are kept afloat by one and a half (or maybe two) dozen literary critics on the staffs of the most important print media and radio stations: kept above water by good reviews, by literary prizes on whose juries they sit, by recommendations to publishing houses, by birthday notices and portraits in weekend supplements. Not only do these reviewers keep these authors afloat; they keep them under their curatorship and, often enough, away from the public at large. Whoever attempts to emulate grand models (models such as, say, Franz Werfel, Lion Feuchtwanger, or B. Traven) gets penalized as a rule. One example of a writer penalized this way is the lyricist and storyteller Wolf Wondratschek.

There are, of course, still a handful of authors who have playfully weathered this kind of punishment because they managed to break through to the public. The best example is Nobel Prize winner Günter Grass, most of whose books since the *Tin Drum* (with the possible of exception of the little book *Meeting in Telgte* and the short novel *Cat and Mouse*) were ruthlessly torn to shreds by critics, yet still went on to register high sales, at least in Germany. Grass has never been forgiven for this accomplishment. Only someone as robust and versatile as Günter Grass could have managed to endure the acid contempt with which this author has been confronted for decades in the feature pages of the major papers.

German literature enjoyed a worldwide reputation under the generation of those born between 1875 (Thomas Mann's birth date) and 1900 (the year Bertolt Brecht was born). It would be easy to fill half a page with names indisputably recognized as formative figures (even if in different fields, with different followings). Today this would be out of the question. Whom could one compare with Norman Mailer, Arthur Miller, Saul Bellow, or Philip Roth? Mario Vargas Llosa and Gabriel Garcia Marquez, of course. But a German?

Two kinds of argument could be adduced in order to explain this situation. First of all, literature is less important in a mass media society. Some of the novel's functions, for example, have been taken over by television. Only: Marquez has succeeded at kneading into his novelistic oeuvre a thoroughly gripping version of Latin American history. Some of his novels are announced in bulletins appearing on advertising pillars along Colombia's sidewalks. In Germany, even to ask about works comparable to these Latin American historical novels is deemed illegitimate and abstruse. Secondly, English and Spanish are global languages; German is not. There is certainly truth in these arguments, and they do at least help to explain why there is no longer a German author whose novels (for example) might be eagerly anticipated by the world. But one should not take too much comfort from considerations like these. Even Thomas Pynchon's books do not enjoy worldwide circulation. Yet he is a great portraitist of modern America. Half a century ago, one could have said without a moment's hesitation: we have authors like this, too. One example might have been Heimito von Doderer. Where would we find today's Doderer? We do not even have any authors who can write short stories, film scripts, and social novels with poise. There are, to be sure, some recent exceptions: Ingo Schulze, Bernhard Schlink.

This cannot mean that there is a lack of diversity in contemporary German literature. There are solitary figures such as Alexander Kluge, Gregor von Rezori, or Patrick Süskind, bit-poetry in the tradition of the aggressively genial Rolf Dieter Brinkmann (1940–1975), a second-generation German-Jewish literature (Esther Dischereit, Maxim Biller, Barbara Honigmann), a branch of German authors of Turkish origin, and even the beginnings of a sensual, popular treatment of German history (Bernhard Schlink, again). What does not exist yet is some new kind of public sound or stylistic intention inherent to the Berlin Republic, some fresh departure or powerful new form. Occasionally, to be sure, a few public relations acts in this innovative spirit are juggled before us. Thus, a troop of sixty younger authors was sent to the Parisian Book Fair in 2001, where they were packaged as the "young Berlin generation." But apart from the fact that half of them came from Hamburg, Munich, and other places in Germany, the only thing that John von Düffel, Benjamin Lebert, Benjamin von Stuckrad-Barre, Alissa Walser, Karen Duve, Felicitas Hoppe, and a few others in this bunch have in common is that they are part of the same age cohort. It could be that one or the other will turn into an important public figure. But Berlin has not given us a new communications setting, a new "school," a group, a paradigm. Naturalism grew up around a periodical, postwar German literature around the "Group 47." So far the new Berlin has not produced comparable centers of power or forums for speakers. For the moment, what is new there are the buildings in the Berlin Mitte district, a dozen posh restaurants, Bonn politicians who get around in Berlin pretty much the same way as they did in Bonn, and an underground indulging in self-pity on the border between the eastern and western halves of the city, in the Prenzlauer Berg district. That's all there is.

The Berlin journalist Claus Koch couched this sorry state of affairs using the following bitter words: "It is curious how uninteresting contemporary Germans have become even to themselves. At least Martin Walser turns the disinterest of these uninteresting people into his subject. Yet, apart from the notorious Maxim Biller, who is unable to take a closer look, there is hardly a writer or journalist dedicated to examining the real moral and political condition of his compatriots with critical, passionate, and affectionate earnestness. There also are no longer any German German-haters, something every healthy nation ought to have. Have the Germans really become so self-evident to each other that they are incapable of summoning up curiosity about themselves? In other words, to acquire some kind of viewpoint about themselves, about their existence at this time? *Anschauung* (viewpoint)—in Greek that means "theory." To have a theory about oneself is no longer desired in this semi- and post-nation."

III

As far as the universities are concerned, Germany has been facing a dilemma for the last quarter century. There has to be an increase in the number of people who will require proper training. Since 1977 the number of students in Germany has doubled, to nearly two million. The Länder are in charge of universities. But they hardly have enough disposable tax income of their own and are therefore compelled to cut university budgets, instead of increasing them as required. At the same time, statist Germany has no tradition of fundraising. Only to a very limited extent do people with major fortunes (who certainly do exist) put their money into universities. That is why private universities, as a rule, are small, offer instruction in only a few subjects, and are not in any position to compete effectively with the major state universities. Yet they are squeezed into the straightjacket of Germany's public service laws, cannot pay their professors properly, have to make decisions in accordance with complicated democratic regulations that prevent them from reacting quickly to new developments in society, and in this way they have lost their academic atmosphere. An American at one of these German universities would not be able to find a lot of the things he takes for granted. There are no faculty clubs there, no alumni houses, no career service, no tuition, no athletic teams, and no university store in which to buy t-shirts with the university logo. As a result, there is no collective emotional identity at a German university. Students do not think over where they want to study;

they study at the "available" regional university, basically wherever their mother's laundry machine is located. The university is a regionally anchored bureaucracy, like a passport office or weighing station. And in the so-called *numerus clausus* departments, restricted majors where the universities have to accept fewer people than the number of applicants, students are allocated to one university or another by a central government bureaucracy. We have long since entered a phase where national educational systems are being transformed into a single international educational market. In this international educational market, the student elite is attracted by Stanford, Harvard, MIT, or Carnegie Mellon, not by Regensburg, Hildesheim, or Osnabrück.

By no means does this require that European universities be reshaped according to the American model. Not all American traditions are suitable for the old continent of Europe. But there is no sneaking around one central insight: whoever wants to train a student well requires enough money. He needs a sufficient number of outstanding teachers from every generation, good libraries, the latest scientific equipment, modern dental chairs for the DDS students, and sufficient funds for excursions by ethnologists or forestry scientists. Since the end of the 1970s it has been plain as can be that Germany has not been able to raise enough money from the Länder for higher education. So Germany should have switched over (as Great Britain has just done) from a government-subsidized system to a system where fees are paid, i.e., tuition. Politicians in Germany (in both major parties) lack the courage to do this. Thus the university system is under-financed to an ever greater extent.

The result of this kind of educational policy has been captured in a sentence uttered by Laron Lanier, who became famous by coining the term "virtual reality" and developing spectacular software programs: "Europe has ceased to think; but it has supplied the software." This is something of an exaggeration. In several German university institutes, and most especially in the Max Planck Institutes, it is entirely possible to find groups of researchers capable of holding their own at the very top of important fields. But it is true that Germany (and almost all of the European countries, with the possible exception of Great Britain and Switzerland) will only have a few isolated individuals who can hold their own in the up-and-coming fields that are going to trigger the next long wave of economic growth. This is especially true when it comes to the links tying genetic engineering to computer science and artificial intelligence. The entire Internet technology—the technology of the World Wide Web, which was developed at CERN (European Organization for Nuclear Research) in Geneva by an Englishman who has long since gone on to work in America—was developed in the United States. The same is true for the decoding of the human genome, stem cell research, therapeutic cloning, and so on. The *Kulturkampf*-like debate that has broken out in Germany over stem cell research has demonstrated that a portion of the country's elites (quite rightly shocked by the crimes of the National Socialists) has abandoned its old Enlightenment vision. In a number of humanities departments an out-and-out hatred of the natural sciences is being cultivated. In both major churches (Catholic and Lutheran), more and more leaders are inclined toward the view that man should no longer mess around with God's handiwork, but should instead stop trying to get to the bottom of nature's secrets. Of course, there are tendencies like this in the United States as well; occasionally among the religious right, sometimes even in an inimitably aggressive manner. Nevertheless, many young scientists, and especially numerous future business leaders, are running away from the Germans and in the direction of American universities.

One should not make out Germany's education system to be worse than it is. The average German university is better than the average American university. Above all, the average German public school is better than the average public school in the United States. Germany's problem has to do with promoting the highly talented and advanced research, with emphasizing special institutions (for example, research universities), and with providing leeway for charismatic types, for people on the ideological cutting edge. In the United States there is a working fluctuation from one elite—political, economic, and scholarly—to another (Henry Kissinger, Zbigniew Brzezinski, Robert Reich, the new Harvard president, Larry Summers). In Germany there is nothing to compare with this. American universities cultivate their stars. Public discussions are shaped by the books of Daniel Bell, Paul Kennedy, Samuel Huntington, Alan Bloom, but also Noam Chomsky, or Paul Krugman. Ralf Dahrendorf, however, absconded two decades ago, to Great Britain (the London School of Economics and St. Antony's College). In the meantime he has become a British subject and member of the House of Lords. Just a bizarre coincidence?

IV

So what is really happening with the new self-confidence of the Berlin Republic noted, above all, by foreign observers? Realistically, one has to say: so far, not much. Of course, German politics is adjusting to the new responsibilities of a reunified Germany, no longer subject to Allied controls. This has been demonstrated by German participation in the Kosovo war. Of course, there has also been this or that courageous (or sometimes loutish) remark by the chancellor or one of his cabinet ministers. Moreover, the new Chancellor's Office (commissioned by Helmut Kohl) is more imposing than its Bonn equivalent. But a new departure for Germany, signaling the Berlin Republic's formative economic and cultural power, cannot be discerned. There are advantages to this situation. There is neither a Johann Gottlieb Fichte holding addresses to the German nation, nor a Heinrich von Treitschke talking up German nationalism. But also missing is that ignition spark that the proponents of moving the capital had promised during the great 1991 capital city debate in the Bundestag. Nobody says anything about scheduling regular discussion rounds bringing together leading politicians with—let us say—Günter Grass, Jürgen Habermas, IG Metall chairman Klaus Zwickel, the chairman of the board of Siemens, Heinrich von Pierer, or Ron Sommer, the former chairman of the board of Deutsche Telekom, at the Paris Bar or Borchardt (two famous Berlin restaurants). No mention of any newfangled ganging up of Germany's strictly segregated elites. The economic elite maintains its distance from Berlin. Politicians still maintain small houses, living in Berlin just as they did in Bonn, in cheap apartments and abandoning the city by mid-Friday at the latest in order to visit their electoral districts. Incidentally, Berlin has three universities and three opera houses, occasionally with brilliant (second-ranking) performances. Daniel Barenboim conducts well whether he is in Berlin or in New York. But we are still waiting for the newfangled synergy, the great leap forward, the new cultural startup that might emerge out of a new communicative link.

Germans might console themselves with two kinds of argument. First of all, more than ten years have passed since reunification, a short period of time. Even after 1871 the country needed more than two decades before anything changed; back then, however, it was a change in a fatal direction, heading toward the Wilhelminian precursor to National Socialism. Secondly, it is equally wrong to expect a major impulse to come out of Germany. This has to come from Europe. Most of the problems with which the Germans have to contend have not been solved any better in France, Italy, or Spain. Julien Green, the great French novelist and diarist (who, incidentally, came from an American family), jotted this down in September 1992: "Europe is like an old lady with a history of serious strokes who, in a feeble state, has to answer a question that no one would have the heart to ask her if one were trying to be fair." This is an illness that Europe has to overcome—and not just Germany or even Berlin.

10. The Architectural Rebirth of a Capital

Peter Conradi

"What belongs together is now growing together," said Willy Brandt in Berlin when communist rule collapsed in the German Democratic Republic (GDR), when the Wall came down, when, for the first time in more than forty years, people from both German states were no longer prevented from meeting each other. Yet growing together has proven more painful, more difficult, and more expensive than we believed it would be in our emotional exuberance back in 1989. The negative aspects of unification, such as the high level of unemployment and the dismantling of social-welfare rights (especially for women) in eastern Germany, and the high financial burden placed on western German workers to cover the costs of unification have given rise to occasional disappointment and even rage about unification. More than ten years after the unification of the two German states, we know that unity—economic, social, political, and cultural—is going to cost still much more money and effort, but above all more time. In Berlin, Germany's capital city from 1871 to 1945 and divided since 1945 (and by the Wall since 1961), the problems of growing together are especially clear.

The 1990 Capital City Debate

Given the pressure from all the problems on the agenda in 1990, the question of Germany's capital city did not yet play a major role that year. The German Unification Treaty between the government of the Federal Republic of Germany (FRG) and the last GDR government of summer 1990 deferred the question: "The question of the seat of parliament and government will be decided after the establishment of the unity of Germany."[1]

Yet by 1991, the debate about the future site of the Bundestag and federal government became the subject of a major national argument. The dispute cut straight through families, friendships, parties, and parliamentary parties. Young people in the west inclined toward Bonn, older people toward Berlin. Southern Germans and those from the Rhine River valley wanted to remain in Bonn, while northern Germans and eastern Germans overwhelmingly favored Berlin as capital. The outcome of the dispute was uncertain at the time. A motion by the Social Democratic Party (SPD) opposition in the Bundestag to have the capital city question decided by referendum was rejected by government majority.

On 20 June 1991, after a suspense-filled eleven-hour debate with more than 100 speakers, the Bundestag decided by a bare majority of 338 to 320 (with two abstentions) to move the Bundestag and federal government to Berlin within four years. Following the Bundestag election of 1994, the 12th Bundestag reconfirmed the Hauptstadt-Beschluß (Capital City Resolution) and passed enabling legislation.

Arguments about cost played a major role in the 1991 debate. The proponents of Bonn had pegged projected costs for buildings in Berlin and for the move at DM 100 billion (50 billion euros). In the meantime, it has become clear that the DM 20 billion (10 billion euros)—spread over ten years—then estimated by the federal government will cover all costs, including for construction.

More than ten years after the Bundestag's Capital City Resolution, the fears that German federalism would be weakened by the move, because of a new centralism emanating from Berlin, have not been fulfilled. In the meantime, an overwhelming majority of both parliament and public opinion agrees that the move to Berlin was the right decision.

Implementing the Capital City Resolution

After passing the Capital City Resolution, parliament and government established a number of commissions to manage the structural,

---

1. Unification Treaty, Article 2, Paragraph 1, Sentence 2.

personnel, organizational, and architectural questions surrounding the move to Berlin. The building commission of the Bundestag was responsible for parliamentary buildings, and the federal building ministry in charge of government buildings in Berlin.

With few exceptions, all of the commissions awarded for the planning of new buildings were handed out on the basis of architectural competitions. On the recommendation of the federal government, though, there was a special arrangement for the Jakob-Kaiser-Haus, the new building complex meant to house offices for members of parliament: five experienced and renowned architectural firms were chosen to plan and build this complex. The amount of time it was hoped would be saved by eliminating a competition, however, did not materialize.

The Berlin city administration and local architects participated in the juries for resulting competitions. In the law regulating the move to Berlin, however, it was decided that the city of Berlin's planning authority needed to take the plans of the Bundestag and federal government into account; in other words, Berlin's planning authority was curtailed.

It was foreseeable that the Bundesbaudirektion, Germany's federal building management office, would not be able to cope with such extensive building measures entirely on its own. Therefore, the Bundestag and federal government established their own building company, the Bundesbaugesellschaft Berlin mbH, which authorized a volume of planning and construction amounting to nearly 1.5 billion euros over eight years.

Old Buildings and New Buildings

Berlin was the capital of the German Reich from 1871 to 1945, and East Berlin the capital of the GDR from 1949 to 1990. There are, therefore, numerous buildings in the city that are the property of the federal government. Federal Minister for Regional Planning, Building, and Urban Development Klaus Töpfer, the federal government's commissioner in charge of the move, decided not to build a new government quarter in Berlin, but rather to use, convert, modernize, and add on to preexisting old buildings. This way a self-contained government quarter, under police guard and deserted by evening and on weekends, would be avoided. Instead, federal ministries are distributed across the entire downtown area, where they are mainly accommodated in modernized older buildings. Only in the Spreebogen (the Spree river bend) alongside the Reichstag building were major new buildings created for the Bundestag and Federal Chancellor's Office, buildings that render visible the political significance of parliament and government.

The Bundestag inside the Reichstag Building

The proposal to have the Bundestag move quickly but provisionally into the former Reichstag building, rent office buildings, and then quietly to plan a new parliament building in Berlin's Mitte district, where the Prussian Palace once stood, did not command a majority. An overwhelming majority of parliament members wanted to move into the historic 100-year-old Reichstag building.

Fourteen foreign architectural firms were invited to submit designs in the architectural competition to remodel the Reichstag building. Two hundred ninety architects from Germany requested application forms for the competition; only eighty actually submitted designs. The names of the architects participating in the competition remained anonymous to the jury. In spite of intense discussion lasting for days, the jury was unable to agree on the first prize. It therefore decided to award three equally ranked first prizes and recommend instructing the designers to make revisions before reaching a decision.

When the envelopes with the designers' statements were opened, it emerged that the first three prizes had gone to three foreign architects: Sir Norman Foster from Great Britain, Santiago Calatrava from Spain, and Pi de Bruyn from the Netherlands. After a difficult phase of revisions and decisions, the Bundestag commissioned Sir Norman Foster with the remodeling of the building.

The turning point in the history of the Reichstag building was marked by an artistic action noted worldwide: in 1994, after a lively and contentious debate, the Bundestag gave the American artist Christo and his wife, Jeanne-Claude, permission to wrap the Reichstag. In the summer of 1995 the "Wrapping of the Reichstag" turned into a gigantic gleeful festival, a peaceful token marking a new chapter in this building's history.

Norman Foster and his architects succeeded in taking a bit of the Wilhelminian severity, a mixture of neo-Renaissance and neo-Baroque, out of the Reichstag building. The building was not restored to its 1894 condition; instead, everything new was panned and built within the architectural language of our time. Thus,

today's Reichstag building reveals traces of history, such as the bul-
let holes in the walls from the violent struggle over the building at
the end of World War II and the graffiti marks by which Soviet soldiers immortalized themselves after storming the Reichstag. Conservatives and liberals achieved their goal of giving the building a
dome once again (even if not the historic dome) and of aligning
the federal government's seats in the assembly chamber so that
they squarely face the other members of parliament (as in the former Reichstag) rather than encompass the government benches
within the circle of parliamentary delegates (as in Bonn).

In the meantime, the Bundestag building (still popularly known
as the Reichstag) has become a first-class public magnet. Hundreds
of thousands of visitors have visited the assembly chamber and the
dome. Even today, several years after the move into the Reichstag
building, people wait in line for hours to visit the renovated assembly. The building's popularity can also be measured by the fre-
quency with which it is used as a background for advertisements.

Compared to the new building that world-famous German architect Günter Behnisch had planned for the Bundestag's assembly
chamber in the late 1980s, Norman Foster's architectural vocabu-
lary is cooler and more reserved. "The cold heart of the republic,"
one architecture critic wrote. Still, the people and their representatives have accepted the building. The building's appropriation
process includes the works of contemporary painters and sculptors,
including contributions from the United States, Great Britain,
France, and the former Soviet Union—the four occupying powers
of a previous era who later became friends to whom we owe a debt
of gratitude for German unification.

The Band des Bundes

The Reichstag building's 17,940 square yards cover about 10 percent
of the space the Bundestag needs. For additional parliament buildings and a new Federal Chancellor's Office along the Spreebogen,
an international design competition was announced in 1992/93, to
which 835 contributions were submitted (of which 481 came from
architects working in Germany and 354 from architects worldwide).
A major international jury awarded the first prize to Axel Schultes
and Charlotte Frank from Berlin for their spacious, linear, urban
structure—the Band des Bundes (Federal Ribbon)—which, by twice
crossing the Spree River, expresses a strong link between east and

west. With this project, parliament and government opted for an audacious, headstrong, and powerful act of self-promotion by the democratic state. This ambitious approach proved sound during the follow-up competitions for implementing the new Federal Chancellor's Office and the parliament's committee building.

The proposal by Schultes and Frank to build a public forum in front of the Federal Chancellor's Office proved problematic. The federal government and Bundestag did not want to implement this idea, especially as the notion that the people might petition the chancellor at this site was unrealistic—in a parliamentary democracy the public does not petition the chancellor, but rather its elected representatives in parliament, now located further east on Friedrich-Ebert-Platz, or at another site for major demonstration just west of the Reichstag, the Platz der Republik. In place of the forum there will now be an empty space between the Bundestag's committee building and the Federal Chancellor's Office, a gap in the Federal Ribbon that turns these two buildings, originally conceived as components of a continuous ribbon, into solitary pieces. It is hoped that, in the future, the Bundestag and federal government might yet allow construction on this spot, perhaps with a museum of parliamentary history, with spaces for public events, restaurants, and cafés.

Federal Chancellor's Office

The Federal Chancellor's Office in Bonn was a modest, sober, utilitarian building from the late 1960s, frequently derided as a "county savings bank." In 1994 a competition for a new Federal Chancellor's Office in Berlin was announced, to which fifty-one architectural firms from Germany and Europe were admitted. There were fierce debates inside the jury, because the "Berliners" favored a design using a rather severe, neoclassical architectural language, while the "Bonners" opted overwhelmingly for a lively, sculptural, expressive kind of work. Since there was no majority for either one of the designs, the jury awarded two equally ranked first prizes and left it up to then Chancellor Helmut Kohl to decide which design would be completed. After a phase for revisions and a colloquium bringing together architects, politicians, historians, critics, and journalists, Kohl opted for the design by Axel Schultes and Charlotte Frank, which had already won the urban design competition for the development of the Spreebogen.

In the daily press the building was frequently criticized as too monumental and overly large. Professional critics, by contrast, were overwhelmingly positive in paying tribute to the new Federal Chancellor's Office as a building of high architectonic quality clearly distinguishable from the all-purpose office containers on display in so many places. The new Federal Chancellor's Office is not showy, nor is it monumental; it is a lively, strongly expressive building with well-differentiated and interesting interior spaces.

Additional Parliament and Government Buildings

The Jakob-Kaiser-Haus, an office complex for Bundestag representatives, was built in the immediate vicinity of the Reichstag building. Because five architects were commissioned with the work, the result was not one large unified building, but rather a project made up of different houses using different architectural approaches. North of the Reichstag building the architect Stefan Braunfels has planned the Paul-Löbe-Haus in the Band des Bundes, a building for Bundestag committees and for additional offices for Bundestag members, and the Marie-Luise-Ehlers-Haus for the library and Bundestag administration. These buildings, too, do not fall under the rubric of postmodern or neoclassical fashions from the 1990s. By the end of 2002 the entire federal ensemble—the Reichstag building together with the Bundestag's assembly chamber, the surrounding office and committee buildings, and the Federal Chancellor's Office—was set to have been completed.

In the Tiergarten district, immediately next to the Federal president's official residence in Bellevue Palace, an administrative building for the president was created—a severe, coolly polished oval building that tended to correspond more to the Berliners' ideas than to wishes of the Bonn crowd. Even where the ministries renovated and expanded by the Bundesbaudirektion were concerned, the tendency prevailed for rather dry, bureaucratic designs.

The Berlin Architectural Dispute

Different tendencies emerged from the competitions to conceive and complete parliament and government buildings in Berlin: whereas the Bonners pushed harder for caution, lightness, and composure, qualities used by the Rhenish Republic to depict itself in the Bonn assembly chamber designed by Günter Behnisch, the Berliners were asking for more earnest buildings with greater pathos and dignity.

The architectural orientation backed by the Berlin *Senat* (city government) was around Karl Friedrich Schinkel's neoclassical architecture from the early nineteenth century, and not around the lively, pluralistic architecture of 1920's Berlin. Thus, in the 1990s Berlin produced a number of new neoclassical-like buildings that have little in common with the spirit of our time. In France and the United States classicism was the architecture of freedom and democracy; in Germany, however, this architectural vernacular is encumbered by the way the Nazis and their star architect, Albert Speer, availed themselves of the form in order architecturally to express their power.

Fierce debates often erupted within the juries because Berlin demonstrated an inclination to revive neoclassicism that seemed rather suspect to the rest of the republic. The architecture critic Tilmann Buddensiek has lamented the "official esteem for Nazi architecture in the middle of the capital" and the "solidaristic upgrading of reactionary building from the Nazi era" for which, above all, Berlin's architecture policy has been held responsible.

Architectural forms display as little arbitrariness as words; they show us what we regard as important. The new Germany—a civil, democratic society—must also be concerned that the architectural character of democracy expresses friendliness and lightness, not a strained dignity, empty pathos, or intimidating solemnity.

For postwar West Germany, Bonn was a good capital city— moderate, modest, inconspicuous, and pragmatic. After the Nazi era, Germans were able to find their way back into the community of democratic states via Bonn. The West German Bonn Republic's forty years were not bad for Germany. Bonn's political style and government architecture were sober, predominantly modest, not power-conscious, and sometimes a bit provincial. Berlin has rarely been about modesty, but rather occasionally about power, greatness, and dignity. It remains to be seen whether government and parliament will succeed in bringing something of the Catholic-Rhenish "lightness of being" and southern German joie de vivre into the Protestant-Prussian, occasionally rather sour Berlin. For a united Germany, which has now become the largest and strongest member of the European Union with new international responsibilities, this would not be a bad mixture, but rather a good position.

The Move

The decision to have a working capital in Berlin within four years proved unrealistic. The opponents of Berlin in the Bundestag and government ministries were not willing to move into provisional quarters in Berlin and placed high demands on the size and standards of their accommodations in the old-new capital. An urban design competition had to be announced for the development of the Spreebogen, and there also had to be architectural competitions for new buildings. All that cost time.

In 1999, when the Reichstag building's remodeling to accommodate the Bundestag had been completed, pressure grew on parliament and government to move from Bonn to Berlin even though numerous additional buildings had not yet been completed. The public would not have accepted allowing the remodeled Reichstag building to stand empty for several additional years until the last Bundestag member's office was finished. So provisional and leasing arrangements were made for Berlin, after all, and in the summer of 1999—a little over a year after the Bundestag election of 1998 and eight years after the parliamentary resolution on moving from Bonn —parliament and government moved to Berlin. The provisional arrangements were hard on Bundestag members and on the government. In addition, the federal government had decided to move ten ministries and the Federal Chancellor's Office to Berlin while leaving eight ministries in Bonn, with each ministry keeping branch offices in the other city. This has placed a burden on the work of parliament and government and, as expected, there have been new demands to move the remaining ministries from Bonn to Berlin.

Altogether, about 4,600 parliamentary staff and 7,600 federal government staff had to move from Bonn to Berlin, along with more than 600 Bundestag members, amounting to a total of around 12,000 people (and about twice that if their families are included). In addition, there were 10,000 people from embassies, interest groups, lobbyists, and the press. For Berlin, with a population of over three million, this was not a disruptive number. Nevertheless, the move has changed the climate in Berlin, and in many parts of the city it has brought about the dawning of a new beginning.

Spreebogen and Potsdamer Platz

In the meantime, less than one mile south of the Spreebogen, Potsdamer Platz has been rebuilt—a concentrated new urban

development with office buildings, a shopping mall, movie theaters, and hotels. The builders included the real estate subsidiary of
Daimler-Chrysler AG, Sony AG, and other corporations. Berlin's
public, and especially numerous tourists in the city, have taken to
the new urban ensemble on Potsdamer Platz.

Potsdamer Platz has become the building site for international
capital, and the Spreebogen for German democracy. It is still too
early for comparison and evaluation. Yet when both quarters have
been completed, they will be assessed not just by architecture critics; the public at large will also be evaluating these two centers.

Schloß, Palast der Republik, and Schloßplatz

The Schloß, or Prussian Palace, in the center of historic Berlin was
damaged during the war and, in a postwar act of barbarism incom-
prehensible today, demolished by the Communist government of the
GDR. In its place was built the Palace of the Republic, an architecturally dry, pompous building in the style of the 1960s whose usage
adopted the tradition of popular and cultural halls from late-nine-
teenth- and early-twentieth-century Germany. With this expensive
building the GDR government hoped to demonstrate its vaunted
productivity. Like the Centre Pompidou in Paris, the Palace of the
Republic combined different uses—a grand hall, parliamentary
hall, museum, library, entertainment, and restaurant.

By the end of the 1980s it became clear that the Palace was con-
taminated with asbestos. After unification, the federal government,
in spite of fierce protests from East Berlin and East Germany,
decided to rid the building of asbestos and then tear it down. The
asbestos removal phase of the building's rehabilitation was to have
been concluded by 2003, at which time only the building's shell will
remain standing, and the new federal government will have to
decide what will happen with it.

An expert commission set up by the federal government and
Berlin Senat recommended a new use of the building similar to
that of the Centre Pompidou in Paris. The new construction
shall house different cultural institutions, for example, the eth-
nological collections of the Dahlem Museum, the technical and
scientific collections of the Humboldt University of Berlin, the
State Library of Berlin, and an "agora" for civic communication
in Berlin. On the whole, in the context of the major art and archae-
ological collections on the city's nearby Museum Island, such use

of cultural information and communication would enrich Berlin's downtown.

Whereas the commission's recommendation was passed unanimously, a bare eight-to-seven majority advocated a reconstruction in the cubature of the former Palace with a reconstruction of the baroque outer façades and the inner court. The commission brusquely dismissed the architects' request to announce an open competition of ideas without creative proscriptions and subsequently to decide whether a plan to reconstruct the baroque façades or to construct a new building in present-day architectural style would be suitable. Even the Bundestag wanted no creative freedom of thought; the conservative and liberal opposition factions and a minority of the red-green majority factions voted so that only plans with baroque façades may be allowed in the competition for the new construction. Whether this narrow-minded decision will remain has yet to be seen. In the foreseeable future, neither the federal government nor the Berlin Senat has the necessary means to reconstruct the damaged Palace.

The question "Prussian Schloß, Palace of the Republic, or new building?" is more than an architectural-aesthetic question. Whatever is built on this important site of German history will influence not only Berlin's consciousness, but also that of the entire republic. In addition to the question of whether architectural, artistic, and historic preservation considerations would permit a historic building destroyed fifty years ago to be reproduced (some say imitated), the question also arises as to the message this kind of reconstruction would send to the outside world. Fallen Prussia is part of German history, for good as well as for evil; the identity of the Federal Republic of Germany, however, does not reside in Prussia and its palace. But restoring the Socialist Unity Party's (SED) Palace of the Republic would be a solution oriented toward the past, too.

There is much to be said for testing different ideas about the future development of the Schloßplatz within a broadly designed architectural competition. Along with the buildings that represent democracy along the Spreebogen and the buildings that showcase capitalism on Potsdamer Platz, the development of the Schloßplatz will shape our country's architectural visage: democracy, culture, and the economy as the keystones of our republic.

11. Berlin's Jewish Community

Andreas Nachama

In 1980 if one had driven from the Victory Column on the periphery of West Berlin's center in the direction of the Brandenburg Gate over the Straße des 17. Juni—which, during Albert Speer's renovation of the city, had been grossly expanded from the Charlottenburger Chaussee—to the Magistral, one would have been almost completely alone on a street empty of people and would have eventually come up against a police barricade. There Berlin police stood guard over British military police, who guarded Soviet soldiers, who in turn stood honorary guard at the Soviet War Memorial for the Red Army soldiers who fell in the slaughter over Berlin. Behind them stood the Reichstag in which no political resolutions had been adopted, but rather an exhibition was on display with a name rich in associations: Questions on German History. As proof that at the time the German question was still open, the Brandenburg Gate was closed. The Jewish Community of Berlin numbered about 6,000 and had with its legendary postwar chairman, Heinz Galinski, a speaker, who, without having to lift a finger, raised his voice in warning against right-wing radicalism and neo-Nazism in the Federal Republic of Germany and in Berlin, and who found a listening ear in the German public far beyond his flock of 6,000 lambs. Behind the Wall there was also a Jewish community, which looked away with embarrassment when it came to questions of the state party's or the government's anti-Zionism; otherwise, the community looked after itself in its little corner to which it was entitled so as to exist in an atheistic state organization.

Ten years later everything was different. The Brandenburg Gate was open, and a six-lane street was jammed. The police directed the traffic; British military police and Red Army soldiers prepared for their departure from Germany. The Jewish community, like everyone in Germany, was in a fever about the notion of unification, not knowing what it could bring about other than the fact that nothing would remain as it was. How could the changes be measured now? On 3 October 1990, the day of the national unification of both German states, a festival magazine came out. Ulrich Eckhardt, director of the Berlin Festival, was the publisher and had asked me to write an account of a Jewish exploratory expedition of the city. Now, twelve years later, Dieter Dettke, executive director of the Friedrich-Ebert-Stiftung in Washington, D.C., has asked me to submit a contribution on "Berlin's Jewish Community." Let us try it with a commentary now expanded upon by events of the last ten years.

> This walking tour is mainly written in the imperfect, only a little in the present, almost nothing in the future, because everything that can be reported here that belongs to the past has been wiped out. The force that tore through Berlin in the past decades also tore through the Jewish community. As of 1953 there were two independently active Jewish community administrative bodies. They had separated even in death: a new Jewish cemetery was established in Charlottenburg across from the old ones in Weißensee. Although reduced to only 6,000 members in the western section and now somewhat more than 200 in the eastern section, the institutional history of the Jewish communities in Berlin mirrored the history of the city. Thus, divided as the city was in the past decades, the present day is also divided for both communities, which these days are discussing their impending merger.

Today hardly anyone remembers that at the time of the division there had been two Jewish communities in Berlin for almost thirty-five years. The office of the president of the Jewish Community has long since been once again situated at its traditional place next to the portals of the new synagogue—officially opened in 1866, destroyed by British bombs in 1943, reconstructed 1988–1995. If that were not enough, the partial ruins that stood shimmering as an emblem of the destruction during the days of the German Democratic Republic (GDR) have in the meantime completely understandably become one of the most impressive emblems of the new Berlin; and besides this, the community residence from the late 1950s in Charlottenburg has become the center of Jewish culture and learning.

> The Jewish communities and Jewish Berliners made city history as citizens of their city, and all sorts of traces of Jewish life can be found in Berlin's old center, between Alexanderplatz and the Brandenburg Gate.

The synagogues and houses of worship, the adult schools and *Hochschule* (colleges) of Berlin's Jewish community stood a stone's throw from Alexanderplatz. Not only did Berlin expand since the 1880s, but rather the Jewish community also exploded because in the years between 1880 and the Golden '20s pogroms in Eastern Europe drove thousands to the West; many sought out the imperial capital as only a short station stop on their way to the New World. But like so many others they remained in the Weimar Republic, the German Kaiserreich that was tolerant in comparison to their homeland. In those old residential quarters in the middle of the city, which were deserted by those Berliners moving to the suburbs, this group of immigrants grew. Whoever might now look at a city map for Grenadierstraße or Dragonerstraße will, however, no longer find them. But not just the names of the streets have been changed: Dragonerstraße became Max-Beer-Straße and Grenadierstraße Almstadtstraße; the people are also gone. The lucky among them have left the city, perhaps through the Brandenburg Gate. Their travel destinations cannot be determined, are unknown, but one thing is clear: they left Berlin, Germany, and Europe in order to escape those who were not just after their blood, but theirs especially. The unlucky were taken out of the city—deported: their "travel" destinations are known: Auschwitz, Buchenwald, Sachsenhausen, Theresienstadt....

There is no travel guide of the new Berlin that does not refer to this city quarter that was once designated by Berlin's Jews as the *finstere Medine*; in the United States of the 1990s, one would probably say "very downtown." At the Hackescher Markt and around the new synagogue, parlor theaters, restaurants, and bars are located that one has to have experienced as a visitor to the city; in them one's sense of Walter Benjamin's impressions being tucked under the arm, Franz Hessels thoughts in the minds, Else Lasker-Schüler's poems on the lips, and Schalom Alechem's stories on the panels of the cabaret stages is so very present that non-local feature writers gladly speak of a renaissance of Jewish culture.

Where Berlin's first synagogue stood—Heidereuthergasse 2-4—at the corner of Rosenstraße, it is not just a street that has disappeared from the city map due to the city's renovation; rather, there is a gaping wound, because where the synagogue—officially opened in 1714—once stood one finds today the parking lot behind the bookstore, The International Book. Down a couple of streets farther, at Oranienburgerstraße 30, rest the rusted ruins of the absolutely most beautiful and also largest of Germany's synagogues. Berlin's Jews, who had lived in Berlin since the 1671 settlement edict of Electoral Prince Friedrich Wilhelm, had erected their temple here in 1866. In the wake of the equality granted for citizenship for all inhabitants of the country, they had emancipated themselves into citizens of Jewish faith, just as other Berliners not equipped with civil rights, such as those Christians who as servants and wage earners made up the majority of the population, had emancipated themselves; the Jews reached for their weapons along with the Christian Prussians in the Wars of Liberation (1812–1815), not to mention the Great War (1914–1918), in which Jewish soldiers carried out their service in the Kaiser's army just as gladly as their non-Jewish neighbors. A lavish memorial bears witness to this in the Jewish cemetery in Weißensee that is dedicated to those Jews who fell in World War I.

Understandably, there is a plaque where the 1714 synagogue used to stand. Parts of the contours of the old synagogue are marked with cobblestones, and a stone's throw away from where the social council of the Jewish community had its headquarters in Rosen-straße there stands a memorial for the heroic non-Jewish women, who, through public resistance, freed their Jewish husbands from the talons of the Gestapo in March 1943. Advertisement pillars document that following the arrest of their husbands, for ten days and ten nights in Nazi Germany, non-Jewish wives demonstrated on the open street, crying "Let our husbands go!" Thus, following the inferno of Stalingrad, the attempt in honor of Hitler's birthday was thwarted to cleanse the imperial capital of Jews. Every year the women of Rosenstraße are recognized on 27 February, the day of the "factory action," as this wave of arrests of Jewish forced laborers at their work places is popularly called.

> Back to Oranienburgerstraße. Next to the synagogue stands an immense crane that bears witness to the ongoing reconstruction. The resurrected parts of the synagogue will become "Centrum Judaicum"— an archive, research center, and museum of Jewish life in Berlin—a future. A couple of steps further another name has been erased from the map of the city: Artilleriestraße, today known as Tucholskystraße. Another Jewish community founded in 1869, "Adass Jisroel," had its headquarters and a synagogue there. The front house in which the community's council was located still stands. And recently Jewish services have begun once again to take place in the synagogue in Ryckestraße and in Prenzlauer Berg and in the three synagogues in Charlottenburg. Even more institutions of Jewish community life would be introduced in this quarter—rabbinical seminars, *Hochschule* for Jewish studies, a Jewish museum, Jewish schools—but Berlin was not the Jerusalem of the East. The field of religious activity was only the one side to Jewish Berliners: the number of Jews in the cultural arena, especially in the center of Berlin, was particularly high. Max Reinhardt, the actor, producer, and theater director, influenced almost all stages in

Berlin's center: the Deutsches Theater, studio theaters, public theater, and playhouses. Also active under his patronage were Max Pallenberg, Elisabeth Bergner, and Fritz Kortner.

Back to Oranienburgerstraße. To the right and left of the reconstructed synagogue sit the best restaurants in the city; just around the corner, newly awakened from its Snow-White-like sleep during the past years of the GDR, one finds the Adass-Jisroel-Community and its Bet-Café—in the Große Hamburger Straße in the building of the old Jewish boys school. This is where the *Gymnasium* (high school) was opened in 1993 as the first Jewish secondary school in postwar Germany; the first students received their *Abitur* (graduated) in summer 2000. Jewish and non-Jewish students study here together topics such as—aside from the curriculum assigned by the Berlin school senator—Hebrew, Jewish history, and Jewish studies. And where once the center of Jewish learning was situated, in the College for the Study of Judaism, the Central Council of Jews in Germany is installed, which, when still under the leadership of Ignatz Bubis, gave the building its name in memory of the great rabbi Leo Baeck. The weekly *Jüdische Allgemeine Wochenzeitung*, the voice of the Central Council, also conducts its editing in this space. Yet not just an organized Jewish presence has found its home in Berlin. Authors such as Stefan Heym (died in 16 December 2001), Hendryk Broder, theater producers such as Peter Zadek or George Tabori, conductors such as Daniel Barenboim or Eliyahu Inbal are completely understandably Berliners—and this number is far from being a full count. No month goes by in which a delegation of significant Jewish organizations does not make a station stop in Berlin on its mission through Europe; even possibly the federal chancellor or the federal foreign minister may be welcomed because the Berlin Republic is sincere about confronting its history so that the present and future Jewish life will be taken seriously. When Israeli Foreign Minister David Levy was a guest in Berlin in 2000, Foreign Minister Joschka Fischer and I, at the time president of the Jewish Community of Berlin, took him on a tour of the streets around the new synagogue to give him an impression of the lively Jewish life in the new Berlin. It became clear during this tour that Joschka Fischer knows the details of Jewish traces in this section better than anyone else—for example, a doorpost on which the outlines of a Mesusa could be seen that apparently had hung there until the inhabitants were deported. This was no showpiece but yet still more than a trace of the past.

Without also only striving for completeness, the great significance of Jewish businessmen should also be addressed: There is James Simon, who, among other things, gave the Nofretiti to the National Museums. Eduard Arnhold, the businessman and patron to whom the Prussian state owes, among others, the Villa Massimo in Rome lives at Voßstraße 28. The Bleichröders, who had substantially financed Bismarck's historical years of industrial expansion, had their office at Behrenstraße 63. Abraham Mendelssohn, son of the philosopher of religion, lived from 1825 to 1851 where today the Prussian Upper Chamber is based, at Leipziger Straße 3. Felix Mendelssohn-Bartholdy was born there and at the tender age of nine had made his first appearance in his parents' home as a pianist and had composed in the garden, where later the Prussian Cabinet met; at seventeen he composed the overture of *A Midsummer Night's Dream*. At a later time the Prussian Upper Chamber was established there, which, utilized by the Academy of Sciences, still stands today in the former no-man's land in front of Leipziger Platz. Straight across, at Leipziger Straße 132–137, was the famous Wertheim store, which was designed by Alfred Messel and opened in 1904; in 1933 the store was "aryanized," although the Wertheims had long since left the faith of their father and had converted to Protestantism. Another Berliner, Hermann Tiez, had his enormous bazaar at Spittelmarkt. Her-Tie, the initials of the founder, hide in the group of stores "aryanized" in 1934. To mention only two from the area of science, Albert Einstein and Max Born were active, among other places, at today's Humboldt University.

The American Jewish Committee (AJC) has its German office a stone's throw from the former Wertheim store, in the new building with the beautiful name Mosse Palace. The AJC office, established by Eugene Dubois, a trailblazer of American-Jewish and German relations since the beginning of the 1980s, and his alter ego, Rabbi Andrew Baker, who is particularly active in Washington, D.C., in regards to transatlantic relations, is—aside from the Ronald-Lauder-Foundation in the front building of the synagogue in Prenzlauer Berg and the European Jewish Congress situated in the Leo-Baeck-Haus—the most visible sign of the return of Berlin to the map of internationally active Jewish organizations. Before the gates of the city, since 1992 a center of German-Jewish learning has developed under the direction of Julius Schoeps at the Moses-Mendelssohn Center of Potsdam University. In November 2000 the Abraham-Geiger-College was opened there, a liberal rabbinic department in the tradition of the College for the Study of Judaism where Leo Baeck used to teach. In the American Academy, a Berlin-American forum founded after the retreat of the U.S. federation of protective forces, Gary Smith established a salon, which would have honored

Henriette Herz and which has become one of the most important transatlantic exchange points that brings together Jewish and non-Jewish intellectuals from the United States and Germany in determining policy for the new century and millennium. We have physically thereby already left the axis between Alexanderplatz and the Brandenburg Gate, on the flanks of which Peter Eisenman will erect a Holocaust memorial out of 2,700 steles under contract of the German Bundestag. Less than half a mile away a place of learning is being established on the grounds where the agents of Nazi terror had their center. There, where the Gestapo, SS, and the Reich's central security office organized the murder of the European Jews, a building is emerging that should provide answers to those who have questions on the history of those twelve years, four months, and eight days. About nine miles away Zwi Hecker has built a practical architectural icon, namely the new building of the Jewish *Grundschule* (primary school). And in the same vicinity is the new Israeli embassy designed by Orit Willenberg-Giladi, which simultaneously includes in the embassy compound a magnificent villa erected by a Jewish businessman. But not only new buildings have emerged: since 1990 two prayer forums have developed into synagogues. Thus, since 1998 in Oranienburgerstraße somewhat under the dome of the new synagogue there has been an "egalitarian" minyan, which has drawn men and women equally to all worship activities; one year later services were also established in the former U.S. Army synagogue of the Chaplain Center in Hüttenweg in Berlin Zehlendorf, which continues in the liberal tradition of the Berlin community.

Let us now close our city tour as we explore Berlin-Mitte at Pariser Platz. In 1926 in the Armin Palace, Pariser Platz 4, in which the Academy of the Arts has been located since 1907, Jakob Wassermann held his speech honoring Hugo von Hofmannsthal. Alfred Döblin, who published *Berlin Alexanderplatz* in 1929, was a member of this venerable institution until 1933. In house number 6a, directly in front of the Brandenburg Gate, Giacomo Meyerbeer (originally known as Jacob Meyer Beer), the composer of numerous operas such as *The African* and *The Huguenots*, lived from 1843 to 1863; his brother, Michael Beer, the publisher of the tragedy *Strünsee* also lived at Pariser Platz. Max Liebermann lived right next door, at Pariser Platz 7, from 1893 to 1933. There he became a witness to the development of Hitler's government fashioned as a takeover of power on 30 January 1933. The torches carried by the SA on their march by kindled a flame in all of Europe, the fallout of which will never pass because millions of people on all sides fell victim to it.

Liebermann's dictate at the witnessing of this first installation of National Socialist power has become a Berliner bon mot: "I can hardly eat
as much as much as I would like to vomit."

The Armin Palace was destroyed by a bombing campaign down to
a small bit of building until the beginning of the 1990s. With the
inclusion of the small bit of building, the Academy of the Arts once
again established house at this place rich in tradition, giving a living
and often fascinating memorial to the exiled, brutalized, deported,
and murdered artists by controversially exhibiting their works and
appointing their successors in spirit to members of the Academy
not just in its archives, but rather also in its public programs. The
Protestant Church is responding to the challenges of the new Berlin
in that, for example, it invited representatives of the Islamic faith,
Buddhism, and Judaism as guests to its nationally broadcasted
Sylvester (New Year) services, led by Bishop Wolfgang Huber, to
introduce the amazed Christians by way of music and words to alternative paths to God. If this had been possible 100 years earlier, the
history of the twentieth century would certainly have been less fatal
for millions of people.

When, shortly before on 9 November 2000, the German people
wanted to send a message of humanity and tolerance in response
to massive and brutal attacks on foreigners and arson attacks on
synagogues, more than 200,000 came. Peter Strieder, chairman of
the Berlin Social Democratic Party (SPD) and Renate Künast, at
the time still federal chairperson of Bündnis '90/The Greens, initiated together with me a silent march from the new synagogue to
the Brandenburg Gate. There the national symphony orchestra
performed under the direction of Daniel Barenboim; Federal
President Johannes Rau and President of the Central Council of
Jews in Germany Paul Spiegel both spoke, and representatives of
all parties represented in the Bundestag, from Petra Pau of the
Party of Democratic Socialism (PDS) to Bavarian Prime Minister
Edmund Stoiber, stood peaceably next to each other. This is because there is one thing that unifies all democratic parties amid
political party competition, even the opposition: the "Never Again"
slogan pertaining to anti-Semitism, intolerance, and politically
motivated violence.

Connecting the Jewish Berliners mentioned in this article, and many of
those not mentioned, is the fact that they lived and were active in
Berlin, were condemned and banned after 1933: they are a piece of

Berlin's history: Berlin's past—its trails are particularly numerous in Berlin-Mitte and can be uncovered, found, and must be maintained: Berlin's present—that Berlin should once again be more than a museum for the activities of the Jewish Berliners is today so utopian as 3 October 1990 was on 3 October 1989: Berlin's future?!

At the beginning, we recounted the tale of the Straße des 17. Juni, where Berlin police stood guard over British military police who protected Soviet soldiers, who, in turn, stood honorary guard at the Soviet War Memorial for the Red Army soldiers who fell in the slaughter over Berlin. Today, Berlin police stand guard over government buildings as in every capital city and over Jewish establishments, because there is worldwide vagabond Middle Eastern terrorism. The Reichstag is no longer a museum, but rather decisions of the German Bundestag are debated and decided there. So much is so different, some good and some still on the way to becoming good through a historical turn.

Apropos museums: in the meantime Berlin not only has a local Jewish museum in the Centrum Judaicum, but on Lindenstraße it also has a new building designed by Daniel Libeskind to represent the history of Jewish life in German-speaking countries. An American Berliner, former U.S. Treasury Secretary Michael Blumenthal has nurtured a gigantic learning center from an almost failed project, which has straight off become the city's most frequently visited museum; this simultaneously makes clear that Berlin is again more than a gigantic Jewish museum. Berlin has its Jewish museum and also a Jewish past, a Jewish present, and, with God's help, also a Jewish future.

12. Berlin's Turkish Community

Faruk Şen

Following World War II, Western European countries entered a phase of rapid development. They thus faced a deficiency in the supply of labor due to various economic and demographic factors and so turned to relatively less-developed southern European countries with labor surpluses to fulfill their demands. Turkey joined the labor-exporting countries at a rather late stage during the 1960s. Turkish immigration to Western Europe began with the signing of the labor recruitment agreement between Turkey and Germany in 1961. Subsequently, Turkey concluded recruitment agreements also with the Netherlands, Belgium, and Austria in 1964, with France in 1965, and with Sweden in 1967.

In the early years of immigration, migrating Turks mostly formed a homogeneous group in Europe—mainly male laborers. After Western European countries stopped recruiting workers—particularly after 1973—significant changes occurred in the demographics of Turks immigrating to Europe. Beginning in March 1974, the Law of Family Reunification, which first came into effect in the Federal Republic of Germany, set up a framework allowing Turkish workers to reunite with their family members in Europe—most notably in Germany.

Presently, there are about 3.5 million Turks living in Western Europe, making them the largest foreign population in Europe. While this figure represents about 5.2 percent of Turkey's population, Turkish workers in Europe comprise 5.4 percent of Turkey's resident labor force. The largest Turkish minority in Western Europe lives in Germany.

There are currently about 7.3 million foreigners living in the Federal Republic of Germany. Three-fourths of them come from Mediterranean countries. Around 1.8 million of them are EU citizens, while the rest are mainly from Turkey, the former Yugoslavia, Morocco, and Tunisia. With a population of 2 million, Turks constitute the country's largest group of foreigners, who can increasingly be deemed a minority. Turks make up almost 2.4 percent of the total population of Germany, which is about 82 million. Turkish immigrants are followed in number by immigrants coming from the former Yugoslavia, Italy, Greece, Spain, Portugal, Morocco, and Tunisia.

Immigration to Europe from Turkey was initially slow, as it was a new phenomenon for the country, but it accelerated from 1963 on, following the signing of the Association Agreement between the European Community and Turkey. The successive Turkish governments supported emigration because it alleviated unemployment and improved the balance of payments through workers' remittances. Although labor emigration from Turkey to Western Europe came to a halt when recruitment stopped in the early 1970s, emigration continued by way of family reunification for the next two decades. Today, Turkish migration to Western Europe can be observed in three different forms. First of all, most of the immigration takes place as family formation. Family reunification of Turks was practically completed by the end of the 1980s; a trend of increasing immigration is now observed by way of family formation, however, whereby young Turkish immigrants in Europe choose their spouses from Turkey. Second, politically motivated immigration, mostly Kurdish since the mid-1980s, continues. Here it must be recalled that economic reasons, along with political reasons, also play a role, particularly in regards to the Kurds. Third, there is some clandestine labor immigration. In all current types of migration from Turkey mentioned above, no mass, managed type of immigration is noticeable, but rather immigration mostly involves individuals making personal decisions.

Although the level of emigration from Turkey is not what it used to be in earlier decades, pressure for emigration remains. Looking at the official figures of emigration and return immigration, not including the numbers of clandestine emigrants and those seeking asylum, the net emigration figure regarding Turkey remains positive. Although throughout most of the 1990s about 40,000 people returned from Germany to Turkey every year—with a total of 60,000 from Western countries—the number of new immigrants to other countries outweighed the number of those who returned to Turkey (though on a decreasing scale). Looking at asylum figures, it is possible to obtain an annual average number of 22,250 applications in Germany for asylum seekers from Turkey during the 1990s. Here it must be taken into consideration that not all applications for asylum are officially recognized.

Today, immigration to Europe from Turkey takes place mainly in the form of family formation: an immigrant or an immigrant's child marries a partner from the immigrant's or the immigrant's parents' country of origin; this leads to the immigration of the partner. This family-forming immigration (partner selection) is embedded in a larger framework. Under restrictive immigration policies in Europe, family-forming immigration is one way to overcome barriers against migration.

Here it is important to note that the values of the immigrant community, though going through a process of transformation and adaptation, remain much the same in the domain of community and family relations. This implies that, very often, traditional marriage patterns are preserved, leading to the active use of community and family relations in choosing a marriage partner. Furthermore, non-immigrants in the country of origin often exert pressure on immigrants with the aim of making immigration possible for other members of the non-immigrant community. The ultimate objective is to seek financial support and assistance through immigration. Since immigration is currently only possible by way of marriage, marriage partners are sought by non-immigrants among the children of immigrants. Parents often yield to these pressures due to the strong commitment to the community of origin. In Germany alone it is estimated that over 90 percent of the Turks choose Turkish marriage partners (less than 10 percent of the marriages among Turks are binational). Within the last several years, about 16,500 spouses migrated to Germany each year because of a marriage.

Berlin's Turkish Community

In Berlin the recruitment of immigrant workers was initially delayed. In the first instance, the growing need of additive manpower could be satisfied with people from the German Democratic Republic (GDR). The situation in the labor market changed in 1961 with the construction of the Wall. It took only five years (1961–1966) to raise the number of Turkish citizens living in Berlin to the same level as during the period before the war—from 1905 to 1938.

In 1964 there were 20,000 open jobs and only 9,000 unemployed. The market mainly needed unskilled workers; women were preferred because they usually earned less than their male colleagues. In 1964 the first female Turks came to Berlin. Many of their husbands were still waiting for permission to go to Germany. By 1968, seven years after the labor recruitment agreement and the beginning of the Turkish immigration to West Germany, the huge influx of Turkish workers had also affected Berlin. In 1973, already 79,468 Turks lived in Berlin. Since the end of 1972, Turks have formed the city's largest group of immigrants. After recruitment stopped in 1973, family-forming immigration led to a differentiation of the Turkish population in Germany, including in Berlin. Young families began to move away from their guest workers' homes and often chose cheap apartments in the districts that are still to be renovated within the near future. These Berlin districts were mainly Wedding, Kreuzberg, and Tiergarten. At the end of 1978 Turkish immigrants amounted to 15.4 percent in Kreuzberg, 11.8 percent in Wedding, and 7.9 percent in Tiergarten. The establishment of a certain Turkish infrastructure in these areas led other Turks to also move into these districts. And within these districts, special areas of higher concentration developed. Houses in extremely bad condition, which were not meant to be rented to Germans or such and which have yet to be torn down or renovated in the near future, were preferentially rented to the guest workers. In some blocks the percentage of Turkish inhabitants was about 60 percent. In 1975 a limit was placed on the number of foreigners allowed to move into districts with a foreign population of more than 12 percent. This limit was abolished in 1989. Since 1980, as in all of West Germany, a new form of Turkish immigration to Berlin—comprised mainly of political refugees seeking asylum—took place.

Today, Berlin is the city with the highest number of residents of Turkish background. At the end of 2000, of 435,117 people (13.1 percent of the total population) with a foreign passport registered in Berlin, 127,335 were Turks. This means that nearly 30 percent of the foreign population in Berlin has a Turkish passport. At the end of 1999, naturalized citizens with a Turkish background numbered 41,369. In the above-mentioned districts of Kreuzberg and Wedding, the percentage of inhabitants with a foreign passport amounts to more than 30 percent.

With the fall of the Wall in 1989 and German reunification in 1990, the situation for Berliners of Turkish background changed significantly. Their preferred districts, which before were in a way "protected" by the Wall, now comprised Berlin's new center. The fear that rising rents could dislodge people with lower incomes remains. New participation by citizens from the former GDR and other Eastern European countries in the labor market and the domination of the service sector make it harder for all Berliners, but mostly for immigrants, to find their place in the Berlin Republic.

Demographic Structure of Turks

Looking at recent data on the demographic structure of the Turkish community in Germany, it can be observed that 54.2 percent of Turks in Germany are male and 45.8 percent female. Of the population, 50.5 percent are between fourteen and twenty-nine years old, whereas among Germans the comparable rate is only 25 percent. In the Turkish population, 33.8 percent are between thirty-nine and forty-nine years old, while 32 percent of Germans are within this age group. Only 15.7 percent of Turks are age fifty and above, while this rate is 43 percent among Germans. So Turks in Germany still make up a younger population than do Germans.

Meanwhile, 16 percent of the Turkish residential population—as it is called in Germany—are born in Germany. Those engaged in gainful employment equal 29 percent, meaning two-thirds of the Turkish population are dependent family members. The average Turkish household is comprised of four persons, and there are 610,000 Turkish households in the country. On the whole, the average net income of the Turkish household in Germany is about 2,075 euros, according to a survey by the Center for Turkish Studies.

Over time, the change in the demographic structure of the Turkish population resulted in a housing problem in Germany and led to a ghettoization of Turks, which became acute in the 1970s and continued into the 1980s. This had its roots in two areas: the general housing policy in Germany and the lack of acceptance of foreigners by the native German population in local areas.

The housing situation for foreigners and particularly for Turks is also negatively affected in two ways by the recent upsurge of xenophobia in Germany since 1990. On one hand, German landlords' prejudices against foreigners result in discrimination, whereby foreigners find it difficult to find an apartment. On the other hand, although a small factor so far, German landlords are afraid of racially motivated attacks (such as the violence a few years ago by the Kurdistan Workers Party [PKK]) on their property.

With the decreasing tendency to return to Turkey, an increasing readiness to integrate into German society at all levels, the unwillingness of German landlords to rent their houses and flats to Turks, and the general housing shortage in Germany, Turks increasingly prefer to purchase flats and houses in this country. As a result, so far more than 125,000 Turks have acquired real estate in the Federal Republic of Germany.

In the face of Turkey's existing economic and political problems as well as the fact that many second and third generation Turks are born in Germany, speak better German than Turkish, and receive their education in Germany, many Turks see return to their homeland as no longer a viable option. Even first-generation Turks who are more than sixty years old and retired do not go back to Turkey for a number of reasons. A 1992 study of the Center for Turkish Studies, commissioned by the Federal Ministry of Labor and Social Order, shows that elderly Turks have personal ties, such as family, in Germany and believe they receive better health care in Germany than in Turkey.

Turkish Immigrant Businessmen in Germany

The number of self-employed Turkish residents has been rapidly rising. According to data collected by the Center for Turkish Studies, presently there are 80,600 Turkish immigrants who have established their own businesses throughout Europe: in Germany, France, the Netherlands, Belgium, and Great Britain. Of these, 55,700 are in Germany alone. Turkish businessmen are no longer found just in the classical branches, such as food services and retail/wholesale trade, but are investing in many different sectors.

The increasing trend of self-employment among Turkish immigrants in Germany can also be related to the fact that, in general, unemployment is a major problem among Turks in Germany. Germany is presently faced with a serious unemployment problem, which affects foreigners overproportionately. As a result of the structural transition and problems in the German labor market, and due also to insufficient vocational skills and discrimination, the unemployment rate among Turks is the highest among all foreigners.

At the end of October 2000, unemployed Turkish workers numbered 149,828 in Germany, making up almost one-third of unemployed foreigners. It is particularly problematic to place young foreigners, and especially school dropouts, in the labor market. Since employment opportunities for young foreigners in Germany are mostly limited to secondary sector jobs, informal job networks play an important role to compensate for lack of opportunities. Jobs found through informal job networks, however, are often less prestigious apprenticeship positions or are dead-end jobs. Since foreign residents in Germany have no political rights, with the exception of secondary political rights such as union membership and representation in work councils, they have few opportunities to shape job networks.

As a result of the changes in the economic structure in Germany, the employment levels of non-nationals have decreased considerably. The downward trend in employment in the fields of mining, raw material processing, manufacturing, production of consumption goods, and construction have had especially negative consequences; the majority of immigrants were traditionally employed in these sectors, and the tertiary sector could not compensate sufficiently for the loss of jobs in the manufacturing sector.

The Economic Impact of Turkish Entrepreneurs in Germany and within the European Union

One important dimension of the social change in the Turkish population in Germany is the development of Turkish entrepreneurship (see table 12.1), which accelerated particularly in the 1990s. Between 1985 and 2000 the number of Turkish entrepreneurs rose from 22,000 to 59,500, an increase of 170 percent. This equals an average annual growth rate of 11 percent for this period.

Table 12.1 Development of the Economic Power of Turkish Entrepreneurs in Germany

	1985	2000
Number of businesses	1,700	2,900
Average investment per business (in DM)	1,600	2,700
Total investment volume (in DM billion)	5.3	8.9
Average turnover per business (in DM)	3,800	6,400
Annual total turnover (in DM billion)	21.8	36.6
Employees per company	13,900	23,400
Total number of employees	11,400	19,100

Source: Center for Turkish Studies (Essen, 2001).

Economic Power of Turkish Entrepreneurs in the European Union

With more than 3.5 million (in 2000), the number of Turks within the borders of the European Union equals seven times the entire population of Luxembourg. This figure is higher than four-fifths of the population of Ireland, more than half of the inhabitants of Denmark or Finland, and nearly one-third of the population of Austria, Greece, Portugal, or Sweden. Moreover, there are 80,000 Turks living in Switzerland.

In 2000, the share of entrepreneurs among the gainfully employed Turkish population in EU countries reached 6.7 percent. In 1995, this quota amounted to merely 4.8 percent. According to the calculations of the Center for Turkish Studies, the number of Turkish entrepreneurs in the EU has increased from 54,300 to 80,600 between 1995 and 2000 (see table 12.2), showing an increase of 48.4 percent. The significance of Turkish entrepreneurs is revealed not only by their quantitative growth, but also by their economic potential.

The total annual turnover of Turkish companies in the EU grew from DM 42.2 billion in 1995 to DM 68.1 billion in 2000. This corresponds to an increase of 59.5 percent, a development that reflects the investment volume and the number of employees. During the same period the investment volume rose from DM 11.0 billion to DM 17.4 billion. The growth rate of the cumulated investment volume amounts to 58.2 percent.

Also between 1995 and 2000, the number of employees in Turkish companies in the EU rose from 232,000 to an estimated 419,000. Thus, the number of employees has nearly doubled. Turkish workers, and especially entrepreneurs living within the borders of the EU, live predominantly in Germany. This implicates a significant

Table 12.2 Economic Performance of Turkish Entrepreneurs in the European Union

	1995	2000
Number of businesses	54,300	80,600
Average investment per business (in DM)	189,700	216,000
Total investment (in DM billion)	10.3	17.4
Average turnover per business (in DM)	777,000	845,000
Annual turnover (in DM billion)	42.2	68.1
Average number of employees per business	3.9	5.2
Total number of employees	212,000	419,000

Source: Center for Turkish Studies (Essen, 2001).

position among the Turkish population living in the EU for Turkish entrepreneurs in Germany.

Turkish Entrepreneurs in Germany and the European Union: Future Projection for 2015

The Center for Turkish Studies has made a prognosis for the first time concerning the development of the number and the economic conditions of Turkish entrepreneurs in Germany and Europe for the next fifteen years. Between 1985 and 2000, the Turkish population in Germany showed a growth rate of 73 percent and attained an average growth rate of 4.9 percent annually. A careful estimation shows an expected average growth rate of 2.5 percent per annum for the future. This takes into account the net growth of the population and the status of immigration. This puts the population in Germany of those of Turkish origin at 3.4 million by 2015. Based on the same estimate, the Turkish population in the EU is expected to be about 4.8 million by 2015.

On the basis of the presently available data, a doubling of the number of Turkish entrepreneurs within the EU can be expected by 2015 (see table 12.3). According to this estimate, there will be 160,000 Turkish entrepreneurs within the EU, and 12,000 in Germany alone. An increase from 327,000 in 2000 to 720,000 in 2015 is prognosticated for the number of employees in Turkish companies in Germany. Also by 2015, Turkish entrepreneurs within the EU will employ approximately 960,000 people.

Economic indicators are also expected to attain a considerable dimension over the next fifteen years. For example, the total turnover of Turkish entrepreneurs in Germany is expected to increase from

Table 12.3 Turkish Entrepreneurs in Germany and the European Union

INDICATORS	GERMANY		EU	
	2000	**2015**	**2000**	**2015**
Number of businesses	59,500	120,000	80,600	160,000
Total investment volume (in DM billion)	13.6	30	17.4	40
Annual turnover (in DM billion)	55.7	130	68.1	170
Total employment (in 1,000)	327,000	720,000	419,000	960,000

Source: Center for Turkish Studies (Essen, 2001).

DM 55.7 billion in 2000 to DM 130 billion in 2015. For the same period, the cumulated investment volume is expected to increase from DM 13.6 billion to about DM 30 billion. Also in 2015, Turkish entrepreneurs within the EU should attain an annual turnover amounting to DM 170 billion and a cumulated investment volume of about DM 40 billion.

When Turkish labor immigration began forty years ago, nobody would have anticipated the present situation. Given a normal process of social, economic, and political circumstances, this trend will likely develop even more positively than estimated.

Outlaw Discrimination against Minority Groups in the European Union

Studies show that in the EU, 31 percent of Europeans agree that discrimination against minority groups should be outlawed in order to improve the relationships between people of different races, religions, and cultures. In Luxembourg and Sweden, this figure is higher, whereas agreement with this opinion is lowest in Austria, Spain, and Ireland.

Discrimination in the Labor Market

In 1994 the International Labor Office commissioned the Center for Turkish Studies to conduct a study in Germany on "Empirical proof of discrimination against foreign workers regarding access to employment." Carried out by a number of institutions in different countries worldwide, the global study as a whole aimed at determining if there was any discrimination against foreign communities regarding entry to the labor market in the industrialized countries.

Parameters were set. Under the principle of equal access, the applicant of the minority population was to have an unlimited and unrestricted work permit; in addition, educational and vocational qualifications were to be considered equally. Against this backdrop, in each situation a member of the majority and a member of the minority populations applied for the same job. In this way equal discriminatory treatment by the employer could most clearly be traced back to the different national origin of the applicants. Since the Turks constitute the largest minority in the Federal Republic of Germany, they were chosen as the representative minority population in the study. Jobs to which the applicants applied were separated into two categories: semi-skilled jobs and higher-qualified jobs.

A complete examination of individual results revealed that, on the whole, discrimination was statistically significant in semi-skilled jobs, but not in higher-qualified jobs. In the category of semi-skilled jobs, among 175 usable cases there were 33 cases in which the Turkish applicant experienced discrimination, which corresponds to a net discrimination rate of 19 percent. In the higher-qualified jobs, from 299 usable applications, in 218 cases both the German and the Turkish applicant received an equally positive response. In total, the Turkish applicant was discriminated against in 55 cases and the German applicant in 26 cases, which gives a net discrimination rate of 9.7 percent against the Turkish applicant. This rate, however, lies below the statistically significant rate of 11 percent obtained by Bernoulli's theory of normal distribution. One can therefore conclude that the empirically obtained data on the net discrimination against the Turkish applicant in the field of higher-qualified jobs was statistically insignificant. A distinction should be made, however, for clerical jobs in which face-to-face contact with customers plays an important role. In this area, the net discrimination rate against the Turkish applicant was found to be 43.2 percent The study also reveals the interesting point that discrimination occurred mostly in large companies in the field of higher-qualified jobs, but mostly in small companies in the field of semi-skilled jobs.

The reactions in each branch must also be considered in connection with the actual need for labor. For instance, the demand for orderlies (male nurses) in Germany is very high. Also, in many areas of skilled labor, not enough German labor is available in the market, which results in a demand for more foreign skilled labor and apprentices.

Moreover, within the Turkish community the study focused on applicants of the second generation, who have a higher degree of integration in German society. Conclusions about the behavior of the employers toward the first generation are not included in the results. Nor can any statement be made about possible discrimination against Turkish women. If these groups had been included, the results would have probably turned out differently, which was the case in the Netherlands.

Among the semi-skilled jobs, discrimination was not only found to have occurred to a significant degree in small companies; discrimination was likewise detected within the services sector, particularly when sales activity called for direct contact with the customers.

In no other profession is personal contact as intensive as it is for orderlies—the area of least discrimination against the Turkish applicant. Some employers might reason that customer contact with foreign employees hinders or prevents business. This may not apply to hospitals, however, since they do not aim to make a profit; and foreign skilled labor has existed for many decades in German hospitals.

In the literature on immigrants, involvement in the social and economic life of communities is defined as social citizenship, which is discussed in terms of exclusion (marginalization) and inclusion (occupational mobility). Exclusion from the labor market leads to marginal employment positions, relegation to dead-end and low-paying jobs, and unemployment and thus income poverty. Inclusion, on the other hand, occurs when there is access to job training, post-secondary education, and entry into jobs with prospects for professional advancement. Access to jobs and education determines not only participation in the labor market, but also the quality of social citizenship—activities in the social, economic, and political aspects of life. Lack of access to the above may lead to socioeconomic marginalization and finally to the emergence of sub-cultural groups in society.

In order to support the integration of immigrant groups into the larger society, to reduce discrimination and combat xenophobia and racism, it is often proposed that immigrant workers be granted the same rights as nationals. These rights would, of course, entail obligations. The present immigration policies in Europe and in Germany are founded on the principle of equal obligations, i.e., for immigrant workers to give full recognition to legislation and other regulatory provisions on the same terms as nationals. Immigrant workers' integration into society, however, is not based on the principle of equal rights and equal opportunities. Although the lives of immigrant workers are as affected by government decision making as any other residents, their participation in the decision-making process is very limited, if not nonexistent. If a substantial number of permanent residents cannot vote, the legitimacy of the political decision-making process is impaired. It must be recognized that throughout Europe the existence of such marginalized groups in significant numbers undermines democracy.

Political participation, such as the right to vote, would be an effective means for integration of non-nationals, for Turks in particular. It would also stimulate action by political parties to become more engaged in matters regarding non-nationals.

Part II

PERSPECTIVES ON THE BERLIN REPUBLIC FROM ABROAD

13. The Berlin Republic's Evolving Leadership Role in Europe

Garrick Utley

No single event at the end of the Cold War has more symbolic meaning and practical potential than the unification of the two German states with their focus in Berlin as the restored capital of Germany. For more than fifty years, since the consolidation of economic and political governance systems in East and West during the late 1940s, and more particularly since the erection of the Berlin Wall in 1961, Berlin stood as an open wound in the heart of Europe. Layers of historical experience stood painfully exposed in the bombed-out streets and barbed wire of a torn city and in the memories of past generations of Prussian and German power lying in barren inner-city ruins. Berlin was also the frontier of America's promise to safeguard human rights, democracy, and market economies against the command economy and political dictatorships of Soviet control. From the implementation of the Marshall Plan through the Berlin Airlift to the formation of the Federal Republic of Germany, American efforts to promote Germany's full integration and membership in the Western community of nations provided a focal point of U.S. foreign policy. The full integration of a unified Germany as part of both NATO and the European Union provides eloquent testimony to the wisdom and courage of that approach. United Berlin remains Germany's central symbol and a key reality for the future of Europe.

For the United States, the Berlin Republic's particular significance lies both in its being the symbol of united Germany and the center of a broader EU integrating Western and Eastern Europe. Despite many remaining problems, Germany alone has experienced the integration of its western and eastern Länder, with their historically divergent systems, and the separate sectors of Berlin. The German unification process has been slow, troubled, and expensive, and it is not yet completed. A deep crisis in Berlin city finances has had considerable fall-out effects for the major political parties there. While it seems unlikely to join a coalition in the federal government in the foreseeable future, the growing popularity of the Party of Democratic Socialism (PDS), the heir of the German Democratic Republic's (GDR's) Socialist Unity Party (SED), and now its inclusion in the Berlin city government, testify to the yet unfinished business of German unification. Germany's friends and allies in Europe and America are following closely the efforts of German political leaders to overcome the remaining social and cultural barriers.

Just as German political leadership in Berlin, including the local, state, and national governments, have sought to overcome these obstacles, so the leadership of the European Union needs to reach out to the new democracies in Central and Eastern Europe. A widespread and largely successful effort is underway to help these countries adjust their systems and political cultures to Western norms and global practices. However, without effective stewardship from the Berlin Republic in broadening the EU, enlarging NATO, and assuring the future of the euro, this process cannot proceed on a steady and sound basis. Berlin's voice within both the EU and the transatlantic alliance needs to be strong and clear in order to achieve the full potential of a united Europe.

How will the Berlin Republic exercise its new responsibilities of leadership in Europe and the world? This remains an unfolding story. The roles and characters of other major European powers such as the United Kingdom and France are, by comparison, more fixed and predictable in their historical patterns. These countries have not faced the challenges of overcoming territorial division or living on the frontier of the Cold War. Nor have they carried the financial burdens of integrating seventeen million of their own citizens once stranded behind the Wall. Germany, on the other hand, is still adjusting to its new role as Europe's largest nation-state, but it has taken enormous steps toward defining that role and implementing the policies to support it.

Many Americans who study Germany understand that it is engaged in a complex process of building its relationships with neighbors to the south and east. These neighbors, no longer kept at a distance by the Iron Curtain, are developing an intensive relationship with the Federal Republic politically, economically, and socially. Central and Eastern European countries have reoriented their economics and politics toward Western Europe, Germany in particular. Trade and investment flows between Germany and these new market economies now surpass by far their levels of interchange with the former Soviet Union. In matters of law and financial systems, many Eastern European countries are adapting themselves to German rather than American or British standards. In corporate relationships, the Eastern countries have responded profoundly to German initiatives and proposals for cooperative ventures. And in the crucial area of immigration, Germany has taken the initiative to identify a just and equitable system for governing the movement of peoples in and out of European Union territory. German leadership has not been perfect or ideal. Clearly, much remains to be accomplished in terms of integrating the nations of Central and Eastern Europe, and major questions remain in agriculture, environmental quality, and energy usage and dependency. Meanwhile, there are worrisome signs of impatience in several Eastern European countries with the pace of the accession process. Nevertheless, German political and business leaders have clearly recognized the challenges and responded to them with energy and vision.

From an American perspective, German leadership is increasingly important in helping to define how the West deals with another major legacy of the Cold War: relations with Russia. German foreign policy has identified Russia as its biggest long-term challenge. And Russia looks increasingly to Germany and the European Union as one its major paths to integration in the global system. The challenges facing both Germany and Russia are enormous. German policy recognizes that a destabilized and floundering Russia can only harm Europe's own sense of security and stability. A weak Russia will not be a good partner of Europe but rather a source of uncontrolled migration, organized crime, and potential social disintegration along the eastern frontier. Russia cannot, however, realistically expect to become a full member of NATO or of the EU in the foreseeable future. Russia may require another generation in order to adjust itself to the EU's rules, procedures, norms, and in general the requisite degree of internal cohesion and standard of governance. But EU leaders increasingly recognize the need to engage Russia in a constructive interchange including business, political, and security relationships. Again, Germany must stand at the center of this interchange to maintain its momentum and assure its eventual success, and there is every indication that its political leaders recognize this imperative.

The Berlin Republic's new importance in international relations reveals itself in other areas as well. Since the end of World War II, the Federal Republic has carefully built a strong and positive relationship with the State of Israel and with the Jewish community in the United States. This has included many projects of diplomacy and political dialogue, exchanges, education programs, financial support, and efforts to resolve and heal the painful legacies of the Holocaust. In the process, German statesmen have established close and trustworthy relationships in the Middle East, and this has recently encouraged hopes that Germany will play a positive diplomatic role in helping that war-torn region move toward peace. Not that it will supplant the crucial American role there. Nevertheless, Germany's voice in the region can become an increasingly positive force.

Regarding transatlantic defense, American-European relations entered a new phase, if not a new era, in the aftermath of the September 11 terrorist attacks on the United States. For the first time in its history, NATO invoked Article 5 of the Washington Treaty calling for a common response in the collective defense of one of its members. It is extraordinary that a treaty provision originally intended to protect the Federal Republic of Germany from a Soviet invasion was first applied to defend the United States as a result of a terrorist attack. Just how NATO member countries, including Germany, will interpret this decision and its meaning for NATO's mission remains unclear. Clearly, though, the transatlantic alliance will provide the core of any larger international alliance to protect civilized society from the horrors of terrorism. The outpouring of support in Germany and other major European powers for the United States provides eloquent testimony to the deep transatlantic community of values and interests that have been created during the last five decades, even though differences and even tensions are bound to emerge.

There are, of course, legitimate concerns regarding a long-term bifurcation of American and European defense interests. Unilateralist sentiments among some leaders of the current American administration have caused many Europeans to question the U.S. commitment to multilateralism in the areas of global warming, the spread of weapons of mass destruction, and the alleviation of world poverty. Meanwhile, in Europe, declining real budgets in defense have caused American leaders to ask whether Europeans are prepared to marshal the political and financial wherewithal for the modernization of their military apparatus, support the future needs of NATO, and strengthen the European Defense Initiative. In Germany, continuing budgetary pressures resulting from support of the Eastern Länder have kept defense spending as a percentage of GDP even below that of France and the United Kingdom. Weak economic growth during 2001 and 2002 worsened this picture further. Nevertheless, Germany's historic willingness to send peacekeeping troops to the Balkans and to take a leadership role in relations with Eastern Europe, Russia, and the Middle East, and particularly the decision to participate in military operations in Afghanistan, signal a sea change in the Federal Republic's foreign policy engagement. The Berlin Republic has moved away from both Cold War and post–World War II identities toward a new and responsible role in a complex multilateral world. This will have positive long-term effects on Germany's relations with the United States.

Nowhere is the interdependence of the transatlantic community more powerfully illustrated than in economic and corporate relations. During the last few years, Europeans and Americans have invested extraordinary amounts in transatlantic ventures. Corporate acquisitions, mergers, foreign direct investment, and portfolio investment have by far exceeded historic norms. Investment flows have replaced trade as the chief motor of the transatlantic economy. Sales by American branches of European companies now amount to five times the amount of European exports to the United States. The year 2000 witnessed approximately $200 billion in net capital flow from Europe to the United States, much of it represented in multi-billion dollar corporate acquisitions such as Deutsche Telekom's purchase of Voicestream. As a result, the American and European economies are now more interdependent than at any time in historical memory. This reality augments and cements the transatlantic community of common interests across the board of economic policy questions. Meanwhile, however, it carries the somewhat unexpected consequence that a downturn in the United States has resulted in a simultaneous downturn in the European economy, leaving the global system without a major engine of renewal. The world market today is highly integrated, particularly in terms of its European-American component.

In the aftermath of September 11, major geopolitical shifts seem at hand. Wherever they may lead, the European-American connection is certain to be the focus and center of the values-based community grappling with the issues. We are destined to work together in global economic, political, and security affairs to secure our common future. Similarly, the Berlin Republic seems destined to play a major leadership role in this evolving endeavor. The last ten plus years of German unification and restoration of Berlin as the capital have prepared the way. This has also been a period of tremendous progress in European integration and in globalization itself. Neither Germany and the EU nor the United States will be able to escape these larger challenges. Only together will we succeed and prosper.

14. Transformed Relations: From the Cold War to a New Partnership between Russia and the Berlin Republic

Andrei Zagorski

Whatever the transfer of Germany's capital city from Bonn to Berlin may mean for German politics, this change has not been widely acknowledged by the Russian public. Nor has there been any significant adaptation of Russian perspectives of Germany—of the Berlin Republic—since the transition was completed. This does not imply, however, that Russian perspectives of Germany have remained static all through the last decade. On the contrary, both the public opinion polls and the evolution of Moscow's policy portray very dynamic and profound changes in how Russians see Germany and what expectations they have with regards to the forthcoming future.

The end of the Cold War made it possible to reverse the adversarial relationship between Bonn and Moscow shaped in the decades after World War II. Much faster and more easily than quite a few other nations, both the Russian public and, largely, the elite have found a way to accommodate themselves to German unification and to abandon obsolete thinking about Germany. Many descendants of the old Soviet political class do still feel that Mikhail Gorbachev and Eduard Shevardnadze sold out East Germany along with other Eastern European countries previously comprising the Soviet "outer empire"; the evolving positive cooperation between Moscow, Bonn, and now Berlin has, however, largely contributed to the enthusiastic feeling that the Cold War is, indeed, over, and that a new partnership is emerging out of the revolutionary changes in Europe of the late 1980s. The gradual recognition of the limits of the new partnership emerged much later and almost do not touch on the popular view of Germany.

Nevertheless, the dynamics of the Russian perspectives of both the Bonn Republic and the Berlin Republic can hardly be deduced from just the changes implied by the end of the Cold War. Those changes were paralleled by the dramatic and profound transformation of the Russian society and polity. Yet uncompleted, the transformation from the communist system to attempted democracy and economic freedom may have provided a much more powerful impetus to the transformation of Russian perspectives of Germany than the termination of confrontation. Russian society was and still is undergoing profound changes, and it has begun to see the world with different eyes. Thus, the shifting perspectives on the outside world, in the first instance, reflect those changes within the Russian society more than they do the acknowledgment of no less significant changes that have taken place in the world.

Still, as a matter of fact, the mutual perceptions of Germans and Russians have evolved dramatically and profoundly over the past decade. And the emergence of the Berlin Republic stands as a symbol for this profound change.

This chapter reviews the evolution of the Russian mindset and expectations extended to the united Germany at different levels. It starts by revealing the changes in the public opinion which, indeed, have been much more profound than anybody would have believed a decade ago. It looks further into the evolution of Russian policy toward Germany with special attention to the trends in the policy by the government of President Vladimir Putin. Although the evolution of both the public opinion and the policy of Russia reveal the same positive trend, they do not entirely coincide.

Changing Mindset of the Russian Society

Although both Russians and Germans had always extended to each other much more warmth than the official propaganda was prepared to admit, the tragic common history, especially that of World War II, as well as the decades of the Cold War played a significant role in shaping the Russian mindset of a revanchist and aggressive Germany. During the last decade, this mindset has proved inconsistent and is vanishing surprisingly fast.

Since 1995, the Russian Independent Institute of Social and National Problems has been continuously conducting polls of the Russian public opinion on behalf of the Moscow Office of the Friedrich-Ebert-Stiftung.[1] The polls clearly reveal that it is predominantly the elder generations of Russians (those over sixty years old) who maintain their dedication to many of the old clichés. Younger people under forty, as well as people with higher levels of education, or such social groups as inhabitants of large metropolises, entrepreneurs, and intelligentsia, reveal an increasingly positive perception of Germany. This trend has proved to be sustainable within the Russian society despite any ups and downs in the attitudes of Moscow's narrower political elite, which waged one controversy after another—either over the costs of German unification in the early 1990s, the extension of NATO eastward in the mid-1990s, or over the air strikes against Yugoslavia at the end of the decade. The controversies have most obviously hurt the attitude of Russians toward the West in general and the United States in particular. They did not, however, do any harm to Russian perceptions of united Germany. Russians continued to think rather optimistically about the prospects for further improvement of Russo-German relations.

This overall enthusiastic vision does not imply, however, that the emerging appreciation in Russian society for Germany is based on a deep comprehension of the domestic developments in Germany, or of German policies. This vision involves a rather spontaneous, often peculiar process of a search for a new identity within Russian society itself. This uncompleted search is, probably, the only possible explanation of the fact that most Russians consistently put Germany into the category of "friendly states" along with such countries as Yugoslavia, Kazakhstan, China, or Iran. In April 2001 France made it into the group of "rather friendly" states, while the United States ended up in the group of "unfriendly" states along with the Baltic states and Afghanistan.[2]

The relevant trends of the—sometimes puzzling—evolution of Russian public opinion with regard to Germany are especially

1. Here and later in this section, unless otherwise specified, I refer to the data collected by the Russian Independent Institute of Social and National Problems (RNISiNP) in *Rossiya na rubezhe vekov* (Russia at the threshold of the centuries) (Moscow, 2000), 49–82.

2. See *Vneshnaya politika Rossii: Mneniya expertov* (Foreign policy of Russia: Experts' opinion), an analytical report on behalf of the Moscow Office of the Friedrich-Ebert-Stiftung (Moscow, 2001), 26.

revealed by the current mindset on World War II, German unification, and the prospects for Russo-German relations.

The Legacy of World War II

During the decades of the Cold War, the picture of a revanchist (West) Germany dominated Soviet propaganda and largely exploited the suffering of the Soviet people during World War II. This negative image only gradually eroded as of the early 1970s when the new Ostpolitik brought about a notable improvement of the climate between Moscow and the Bonn Republic.

In the 1990s, with the transformation of the Soviet Union into Russia, the experience of World War II still dominated the concept of Germany in the Russian mass consciousness. Until now, 53.5 percent of Russians have thought first of the war when polled about Germany. For a much smaller number of Russians the image of Germany is primarily associated with either the names of big German companies (11.3 percent), the German way of life (15.2 percent), or with the great German thinkers or artists (8.7 percent). Until now, 37 percent of those polled are convinced that the legacy of the war divides the German and the Russian peoples, while 32 percent believe that the negative lessons of the past should rather unite the two peoples.

The importance of the recollections of war, however, is significantly lower among the younger generations of Russians (under 40 percent of those younger than twenty-five think of the war when polled about Germany) than among older Russians (over 74 percent of those over sixty years old). More than one-third of Russians consider the Germans victims of the Nazi regime, while only 10 percent see the Germans guilty of the emergence of that regime.

German Unification

All through the 1990s, the idea of German unification remained a controversial issue within the Russian political elite, as it has been during the actual process of unification. Many accused the first president of the Soviet Union, Mikhail Gorbachev, as well as the former Soviet foreign minister (the current president of Georgia), Eduard Shevardnadze, of unnecessarily relinquishing Moscow's geopolitical interests while pulling out of Central Europe and allowing Germany to unify—all this without getting appropriate concessions from either Germany or from the West in general. In the eyes of many in the Russian political elite, this was the beginning of the demise of not only the Soviet outer empire in East Central Europe, but also of the Soviet Union.

The resentments inherited by the Russian political elite during the period of German unification seemed to remain entrenched well into the late 1990s when the Berlin Republic was emerging. As of the end of the twentieth century, however, about 10 percent of the Russian population believes that allowing German unification in the way it had taken place was either a fatal political failure by Gorbachev, or the biggest defeat of the Soviet Union. Again, this perspective is most common for the older generations of Russians—for those over sixty years old. The approval of German unification is, generally, much stronger within Russian society. Almost 58 percent consider it inevitable, and 38 percent a fully legitimate development. German unification is approved by over 50 percent of those who have a secondary education, and by 72 percent of those who have a higher education.

Looking Forward to a Common Future

More importantly, the remaining resentments of the past history are being overtaken by a generally optimistic popular perception of both Germany and of the future of Russo-German relations. Fifty-seven percent of Russians think optimistically about the future of Russo-German relations, while only 23 percent do not expect the bilateral relations to bring about any good. More than 35 percent of the population (especially younger and middle-age people with higher education) consider it worthwhile for the Russian leadership to pay more attention to further development of the cooperation with Germany. About 34 percent believe that the current level of Russo-German relations is sufficiently good, and only 13 percent (predominantly those over sixty years old) do not feel it necessary to further stimulate Russo-German relations.

These data reflect some general but certainly no specific popular expectations toward Germany. Although Russian society has become intensively acquainted with Germany during the last decade (more than 27 percent of the Russian entrepreneurs polled have visited Germany, about 15 percent of the intelligentsia, almost 14 percent of pensioners, 8 percent of students, and 6 percent of pupils), the comprehension of the realities of and the objectives pursued by either the former Bonn Republic or by the Berlin Republic remains rather vague.

Twenty-six percent of those polled believe that Germany seeks to dominate Europe in order to serve its economic interest. About 19 percent think that Germany's objective is to achieve by peaceful means what it failed to achieve by military coercion earlier in the twentieth century. Only 14 percent of Russians see the goal of the Bonn Republic and the Berlin Republic as uniting Europe— with the essential purpose of rendering impossible new wars on the continent.

The conclusion from the recent polls in Russia is relatively simple: Russians like Germany despite the residual legacy of the uneasy and controversial history. They had extended their appreciation to the Berlin Republic even before they realized that the Bonn Republic was no longer. Most Russians would find it quite difficult even to distinguish the former from the latter since they have never had any serious exposure to the Federal Republic before unification. And, less than a decade from now, a new generation of Russians will graduate from universities—a generation for which the Bonn Republic is nothing more than just a few paragraphs in a textbook. Although most Russians really do not care much about what is going on in Germany and the direction of its policy, they generally expect relations and exchange between the two countries to improve and expand, thus opening opportunities for further mutual exposure and learning in the years to come. Particularly the younger generations of Russians look forward to benefiting from these opportunities.

Policy Issues

The transition from the Bonn Republic to the Berlin Republic did not have any direct effect on relations between Germany and Russia. The continued evolution of these relations reveals a great deal of continuity from the earlier 1990s. This transition has, however, almost coincided—in a symbolic way—with the changes in the government of both countries and thus with the transition from the Helmut Kohl-Boris Yeltsin era to that of Gerhard Schröder-Vladimir Putin.

The Late Bonn Republic and the Yeltsin Era

In the first half of the 1990s, the close and friendly relationship between Russian President Boris Yeltsin and the German Chancellor Helmut Kohl picked up on the positive dynamic of the latest stage of Soviet-German relations, and helped improve cooperation despite internal controversies within the Moscow elite regarding the general course of the Russian policy: Should it pursue the goal of rapprochement with the West, or rather that of a consolidation of Eurasia under Russian leadership? Moreover, in particular regarding the policy toward Germany after unification, should there be some sort of special relationship between Moscow and Bonn, or should the Russo-German relationship be rather imbedded in the general network of Russo-Western relations?

All throughout the Bonn Republic of the 1990s, Germany was largely perceived in Moscow, and, indeed, has performed as an advocate of Russian interests in its attempts to achieve closer integration of Russia into the dense network of European and Western institutions and organizations. Bonn played a significant role in facilitating the expansion of the G7 to include Russia, thus transforming the institution into what has now become the G8. Germany also helped to mediate the terms and framework of the Partnership and Cooperation Agreement between Russia and the European Union in 1994. Moreover, Germany initiated a general vision of an eventual association between Russia and the EU—a vision that has not yet come true but regularly appears on the political agenda. The Russo-German relationship was not harmed in anyway even after Bonn initiated the discussion of a first wave of NATO's eastward expansion —this despite the fact that the issue became one of the most controversial items in Russo-Western relations in the mid-1990s. Furthermore, Bonn played a significant role in facilitating a compromise to overcome the controversy between Moscow and NATO by developing an enhanced mechanism for consultation and cooperation embodied in the Russia-NATO Joint Permanent Council.

Until Russia's severe financial crisis in 1998, Bonn was regularly helping out the Yeltsin regime through generous loans, or through support of Moscow's wishes in international financial institutions at anytime when the fate of Russian reforms and the fragile democracy seemed to be at stake. This was especially the case in 1996 when Boris Yeltsin was reelected President of Russia.

The dense network of enhanced bilateral political consultation and interaction developed throughout the 1990s and has survived both the end of the Yeltsin era and the emergence of the Berlin Republic. This close relationship has proved to be an important asset for both countries in particular to overcome the crisis in Russo-Western relations during the NATO air campaign against Yugoslavia in 1999.

The Transition to the Berlin Republic and the Putin Era

An obvious change has been evolving with the transition of political generations in the governments of both countries. Maintaining the positive momentum from the previous years, Russo-German relations have become calm and pragmatic, business-like, and, certainly, much less spectacular. During his first year in office—in 2000—President Vladimir Putin gave explicit priority to developing closer relations with Germany and the European Union; the strategy of the Kremlin appears to have changed in 2001, not least because of a series of disappointments Moscow experienced in its relations with the main European powers individually and with the EU as a whole.

At the beginning of his term, Putin tried his best to overcome unfavorable trends in the relationship with the West, overshadowed by the protracted war in Chechnya, worsening relations with the Council of Europe, the consequences of the severe financial crisis of 1998, and an increasing reluctance of the international financial institutions and the Western governments to continue generously subsidizing the Russian government, easing the debt burden for Moscow. Further complicating his mission, however, concerns arose as to whether Putin would continue democratic change in the country and decentralization in relations with the constituent parts of Russia, or if he would rather consolidate an autocratic rule. The West hesitated to engage Putin's Russia on any other ground than a reasonable pragmatic arrangement. The new German government did, too.

Putin did his best to build a closer cooperative relationship with Europe, and Germany again became the focus of his efforts. During the semi-annual summit meeting between Russia and the EU in May 2000, and during his subsequent trip to Berlin in June of that year, Putin boldly emphasized the European option as the main thread of Moscow's foreign policy and suggested developing some sort of strategic partnership between Russia and the

EU. The declared goals of both Russia and the EU coincided largely by foreseeing gradual development of a common economic and social sphere with a prospective goal of establishing a free trade regime.

Especially during an unsettling period with regard to the energy markets, Putin offered to complement the evolving partnership with the EU by strengthening cooperation in the energy sector and by significantly increasing energy supplies from Russia to European markets. In October 2000 the regular EU-Russia summit meeting in Paris settled on institutionalizing dialogue between two parties on the energy issues. From 1999 on, Moscow has also sought to encourage the development of the common security and defense policy of the EU, offering cooperation regarding armaments policy as well as crisis management. Again, in October 2000, the EU-Russian summit adopted a special joint declaration on the enhanced dialogue and cooperation in security policy that gave priority to the institutionalization of the security policy dialogue.

Especially since the summer of 2000, Moscow has obviously been seeking support from Germany for the ambitious projects aimed at bringing about a closer affiliation between Russia and the European Union. Moscow signaled that it would appreciate it if Berlin resumed its role as an advocate of Russia's interests in the West and, particularly, within the EU: "We would welcome it if Germany would retain the leadership in shaping the partnership between the West and Russia," so Putin in Berlin in June 2000. "We would be happy to continue seeing Germany among the leaders of the group of 'Friends of Russia.'" Putin reiterated this message during his first official visit to Germany in September 2001. "Germany is our key counterpart in foreign policy issues," so Putin in the German Bundestag on 25 September 2001.

Although no personal relationship has developed between Putin and Schröder like the one between Yeltsin and Kohl, both current leaders have been seeking a pragmatic cooperative mode, and have been open to paving the way for improved relations between Russia and the West, and the EU in particular. Since summer 2000, both the German and Russian leaders have been speaking of a strategic partnership and strategic dialogue between the two countries to be extended in particular to issues of economic and financial cooperation as well as to issues of European security. For that purpose, the already dense network of consultations was to be strengthened by establishing a strategic working group composed of senior representatives of the two governments.

For several reasons, however, the promise of an enhanced dialogue between the European Union and Russia, supported and driven by Berlin and Moscow, apparently did not live up to initial expectations. At least this is true in the eyes of Moscow leaders. Increasing disappointment in the capacity of European leaders to take on a leadership role and to achieve breakthroughs in the relationship with Russia has been notable in Moscow since spring 2001. The high-level strategic group established by Schröder and Putin in 2000 failed to elaborate on a proposal to ease the Russian debt burden. As a matter of fact, most of the issues on the agenda of Russo-Western relations awaiting resolution, such as the admission of Russia to the World Trade Organization (WTO) or the Organization for Economic and Cooperative Development (OECD), or solving the debt issue, certainly require a longer-term approach and cannot be quickly resolved in a similarly spectacular way as was the political agreement concerning the extension of the G7, Russia's admission to the international financial institutions, or the negotiation of cooperative frameworks with NATO and the European Union. The failure of the EU-Russia summit in the spring of 2001 to achieve any visible progress in an elaboration of the specifics of the EU-Russia dialogue on security and defense policy, or on the energy dialogue, again contributed to a further cooling off of the Russo-European and Russo-German strategic dialogue.

Moscow's increasing disappointment in the European leadership capacity was complemented by the gradual return by Russia to a greater emphasis on the relationship with the United States. The evolving dialogue between Putin and U.S. President George W. Bush, initiated in the summer of 2001, was only strengthened by the unequivocal support Moscow extended to the United States in its campaign against international terrorism after the September 11 attacks on New York and Washington, D.C. Most boldly, the new trend in Russian policy was revealed precisely during the short stop by Chancellor Schröder in Moscow on his way back from a trip to Pakistan, India, and China early in November 2001. Listening to concerns of the Chancellor that the anti-terrorist military operation in Afghanistan might run into problems, Putin unequivocally took the side of President Bush and supported his campaign.

Thus, the transition from the Bonn Republic to the Berlin Republic may have at least tentatively coincided with a gradual shift in Moscow's policy orientation, shifting from Europe toward the United States.

Conclusion

The 1990s witnessed an unprecedented increase in the sympathies that the Russian public opinion extended to Germany. The positive image of both the Bonn Republic and the Berlin Republic has survived all the ups and downs in the relations between Russia and the West in the last decade.

The Russian political elite has certainly maintained more differentiated perspectives on German politics and prospects for Russo-German relations. In part, Russia has revealed an even more skeptical approach to its key partner in Central Europe. Nevertheless, despite a series of controversies within the Moscow elite, the strong impetus for the improvement of political relations that was provided at the beginning of the 1990s has been maintained through the transition to the Berlin Republic. Russo-German relations have maintained their role as a factor for stability and for shaping a new European security architecture that seeks full, equal, and cooperative participation by Russia.

This role has, however, been unevenly performed at different times. Russo-German relations have not been without failures and have missed several opportunities. The Berlin Republic, still in the initial years of its emergence, has also failed to raise its profile in the relationship between Moscow and the West, as once the Bonn Republic did. Does this have to do with any differences between Bonn and Berlin? Or is it due to the coincidence of the change in government in the two countries, which need time not only to adjust to each other, but to also go through a series of common experiences? Is the focus of Russian foreign policy shifting back to reemphasizing the U.S.-Russian partnership, or will the European option for Russia prevail following a tentative step backwards?

15. In Search of a New Balance: France, Germany, and the New Europe

Philippe Moreau Defarges

For France, German reunification in 1990 was certainly the most important diplomatic event since the end of World War II. France's eastern border has always been a focus of anxiety. So many invasions, so much suffering! Under Louis XIV and Napoleon I, France dreamed of ruling the continent. But each time the imperial dream turned into a disaster. What France could achieve when it was a demographic colossus (seventeenth to the eighteenth centuries), in any event became impossible to reach because of a declining birthrate. From the defeat of the war of 1870/71 to the end of World War II in 1945, French foreign policy has turned on one issue: how to live with a neighbor more populated, economically more vigorous, and very restless. In 1945, even after the crushing defeat of Nazi Germany, the question remained. France's next "war" should have taken place with Germany in 1946/47.

The Cold War divided Europe and Germany, however, between two alliances and systems. Western Europe was put under U.S. protection. The United States was determined to rebuild its Germany, to make it a democracy—similar to the United States—and even to provide it with an army under the Atlantic umbrella. France had no other alternative than to find a kind of partnership with its old enemy. From the early 1950s to 1990, a balance, although a bit awkward, was reached between Paris and Bonn. All went well. First, Germany stayed divided. Its definitive future remained open, with no peace treaty being signed. Germany had a long way to go to be recognized as a "normal" nation. West Germany had to be friendly. Second, West Germany was a new Germany: peaceful, democratic, and cured from Eastern-oriented ambitions and nationalist passions and giving priority to its Western roots. Third, France proposed a common project that could unite the countries and strengthen the ties between Paris and Bonn: the construction of a united Europe. West Germany or, more precisely, its leaders were clever enough to accept a subordinate position. During those decades, France was more equal than West Germany. France was a fully sovereign state, one of the founding members of the United Nations Organization. West Germany, even if, step by step, it extended its area of sovereignty, was not a normal state: its situation was provisional, West Germany being only a part of the German nation, its ultimate future having to be settled by a kind of peace treaty.

But human and political relations are never perfect. West Germany was ready to play second fiddle to France but not to forget its special relationship with the United States. France would have probably liked to be the first priority but it could not ignore that, to a certain extent, the new (West) Germany was a child of America. In one way, France wanted an immaterial Germany, deprived of any national interest. But West Germany was a country with a national problem. French President Georges Pompidou was uncomfortable when Ostpolitik was initiated in the late 1960s. For each time that Germany moves, France becomes anxious, because the past is not so far away. Nations' memories fade very slowly.

A Multi-tiered Shock

France views German reunification as embodying three distinct but interrelated upheavals:

The World Upheaval

During the Cold War, with the European order being shaped by the East-West divide, France gained status as a world power. It could define itself as the Western ally having its own way. France had three assets, which at that time were decisive: permanent membership in the United Nations Security Council, nuclear deterrence, and a sphere of influence in Africa. The East-West struggle being global and mostly strategic, the French advantages were very effective. France was an important player at least in the three areas of the Security Council, nuclear management and disarmament, and western

Africa. The post–Cold War game is quite different; it is principally economic and is geographically fragmented. The East-West strait-jacket having vanished, regional factors that had been repressed have now come to the fore. The East-West order is not the only one to disappear; other orders are crumbling (the postcolonial order in Africa) or are at least jeopardized (the atomic order). France cannot continue having its own way; it knows that it is the status quo power. And in this new game Germany has two great assets: its economic weight but, more decisively, its geohistorical position.

The European Upheaval

The post–East-West world is fragmented, each continent confronting its own liberated forces. Formerly, Europe was frozen, neatly divided between two hostile blocks, each one fastened down by its own system of values and its own big protector. Today, the old continent is under complete renovation. The two Germanys were border countries, each camp facing the other. The new, united Germany is, first of all geographically speaking, the center of Europe. Now a "normal" nation, Germany stands, however, at the crossroads of being the bridge between Eastern and Western Europe in more than just a geographical sense. France views the moving of the German capital from Bonn to Berlin as symbolizing the shift of the European perspective toward the East. Germany gains all the advantages of being the center (for instance, proximity with low-wage countries) but also the drawbacks (for instance, influx of refugees). In a Europe divided by the Iron Curtain, France was the center of Europe (at least of the free, capitalist, or Western Europe); this central position was strengthened by Great Britain remaining on the margins of European politics (at least until the rise of the Labour Party under Prime Minister Tony Blair). The European project was French, Germany being the junior partner or, in a way, the best friend. The European axis has now shifted from France to Germany.

The Franco-German Upheaval

During the Cold War, France carried more weight politically than West Germany. France was more equal than West Germany: France could take provocative initiatives, say no to the United States, something which West Germany could not do. It is no longer the case given a united Germany. With the end of the Cold War, the two countries are undergoing very different experiences. France is rediscovering the Atlantic community as a balancing and securing factor in Europe, while Germany is learning to be involved in international interventions.

Is Germany today more important for France than France is for Germany? Germany's relationship with France is carefully watched. If Germany becomes distant from France, other countries will have cause for alarm. France knows that Germany is its indispensable partner in the promotion of European unity.

Three Policies in One

Throughout history France has pursued three types of policy toward Germany, which are not mutually exclusive.

The first policy was the simplest: Be stronger than Germany. This policy was possible from the Thirty Years War until the Napoleonic era. France was the biggest power in Europe, and Germany was divided into about three hundred principalities. The constant French goal was to keep Germany fragmented, which became impossible in the nineteenth century. France was the first European country to implement birth control and was slow to mobilize; it lost demographic and economic weight, while Germany emerged as a new colossus. Reacting to France and imitating it, Germany became united in 1871 under Chancellor Otto von Bismarck.

The second policy was: Balance Germany through alliances. The lesson of the 1871 defeat was clear: France was not able to defend its territory by itself. The Third Republic sought alliances with Russia and Great Britain, which made for an insecure policy. Allies are never permanently secure: they can crumble (Russia in 1917) or disappoint (Great Britain in the 1920s, looking for better relations with the Weimar Republic; or the Soviet Union in 1939). Allies are not always friendly: Great Britain considered France, at times, to be a troublemaker that needed to be reined in. France had to pay the very heavy price of more than two million casualties during World War I and a terrible defeat in June 1940. This policy of alliances was probably the only one possible in the Europe of 1871–1941: Europe was the world leader; all the world diplomatic game was European; war was "natural" between sovereign states.

The third policy evolved from the Cold War: Monitor and guide the new Germany. The policy of alliances had become impossible: One of France's traditional allies, the Soviet Union, had become the great enemy; the other key power, the United States, was rebuilding, protecting, and rearming West Germany. France had to reconcile with at least West Germany. The basic condition laid down was the establishment of mechanisms to watch and guide the new Germany, such as the Atlantic Alliance or the European Community. The third policy was made possible by way of the completely new European landscape: the Cold War and the Soviet threat; U.S. protection; and, in the words of Josef Joffe, America as "the great European pacifier." But this policy also had a cost: equal status and rights between France and Germany, a standing request of any German government since the inequitable Versailles Treaty. In this treaty, which was imposed by the victors onto the Weimar Republic, Germany was declared guilty of World War I and, for that reason, was unequal; especially its military forces were severely limited, under the scrutiny of an Allied Commission. Gustav Stresemann, Adolf Hitler, and Konrad Adenauer would have all agreed: no peace, no reconciliation with France, if the two countries did not have equal rights and obligations. In the French subconscious, an inequality of rights could compensate for an inequality of political weight. In 1951 France was ready to accept a European unity in terms of coal and steel (with the European Community for Coal and Steel). But in 1954 France killed its own creation, the European Community of Defense, because it could not envisage such an equal system of defense.

In fact, from 1950 to 1990, France combined the three above-mentioned policies. The prevailing one, of course, was the policy on European integration, driven by the Franco-German engine. But in the three specific areas of the UN Security Council, nuclear deterrence, and policy toward Africa, France was stronger than West Germany and could claim an avowed autonomous foreign policy. As for the policy of alliances, France could rely on it from time to time (for instance, the strong Franco-British axis between French President Georges Pompidou and British Prime Minister Edward Heath in the early 1970s, just when Ostpolitik was starting). But this delicate tripolar balance was irreversibly rocked by the historical upheaval of the European landscape in the period of 1989–1991.

In Search of a New Balance

Foreign policy does not change easily. More precisely, the geographic dimension cannot be changed. Germany is France's more important neighbor. (With Great Britain, there is the Channel; and the power rivalry between the two countries was settled at the end of the Napoleonic wars.) After unification, Germany carries more political weight than ever. France must look for a new balance between the three elements of its diplomacy.

First, what made France stronger than Germany has lost some of its value. France remains one of the five permanent members of the UN Security Council, but at some point in time serious reform of this system, inherited from 1945, will take place. France retains its policy of nuclear deterrence, but needs to determine how to use it as a political tool, in light of nuclear weaponry being strongly criticized and the old order being destabilized by states denouncing the rules as illegitimate (e.g., India and Pakistan). And policy toward Africa appears unmanageable. In any event, time has passed, and new generations are now coming to power.

Concerning alliances, the key player remains the United States. Confirmed by its immediate and strong support following the September 11 tragedy, Great Britain is, for the United States, an intimate friend. Friends can disagree, but in times of crisis they stick together. Germany is the biggest European state (Russia not being a part of the old Europe), the center of the new Europe, and the bridge between East and West. In sum, for France, the game is much more difficult. What can it do? First, despite anti-American sentiments occasionally given voice, at the end of the day France has shown itself to be a very reliable friend, as witnessed by its support during the Gulf War and the Bosnian conflict, for example. Second, France is one of the two European states (along with Great Britain) that has kept alive a system of special operations. This can be very useful in an unstable world. The post–East-West world requires France to rediscover its membership in the Atlantic Alliance. Paradoxically, the relationship with the United States is more important than it was during the Cold War: during that period, the United States was to stay in Europe forever; today, that is not so certain.

In today's world, the European dimension is more and more dominant. France recognizes that German unification fulfills a basic right of the German people. How could a democracy deny such a right? But France insists on two conditions: a clear and definitive agreement on German borders and a substantial move forward in European integration. The Maastricht Treaty but first the single monetary currency, the euro, might alleviate the heaviness of Germany's new political and economic weight.

The French Dilemma

Here the French dilemma returns. For France, European unification can settle the German question by integrating the small giant into a community with rules and procedures. But egalitarianism demands the same of France. To see a more European Germany, France must also become more "Europeanized."

All during the Cold War, France was able, from its viewpoint, to strike the right balance between its European commitment and its desire to continue an independent foreign policy. European integration was focused on "technical" advances: the Common Market and, in following, the Single Market. Political issues (foreign policy or defense) either remained national or were dealt with on an intergovernmental basis. The balance was supported by many converging factors: Europe seemed to be locked in place; West Germany was not a "normal" state; East-West politics had many faces. Moreover, French leaders could not feel at ease with the idea of a German foreign policy. To them, European and German division was there to last forever.

A united Germany being much weightier, the price for France in European integration would seem to be much higher. But through the Maastricht Treaty, Germany looked to be making the biggest sacrifice: its own currency, the deutsche mark, symbol of its renaissance. And France? For it, the Maastricht Treaty, behind its incredible complexity, is a considerable move forward. The European Union is an international institutional framework, including economic and monetary integration, foreign policy and defense, law and order. The proceedings are different in the three systems. But what is the most important: the differences between the systems or the creation of a single union? As part of integration, many small changes produce incrementally a kind of European federation: European citizenship, the Council of Ministers, and the European Parliament on an equal footing.

It is not just an issue of power for France: European integration also affects state structures, the relations between Paris and the country's regions. The balance reached in the period between the 1960s and the 1980s has shifted, not only at the European level but also inside the member-states. Such a shift can maybe be more easily cushioned by a federal state (Germany) than by a unitary state (France). But Germany has its own difficulties in the form of relations between the Bund and the Länder.

France, Germany, and the New Europe

Franco-German relations cannot be considered separately from European unification. A strong link between two persons or two states requires a common focus. European unification is this common focus.

For France, the new Europe, the post–East-West Europe raises many questions. The old Europe (the European Community, between 1951 and 1990) was, to a certain extent, French. After World War II, Great Britain should have been the leading power in Western Europe, but it refused to play the role. France, seizing the historic opportunity, successfully filled the vacuum. From 1950 to 1990 France played a central role in unifying Europe. Many key ideas came from France: Jean Monnet's supranationalism and Charles de Gaulle's intergovernmentalism. The institutional European debate was a French debate. The successive enlargements did not fundamentally alter this, first because Great Britain joined the club without being ready to become a full member. And last, but not least, West Germany agreed to be a junior partner.

The new Europe will be considerably different: around twenty-five member-states, significant inequalities in economic development, very diverse political and cultural traditions, and important challenges in the East (the Balkans, Ukraine, Russia). Moreover, the old partners are becoming more assertive: Germany, because it is now a "normal" state but also because it is required to become more involved in international affairs; Great Britain, Tony Blair wanting to place his country at the heart of Europe; even Spain rediscovering its national grandeur.

Today, as before, European unification remains the greatest common ground between France and Germany. At first glance, the two countries have very different visions of the future Europe: Germany imagines a federal structure; France would like to continue with an intergovernmental Europe. Is this the most important? Germany knows or will come to know that a European federation cannot be similar to a national federation. As for France, the word "federation" is no longer taboo: France can say yes to a federation of nation-states. Is there something contradictory in that formula? The same flag can represent different and changing goods. French European policy is steered by the major objective of keeping equal relations with Germany. In 1950, when West Germany was rapidly recovering from the war, and in the early 1990s, when Germany became reunified, the solution was a more supranational Europe. Why not the same for the future? France and Germany cannot go backwards; they must move forward. The great institutional debate in the European Union is open. Many unforeseeable factors will affect it, but a discussion on the question of a European government will take place. If France and Germany remain ruled by the same kind of leaders they have today, they will not separate. They have too much to lose. And Europe is no longer the center of the world.

References

Jospin, Lionel. "L'avenir de l'Europe élargie." Speech of 28 May 2001 at La Maison de la Radio, Paris.

"La question du gouvernement européen." *Le Débat,* no. 118 (January–February, 2002): 78–89.

La Tribune franco-allemande, 1998, 35ᵉᵐᵉ anniversaire du Traité de l'Élysée. November, 1997.

"Le couple franco-allemand." *ENA mensuel,* no. 286 (November, 1998).

Le Forum franco-allemand. 1st semester, 2000.

Moreau Defarges, Philippe. *Les institutions européennes.* 5th ed. Collection U. Paris, 2001.

16. Enduring Affinity? From Old Tensions to a Promising Partnership between Germany and the United Kingdom

Kerry Longhurst

The relative shifts in the power positions of the United Kingdom and Germany that have occurred over the past fifty years form the overall context that shapes current British perspectives on the Berlin Republic. As one of West Germany's mentors during the Cold War, the United Kingdom sunk from being a global colonial power to a middle ranking power in decline, and subsequently, as noted by Dean Acheson, failed to find a role for itself in the postwar era. Although the "special relationship" with the United States helped the United Kingdom maintain a certain status as a global actor, as William E. Paterson noted, this relationship served only to partially hide the United Kingdom's decline as a key international player in the age of superpowers.[1] The importance of the United Kingdom's role and status was further eroded by West Germany's postwar economic recovery, which London realized could never be equaled; it thus sought to sustain and manage a role throughout the Cold War aimed at maintaining an influence at least as equal to both the Federal Republic and to France, grounded in a strong political role and global presence.[2]

---

1. William E. Paterson, "Britain and the Berlin Republic: Between Ambivalence and Emulation," in *Continuity and Change in German Politics: Beyond the Politics of Centrality*, ed. Stephen Padgett and Thomas Poguntke (London, 2002).
   2. Ibid.

The ascendance of Germany's political significance posed by unification in 1990 challenged this concept of role and status that British foreign policy had sought to manage and sustain throughout the Cold War period.[3] Crucially, although the United Kingdom had already yielded economic primacy to the Federal Republic, the overriding perspective from London was that the enhancement of Germany's geopolitical importance and international role to ensue from unification would potentially fundamentally question the United Kingdom's political primacy and international status.

"Unification Is Not on the Agenda"

This reading of the situation taken in 1989/90 translated into a status quo-oriented policy pursued chiefly by Prime Minister Margaret Thatcher, though not fully shared by the Foreign and Commonwealth Office, which sought to keep the prospect of German unity off the agenda. The background and rationale to this strategy was twofold and related to what had been a key aspect of Thatcher's agenda over the 1980s: Primarily, to restore the United Kingdom's global role, status, and prestige. The second strand behind Thatcher's grudging attitude toward German unity was highly emotional and drew from her own preconceptions about Germany and the Germans, which had developed during the war. As seen from Number 10 Downing Street, the prospect of German unification posed a threat to key British interests and challenged the very pillars of British foreign policy and place in the world; in short it challenged "Thatcher's life work."[4] Consequently, although the unification of Germany had been a declared goal of British foreign policy since 1949, on the eve of the actual event there was a profound lack of support for it on behalf of the British government, but especially by the prime minister.[5] By seeking to maintain the status quo, containing German power and thereby sustaining Britain's status and role, Thatcher argued in 1989 that the prospect of German unity would only be discussed in ten or twenty years' time and that too speedy a move to unification would endanger stability in Europe. To hinder the pace

3. Paterson, "Britain and the Berlin Republic."
4. Yvonne Klein, "Obstructing or Promoting? British Views on German Unification 1989/90," *German Politics* 5, no. 3 (1996): 407.
5. See Sir Julian Bullard, "Great Britain and German Unification," in *Britain and Germany in Europe 1949–1990*, ed. Jeremy Noakes, Peter Wende, and Jonathan Wright (Oxford, 2002).

of change Thatcher also sought to nurture closer relations with France and the Soviet Union, a strategy that neither prevented unification nor slowed it down.

In keeping with Thatcher's position on the German question in March 1990 the prime minister convened a now infamous closed-door seminar at Chequers, which brought together experts working on Germany with the aim of assessing the possible implications of German unification. The memorandum from the meeting, which was subsequently leaked to the press, acknowledged that the Federal Republic was a totally different state to previous German states, but claimed still that German national characteristics such as angst, aggressiveness, assertiveness, bullying, and egoism remained. The memorandum cautioned also that although stability and prosperity had been accomplished by the Federal Republic, the system had not been "seriously tested by adversity such as a major economic calamity," it questioned also if in the long term stability would endure and posed whether characteristics of the past would reemerge with the same destructive consequences as before. The furor caused by the Chequers memorandum was subsequently exacerbated by an interview in *The Spectator* in July given by then Trade and Industry Secretary Nicolas Ridley in which he charged that the plans to create an Economic and Monetary Union were a "German racket designed to take over the whole of Europe." Ridley's anti-German sentiments went further when he declared that if you were prepared to give up sovereignty to the Commission of the European Communities "you might just as well give it to Adolf Hitler."[6]

While the Chequers memorandum was swiftly condemned in the House of Commons and, following the article in *The Spectator,* Ridley resigned, the two incidents did serve to illustrate the strong current of thinking present in the government, which made an explicit connection between the demise of the United Kingdom's international role and Germany's potential ascent. More fundamentally, it showed that Thatcher's understanding of international politics was viewed through a realist prism, grounded in the belief that "the increase in power of one state necessarily involved the diminution of another."[7] As Yvonne Klein lucidly concludes, Thatcher's "evident attachment to the institutions of the Cold War and her resistance toward any fundamental changes in Europe, of which German unification was the clearest symbol,

6. *The Spectator,* 14 July 1990.
7. Paterson, "Britain and the Berlin Republic," 206.

did not arise from ignorance but from the fear of a decline in Britain's international role."[8] Four specific challenges to the United Kingdom's position and status were seen to arise from German unity. First, the increase in Germany's economic position, which would result from unification, questioned Britain's postwar status as a significant power. Second, the proposition voiced at the time that Germany should have a permanent seat on the UN Security Council was viewed as a challenge to the United Kingdom's global profile. Third, the American initiative to forge a new relationship with Germany as "partners in leadership" in May 1989 was viewed as a clear indication that the United States expected the new Germany to play a more substantial role in international affairs and was seen in London as a challenge to the United Kingdom's cherished special relationship with the United States. Fourth, the debates and discussions that appeared at the close of the Cold War surrounding the future of security governance in Europe, questioned the centrality of NATO, within which the United Kingdom had always been the main European player.[9]

The policy of further enmeshing the united Germany into a more deeply integrated European Community was to prove to be the most significant factor to determine Thatcher's ambivalent stance on German unity. Crucially, the policy that prevailed of sanctioning German unity via containing its power through an enhanced state of integration in Europe cut across the grain of Thatcher's stance on Europe. Thus a powerful conflation of anti-Europeanism twinned with a fear of German hegemony pervaded and shaped Thatcher's thinking throughout the unification process. A great deal of the Conservative Party's intransigence toward Europe in the post-Thatcher era continued to be heavily flavored by her atavistic approach to Germany, which was to show itself at various crisis points in the early 1990s.

When John Major became prime minister of the United Kingdom, the British-German relationship entered a warming period, which was greatly facilitated by the more congenial state of relations between the two leaders that emerged. Despite this, the United Kingdom's ambivalence toward Germany continued to be fueled by developments in the EC, which were seen to be detrimental to core British interests by most in the Conservative Party. Developments toward the deepening of integration served to expose ever more

---

8. Klein, *German Politics*, 409.
9. Klein, *German Politics*.

acutely the contradictions between the British vision of European integration and what was actually happening on the ground, particularly with the moves to transform the EC into a European Union. The pro-deepening agenda pursued with great gusto by Chancellor Helmut Kohl at the time served to excite British Euroskeptic voices, which again were heavily tainted by an anti-German flavor. This was to peak in 1992, when the sterling was devalued and the United Kingdom forced out of the European Exchange Rate Mechanism in the wake of the Danish referendum on the Maastricht Treaty. The condemnation in the United Kingdom of the role of the Bundesbank in particular, and Germany more broadly for causing this, served to illustrate that Euroskepticism was still very much being conflated with a fear and resentment of Germany inherited from the Thatcher years.

Post 1997: Toward an Enduring Affinity?

A critical juncture in British-German relations emerged in the late 1990s when in 1997 and then 1998 center-left parties came to power in Germany and the United Kingdom. The arrival of New Labour in the United Kingdom and the Social Democratic Party (SPD) in Germany signaled the emergence of a far closer ideological affinity between the two states, which was harnessed and nurtured under the mantle of the *Neue Mitte* or "Third Way." What Chancellor Gerhard Schröder and Prime Minister Tony Blair had in common, aside from belonging to the same postwar generation, was a desire to renew and realign some of the central tenets of social democracy, through a program of modernization. Exhibiting this proximity, the so-called Blair-Schröder paper of 1998 entitled "The Way Forward for Europe's Social Democrats" addressed such themes as social justice, civil society, and citizenship, detailing points of convergence, a common agenda, priorities, and global visions shared between the British and German center-left parties.

Significantly, the renewal of the Labour Party in the United Kingdom entailed a more proactive stance toward the issue of Europe, with a swift and decisive move away from the former obstructionist character of the United Kingdom's European policy. Dubbed a "step-change," this strategy placed great emphasis upon developing bilateral relationships and partnerships on key European issues, thereby taking the traditional form of "multiple bilateralism" and assigning it a more strategic, less tactical, visionary mission. The defense agreement signed between the United Kingdom and France in 1998 at St. Malo, France, was one of the first and most sensational manifestations of this step-change; unsurprisingly, the realization followed after its federal election in 1998 that Germany, with Gerhard Schröder in power, would be a promising partner.

Crucially, a key change that enabled this shift in British European policy toward Germany to occur was a change of mindset in London, from viewing relations with Germany in terms of balance of power politics and a fear of German hegemony, toward a mode of thinking more accepting of Germany's power and the need for it to be used. Ultimately, Germany was now viewed not only as a potential strategic partner, but also as a model in some specific policy spheres.

Policy Transfer and Multilevel Governance

By 1997, after eighteen years of Conservative rule and the centralization of power in the United Kingdom, declining levels of attachment and external prestige associated with the Westminster model were becoming apparent. Crucially, the unitary framework of governance in the United Kingdom, which had remained unchanged, came under acute stress, seen most vividly in the case of Scotland, where the supporters of change pointed to the example of the German form of multilevel governance as a fresh alternative. As noted by Paterson, in this context the Federal Republic's "consistent success rendered the institutions of the Federal Republic potentially worthy of emulation."[10] Subsequently, in the processes of devolution in the United Kingdom, with the formation of the Scottish Parliament and the Welsh Assembly direct lessons were drawn from Germany, with some key features of the German system being emulated, though not always directly copied. Scottish and Welsh policy makers used Bavaria and Baden-Württemberg as positive examples of how to forge effective multilevel governance in a European context.

The United Kingdom, the Berlin Republic, and European Integration: Toward Common Ground?

Behind much of the tension in British-German relations in the period during and after unity lay severely contrasting visions and

10. Paterson, "Britain and the Berlin Republic," 211.

strategies vis-à-vis European integration. Although on the fundamental issue of the future of the European Union, British and German perspectives remain poles apart, in some specific policy spheres and also in policy style a detectable closeness has transpired between the United Kingdom and the Berlin Republic since 1997/98.

This greater synthesis of perspectives emerged when the UK's step-change in foreign policy matters gelled with the red-green coalition's less reflexive, more considered approach to EU matters. Although many commentators had indicated that the post-unification Germany's European policy may or indeed should take on a more British character, meaning a less unconditional form of support for integration,[11] it was not apparent until the arrival of the red-green coalition government that the habitual, predictably reflexive German take on Europe had somewhat abated. Demonstrating this, soon after becoming chancellor, Schröder spoke of a new self-confidence in Germany and of the need for Germany to watch over its own interests. Certainly, the distance between British and German European policy has narrowed on a number of counts; this is seen in the synergy that has transpired in certain policy sectors, though, as mentioned above, on the issue of the future of Europe their perspectives remain divergent.

The most crucial areas where the United Kingdom and Germany concur are EU enlargement, the need for the reform of the Common Agricultural Policy (CAP), the development of the European Security and Defense Policy (ESDP), as well as some general reforms in the EU budget and improving the transparency of such processes. Both states have always been in favor of EU enlargement, though until 1997 there was a divergence since the United Kingdom explicitly pursued the widening of the EU as a means to dilute its deepening—the policy of which Germany was one of the chief advocates. Since New Labour's arrival to power, the deepening versus widening divide has become less pronounced as a point of discord; consequently, on this point the United Kingdom and Germany are much closer to each other than to France. Similarly, on the issue of CAP and the need for reform, greater convergence emerged in the late 1990s, when the red-green coalition came to power. This synergy would, however, discontinue in the context of the Christian Democratic Union/Christian Socialist Union (CDU/CSU) returning to power, given that they have a large farming constituency. The

---

11. See Arnulf Baring, ed., *Germany's New Position in Europe: Problems and Perspectives* (Oxford, 1996).

reform-minded nature of current British and German European policy found its expression in a joint call made to the Spanish EU presidency in February 2002 for greater transparency in the EU's decision-making processes, to address the democratic deficit, and to end closed door sessions, except on foreign and security policy issues. The declaration also stated that heads of state should focus on EU "strategic and overarching issues" rather than petty technical matters. The paper was to signal the two countries' desire on reform issues, to set the pace of reform especially in the context of the convention on the future of Europe and the enlargement of the Union. Beyond these broad areas of synergy, it has been argued that further scope exists in the field of Justice and Home Affairs for British and German perspectives to converge, depending largely upon the United Kingdom joining the Schengen Area.[12]

This context suggests that by 2004 there may be a far greater convergence on European matters in Berlin and London's perspectives. However, at the same time serious conflict pervades regarding monetary union, economic reform, and in the area of tax harmonization.[13] More significantly, German and British perspectives are fundamentally opposed on the issue of the future of Europe. Berlin's commitment to realizing its vision of a truly federal Europe, with a stronger commission and parliament stands in contrast to the type of Europe Blair wishes to see, involving an increase in the role of the European Council and national parliaments.

Conclusions: Germany's Normalization and the United Kingdom

The British perspective on the Berlin Republic has fundamentally altered over the course of the previous decade. At the start of the 1990s Germany was viewed with resentment at worst and suspicion at best, a standpoint that manifested itself in a reluctance toward German unity, twinned with a posture toward European integration dominated by Euroskepticism. This perspective shifted after 1997, when the Berlin Republic became increasingly viewed by the new British government as both a potential partner and also as a model for the process of devolution and constitutional change about to

12. See Heather Grabbe and Wolfgang Munchau, *Germany and Britain: An Alliance of Necessity*, Centre for European Reform (London, 2002), 5.
13. See Grabbe and Munchau, *Germany and Britain*.

take place in the United Kingdom. The great distance that British-German relations have traveled over the past decade is most evident in the sphere of European integration. As discussed above, synergy now exists between the two states' perspectives on key policy areas, including enlargement and security, and both Berlin and London are dedicated to overcoming the inertia in the EU and to enact the necessary reforms to facilitate a larger Union.

Although British-German European initiatives are still very much a "novelty,"[14] the scope and necessity of London and Berlin working together is immense, and the clear need for the big states to drive the EU forward has already been shown on a number of occasions, not least in the form of the *directoire*. Certainly, the contrasting visions of the future of European integration held by London and Berlin impedes the emergence of a fuller strategic partnership, on a par to the traditional Franco-German double act; the slowdown in the Franco-German engine renders British-German cooperation on Europe as a practical partnership even more valid and important.

As seen from the United Kingdom, the spirit of the Berlin Republic implies a Germany more similar to the United Kingdom than has ever before been the case. A host of factors has contributed to this appraisal. Perhaps the most overwhelming of these, as far as the United Kingdom is concerned, has been the transformation of governance in the United Kingdom and the step-change in European policy. As far as Germany is concerned, it has been the development of a more active foreign policy and adoption of a less reflexive stance on every single European issue that have helped foster better and more productive relations with the United Kingdom.

In essence, the spirit of the Berlin Republic implies a more normal Germany, which, from the United Kingdom's perspective, makes it more understandable and therefore a more promising partner.

14. *International Herald Tribune,* "EU 'Democracy Deficit' Cited," 26 February 2002.

17. The Berlin Republic from a Polish Perspective: The End of the German Question

Anna Wolff-Powęska

The image that individual nations have of each other depends on many factors, the most important of which include historical experiences, their state of knowledge about each other, and each nation's estimation of itself and its situation. The process of German unification and the changes that have taken place between the Oder and the Rhine rivers over the last decade represent a unique historical process, which neighboring countries have, of course, followed with keen interest. Because of how the neighborhood has been marked by the tragic history of the last century, Poles pay close attention to developments on the western side of their border. They are conscious of the fact that the changes emanating from Germany will consequently affect the quality of Polish-German relations and future prospects for European integration. On what is this specific historical Polish angle based, and what does the Berlin Republic mean to Poles? These are questions worth pondering, even if there cannot be a clear and simple answer.

The reunification of Germany and the democratic change of power in Poland have placed relations between these two neighbors on an entirely new foundation. The period of 1989/90 was an important turning point in postwar European history. Germany no longer supplies two frontline states on the border between two blocs. For the first time in the thousand-year history of their relations, both peoples are guided equally by the principle of recognizing universal democratic values. This perspective opens up new opportunities, but at the same time it brings to light the whole complexity of the neighborhood. There is reason enough—based on the creation of an international legal framework for Poland's territorial integrity, on the country's admission into NATO, and on the prospect of membership in the European Union—for an entirely new perspective on Poland's neighbor to the west. The decisive question for Poland resides in uncertainty about whether there is more continuity or more change in the policy of the new Germany. Might a bigger, stronger Germany succumb to the temptation of power politics after all? What role will Germany play in the process of deepening and widening the EU?

After the Solution of the German Question

The new Germany represents the solution of the German question. For Poland, this means recognizing the inviolability of its western border and the reunification of Germany in democracy and freedom without impairing the process of European integration. Although communist rulers had deployed the specter of German reunification for years and years as an effective instrument for intimidating their own population, the fact that the two halves of Germany were reunited was received with greater equanimity along the Vistula River than it was among Germany's sworn partners in the West. Meanwhile, mixed emotions were aroused by the eastward extension of the space for democracy and security and by the proximity of Berlin as capital city. Owing to their historical memories, Germany's neighbors (and especially the Poles) have reacted to their large neighbor with great sensitivity, ambivalent expectations, and moral valuations. Objective asymmetry plays no small role here: Poland borders on a neighbor with twice as large a population and with a much higher economic potential and degree of civilization. The inferiority complex that so many Poles have vis-à-vis their large neighbor determines the scope and character of the attention they pay the German republic.

Like other nations, the Poles are convinced that a larger Germany will also have a bigger responsibility for the lot of Europe and the world. On the other hand, when remarks to this effect emanate from Germany itself, Poles are quick to find the attitude arrogant. Owing to a fear of German dominance, confidence in the stability of German democracy has its limits. The inclination to rely on a strong

Germany is accompanied by the fear that the Germans might abuse their superior status. Thus, the Germans are too strong for some and too weak for others. In the past, their commitment to widening the EU was positively received by some; for others it was an occasion to recall that Eastern and Southeastern Europe had traditionally been within the German sphere of influence.

The transformation that took place in Germany over the last decade also suggests a need for scrutinizing the country's self-image. Reunification is opening up an opportunity for both halves of Germany to write history jointly and, in so doing, to shift the historiographic perspective. At the same time, however, there are different consequences resulting from the fact that Germans are being watched from all sides with a certain suspicion. When the Sonderweg is repeatedly ascribed to the German nation, it can arouse defensive reactions, which drive some people to take refuge in radical political thinking.

The German public must constantly come to terms with a persistent tension between different objective facts about Germany's situation: between the potential of a united Germany on the one hand and the power of collective memory on the other. Among Germany's neighbors, this tension is the source of a lack of trust that, in turn, evokes conflicting emotions among the Germans. Transferring the capital from Bonn to Berlin does not imply any fundamental change; rather, it means continuing previous policy, with certain corrections. The Germans have managed, however, to draw lessons from their history. Thus, it is an exaggeration to worry that they might be tempted to go it alone in some fashion. Foreign policy conceived as a policy of self-restraint, unconditional priority for the European Union, deepening those values commonly designated as Western—these are the basics of German foreign policy today.

Reuniting in peace and freedom has allowed the Germans, for the first time in their recent history, to overcome the various domestic tensions to which they had repeatedly been subjected in the past:

1. *The tension between geography and politics:* The fact that Germany has the largest number of neighboring states along its borders and is centrally located on the old continent no longer serves as an argument for Germany to break out of its constricted space and from its encirclement; instead, having all these neighbors constitutes a pledge for Germany's bridging function and for deepening cooperation with all of its neighbors.

2. *The tension between freedom and unity*: The Germans have been united democratically and in a spirit of freedom; this event was not accompanied by any eruption of nationalism or by a global missionary consciousness.
3. *The tension between liberal democracy and the nation-state*: A reunited German state was turned into a catalyst for a policy of integration in Europe, providing an opportunity to end the German question that used to strike terror into the hearts of neighboring states; this German question was now essentially transformed into an internal matter for the Germans.

On the other end of things, the Poles were able to use membership in NATO as a way to overcome most of their Russo-German complex; over the last two centuries, "geopolitical fate" had shaped political thinking and the prevailing interpretation of *raison d'état* in Poland. For almost every quiet rapprochement between Germans and Russians enacted over the heads of the Poles was also, practically speaking, directed against Poland. The new circumstances create preconditions for overcoming these tendencies and the fears associated with them.

Rupture or Continuity?

Under these new circumstances, after the opening of the Iron Curtain, Poles and Germans were immediately confronted with the everyday politics of diverging attitudes toward the state, various ways of comprehending the nation and patriotism, and different visions of Europe's future. The shift in Berlin's governing coalition in 1998 aroused mistrust in Warsaw. The center-right coalition then governing Poland feared a turn toward the left in Berlin and an end of the support for Poland's entry into the EU announced by the Christian Democratic Union/Christian Social Union (CDU/CSU). In the red-green coalition in Germany, however, there emerged a new governing style for this younger generation of politicians. The fact that this generation had been born after World War II lends a new character to its actions. Chancellor Gerhard Schröder values the opportunity to underscore the new approach by changing the governing style that had prevailed for sixteen years of Christian-Liberal rule, with all the wear and tear that went along with that coalition's lengthy tenure in office.

At the same time that this new generation of politics has acceded to power, the least idealistic, least heroic phase in the history of German foreign and European policy has begun. A gradual accommodation to the new situation is discernible in the constant search for balance between the outside world's expectations and Germany's own interests; for a fundamental change in the conditions affecting foreign policy transpired in the last decade of the twentieth century. As long as foreign policy was determined by the Cold War's East-West conflict, its contours were clear. During the first forty years of the postwar era, foreign policy was primarily security policy. External circumstances forced the parties toward consensus. Today foreign policy among nation-states has been enriched by new social, cultural, ecological, and economic components; hence, foreign policy constantly confronts the challenge of finding a balance among global, European, and national interests.

In Poland, the pragmatism of the new governing coalition—which, reacting to the romantic and emotional phase of European policy as the 1980s gave way to the 1990s, displayed a matter-of-factness bereft of pathos and a return to "normality"—was watched with mistrust. In contrast to the era of Chancellor Helmut Kohl, which had still been shaped to a great extent by wartime and postwar experiences, Schröder wanted the world to see the maturity of a normal nation. On 10 November 1998, the chancellor spoke to this issue in a policy statement: "It is the self-confidence of a grown-up nation that does not have to feel superior or inferior to anyone ... that faces up to history and its responsibility, but looks ahead.... Our neighbors in Europe, too, know that they can have more trust in us the more we Germans trust in our own strength. In the past it was always those moments of precarious instability in national self-confidence that led to extremism and discord."

Today, national agreement on foreign economic policy is hard to produce, because clear-cut interests are hard to define; calculations in the fields of foreign, security, and economic policy are in a state of flux. Thus, for example, the West German state's prosperity used to depend, not least of all, on its particular brand of solidarity. Today, because interests are subject to an extensive process of differentiation, it is hard for them to be satisfied either by the state or any other institution in Germany. Business people who think in European and global categories, but whose views cannot be sustained by a national consensus, are speaking up. By participating in the founding of the European Monetary Union, the

German government voluntarily renounced one of the attributes of pride and national identity represented by the deutsche mark. Current circumstances in Poland favor extreme reactions. In a situation where too much is changing all at once, it is easy to revive old prejudices. In this phase of upheaval, politics is conducted emotionally; when this happens, economic knowledge easily loses value. Right now, conventional wisdom and categorical judgments are en vogue. An increase in spectacular outrages and acts of violence against foreigners in Germany is arousing unrest and a suspicion that neofascist tendencies are intensifying there. Swastikas on walls in Paris, Brussels, and London arouse understandable discontent, but setting a synagogue on fire or murdering foreigners on German streets awaken other associations: reflected in the faces of these persecuted foreigners is the fear of women and children being driven into gas chambers at concentration champs.

Previously, international public opinion was able to take solace in the fact that no right-wing extremist party in Germany was able to ensconce itself in the parliamentary system or score any triumphs at the federal level. The question arises, however, as to whether the persistence of structural unemployment, an increase in the number of nasty financial scandals within the traditional major parties, and a rise in other unsolved social problems might not lead to a point at which a section of society previously immune to neofascist propaganda might not fall victim to extremist ideologues and groups. How long will the armor forged by the permanent debate on the National Socialist past last?

The Germans have entered the twenty-first century with inner unity in short supply. This new German question grows out of the complicated processes of transformation and unification in Germany. Transferring government and political structures from the West to the territory of the former German Democratic Republic (GDR) could not, on its own, bring about the development of a political nation and a feeling of togetherness. Such a process requires several generations' time. The complicated mutual relations between people in the old and new federal states conceal an emotional and psychological explosive charge. Even if there are plenty of objective facts capable of arousing a feeling of discrimination among East Germans, their mood conceals a number of unfounded complexes, a masochistic cultivation of a sense of injustice, and a need to shift the blame for everything unpleasant onto the West Germans.

The people who have encountered each other atop the ruins of the former Wall have not only brought along different past histories in their personal baggage; they have also, above all, met each other carrying diverse notions and expectations about the future. To be sure, they believed they were keeping each other in view across the Wall. Yet after unification it was frequently revealed how little, how superficial, and sometimes even how mistaken their knowledge had been. During the unification process, a decline in prestige, a dismantling of mutual conceptions about each other, gradually took place. One's own utopias proved to be sources of major disillusionment.

Many Poles still have a different attitude about citizens from the old and the new Länder. The fall of the Wall had the effect of getting people who had never really been neighbors to face each other. For decades, the "friendship border" was as good as impenetrable. Poles and citizens of the GDR never cultivated an authentic dialogue about essential topics for these two peoples. Polish opposition groups had no contact with opposition forces in the GDR, and the only common language both sides knew how to use was Russian. The mistrust with which the citizens of these two "fraternal" countries encountered each other after the fall of the Wall demonstrated how small the potential was for the kind of friendship decreed by communist rulers. While, as early as the 1970s, groups from the intelligentsia in Poland and in the old western Federal Republic cultivated contacts with each other, relations between citizens of the former GDR and of Poland have to be newly created from the ground up.

National identity is just as hard to privatize as morality; and so the Germans in both parts of a country divided for decades by the Wall have little choice but to develop, gradually, a feeling of togetherness. They have to seize upon reunification as their great opportunity. To be sure, there is concern on both sides of losing something in the process; yet they have to try harder to understand each other, practice solidarity, and arrive at the conviction that they have a lot to gain from doing so.

The new Berlin Republic needs time for the democratic institutions implanted on the territory of the former GDR to take root there and gain acceptance. The example of the old Federal Republic can have a motivating effect in this regard; for the democratic order that the three Western powers imposed after the war initially generated little enthusiasm there as well. It took decades there until passive acceptance—bolstered by growing prosperity—spilled over into active dedication, and until the citizens of the Federal Republic transformed themselves from extras on the political and societal stage into full-fledged live actors.

A New Normality

One of the important things that can help to prop up a feeling of self-worth is the outside world's positive assessment. Every nation has the need to be recognized as normal. But few demonstrate this need quite as obsessively—though for different reasons—than do Germans and Poles. Declaring "We are a normal nation" has a therapeutic, self-calming character. This seems suspicious—ultimately, normality cannot be decreed. If one wishes to view democratic political culture as the decisive criterion, then the Germans have stood the test. No nation in Europe summons up as much empathy for the fate of other peoples and translates this into acts of humanitarian assistance for those who suffer from wars and catastrophes or human rights violations; in no other country are asylum seekers and poor refugees from all four corners of the earth as likely to find a place as they are in Germany. This fact—regardless of whether it serves Germany's own purposes or is intended as a concession to the outside world—amounts to more than an occasional slip. (The Germans are held to higher standards than others owing to the incredible harm they inflicted on others under the National Socialists.)

In the course of just a few decades, the Germans have traveled a long distance—from morally crushing defeat, being ostracized by world public opinion, and isolation all the way to recovery of prestige and trust, even if under constant special and attentive scrutiny. To be sure, for a long time to come, the Germans will have to put up with the rest of the world making moral assessments about everything that takes place inside their borders. The touchstone for the Germans' political morality will continue to be their attitude toward National Socialism. Every normal nation has its past, for good and for evil. Any attempt at withdrawing from history would be judged as an escape and a refusal to draw lessons from the experience of the past.

Germans are in a transitional phase between the Bonn Republic and the Berlin Republic. It is still too early to answer the question of what Germans understand as normality in their republic. How far does change go, and how far continuity? Just the fact that reunification has not been accompanied by nationwide reflection validates skepticism and questions. But today, after decades of living with two states, a condition that implied a certain element of the provisional, there is certainly a consciousness about the need to construct sound structures for the future.

There can be no talk of any "zero hour." The new republic, without any false modesty, needs to relate to the best traditions of the Bonn Republic; the old republic had developed virtues that earned general respect. Their continuation means holding onto the republic of Konrad Adenauer and Willy Brandt, that is, to the same constitutional principles, and remaining loyal to the idea of peaceful coexistence in international relations. The post-Wall transformation requires establishing a new geopolitical situation and adding postcommunist countries to a widened European Union, in order to do justice to the founders' legacy of unity on the old continent.

The Berlin Republic means greater obligations toward the eastern Länder. This is not just a matter of solidarity or a readiness to make sacrifices in order to compensate for differences in living standards. Required, above all, are greater understanding, empathy for this special situation, and sensitivity to difference and to another way of approaching the way people exercise responsibility. The transfer of the capital city signifies an opportunity to get closer to everyday life in eastern Germany and to get better acquainted up close with things that could not be perceived from afar. The significance of the city and its history is anything but unequivocal. It is a city that embodies all the highs and lows that flow into the new republic's normality.

The geographical shift of the capital city and of the country eastward, from the provincial Rhenish city to the metropolis just around forty miles from the Polish border went hand in hand with a united Germany's opening toward the world behind the Oder and Neiße rivers. This signifies a departure toward new shores. The Germans are a free and democratic partner of all their neighbors, a partner making an effort at more intensive cooperation and at an all-around exchange of ideas, people, and capital with every European country. This is a fundamentally new situation.

The post-Kohl era is not one of stability. The Kohl government's sixteen years, in which the Federal Republic of Germany (FRG) solidified its leading position in Europe and which are identified with an increase in stability and trust in the Bonn Republic, have simultaneously proven to be a phase of growing corruption and slush funds of the major political parties. Exposing these facts, which contradict Kohl's assurances about the spiritual and moral upheaval in Germany, has called into question the credibility of German public order, which (as in no other place in the world) was equated with the rule of law. Confidence in the civic values of Germany's political right was undermined. There is a flip side to the scandal, though: it compels thoughtfulness, critical reexamination of reality, and a search for paths toward new beginnings.

The problems that result from the appropriation of democracy by parties and the negative effects of globalization, problems that are becoming increasingly noticeable for a number of citizens, have stirred up a discussion about the range of individual governments' capacities to act. It is hardly possible today to revive the enthusiasm and pioneering spirit that accompanied the incorporation of the old Federal Republic into Western Europe. The reality of a unified Germany looks completely different and, accordingly, demands a different approach. In taking on this overwhelming, ambitious assignment, the Germans are dependent on the trust and cooperation of their neighbors.

The impossibility of doing justice to the outside world's expectations results in a kind of split consciousness. Worrying about whether German intentions for policy toward Europe might be reinterpreted or even completely misunderstood necessitates a kind of caution that can be interpreted as shrinking from responsibility. The peculiar stigmatization of the German nation springs, among other things, from an inclination that has prevailed for decades among Germany's neighbors to make the Germans collectively responsible for the crimes committed during World War II. Thus, the Germans, if they wish to liberate themselves from being afraid of themselves, also have to make sure that other nations can liberate themselves from this fear. Only on this basis can a European community be built.

Today the Berlin Republic is chiefly judged according to how it behaves with respect to the expansion of the European Union. Its attitude toward Poland's membership will be viewed as a litmus test for how Poland's western neighbor sees things. In Poland there was criticism of the German demand for a seven-year transition period before introducing freedom of movement for Polish workers. It was dubious to argue, as was repeatedly done with persistent unemployment in mind, that Polish workers would flood the German labor market. A constant source of irritation, however, is the fact that politicians and the mass media do not even make an effort to analyze the situation objectively, which would inevitably lead them to the conclusion that masses of workers would by no means be pushing across Poland's western border. On the other hand, one may expect Germany to witness an ominous decline in its population, a serious increase in the proportion of retired people, and an enormous decline in the numbers of those of working age. Thus, Germany in the future will be dependent on the absorption of foreign workers if economic life and public order are not going to collapse.

The red-green government's initiatives in the field of European integration encourage questions and arouse skepticism. The vision of a European federation presented by Germany's Foreign Minister Joschka Fischer and Chancellor Gerhard Schröder means sticking to the CDU's old concept. There has been a narrowing in the area of agreement between Germany and France, the tandem that had previously taken the initiative in pointing the way to Europe's future. The paper of the Social Democratic Party (SPD), "Responsibility for Europe," has upset Poles by the way that the Germans, among others, have called for joint European surveillance of the EU's future borders. At the same time, the Germans want to maintain controls at their border to Poland. Here the Poles see a clash with the concept of a Europe without internal borders.

After the fall of the Wall, Poles and Germans turned out to have a different understanding of what patriotism means. The West Germans, almost half a century ago under pressure from World War II's victorious powers, had shifted a portion of their sovereignty downward, toward the federal states, and then later, in the course of European integration, transferred another portion to supranational institutions. For Poland, which had waited for decades to regain national sovereignty, it is hard to get acquainted with the notion that nation-states will no longer have absolute sovereignty in the integrated Europe they wish to join. Their mantra "We are a sovereign state" is greeted with incomprehension by other nations and places Poland under suspicion of being nationalistic.

The Balkan conflict, the barbarism of totalitarian systems so close to home, and even the Poles' own problems coming to terms with communism have made it clear that the Germans do not have a monopoly on misdeeds; that misdeeds can reoccur is demonstrated by these events. A democrat is distinguished from a rabid nationalist by the way he subjects himself to the moral norms he expects his opponent to observe. Every moral evaluation of the past is simultaneously a moral characterization of the present. We therefore have to pose the question of whether democracy in Poland exists only in a formal, declarative sense, or whether it also prompts us to take an equivalent stance in our political dealings with other nations.

We expect European integration to remain the leitmotif of policy in Berlin. Meanwhile, in Poland as in Germany—partly for different, and partly for the same reasons—a discussion has opened up on national identity and national pride. In Poland the starting point for the discussion was articulating the untold stories of the crimes committed at the end of the war against Jews, Germans, and Ukrainians resident there. While the Poles had previously always viewed themselves only as victims, they now had to become acquainted with the recognition that Poles had also been perpetrators. Thus, some saw themselves being robbed of the right to have pride in their own history; this is painful and hard to accept. It rouses a need for catharsis and for seeking evasion in radical thinking.

In Germany, the new wave of reflection about the past and German guilt proceeded from the controversy between Martin Walser and Ignatz Bubis and the exhibition on the Wehrmacht's war crimes. At issue here was a debate between participants in the war and contemporary witnesses, a debate that was highly personally colored and conducted emotionally. Some of the participants in the debate are ready, after all these years of silence, to stand up publicly for their point of view in the hope of gaining sympathy for their position. Others attempt, eagerly, to prove their innocence, to cast off the ballast of the past, in the hope of being able to spend their last years liberated from the nightmare of history and the encumbrance of shame. Every word is carefully ventured in order to leave their grandchildren a trustworthy spiritual legacy. Incidentally, for Polish forced laborers during the Third Reich and for those who can recall the massive theft of art works, this is the last chance to receive at least symbolic compensation, a settlement for misdeeds suffered, and moral satisfaction. For both sides it is a race against time. The more the war recedes into the past, the more intensively do memories and confessions speak up.

In different ways, Germans and Poles are discussing whether they have the right to be proud of their nation. A lack of a feeling of self-worth elicits negative reactions that, as history has shown, can have fatal consequences. For the Greens, with their traditional skepticism about the national question, patriotism (or even its very mention) used to seem unwelcome (or even a disgrace). For many, what counted was *ersatz* patriotism: constitutional patriotism or economic success. How can one create some kind of national pride after Auschwitz? But citizens have a legitimate claim upon national pride, just as they have a right to self-respect. What is decisive is the degree; this is not so easy to define, since the limits are not so easy to demarcate. What matters are tact and restraint; it is by these things that a political culture is measured.

Perhaps the Poles, sadder but wiser to the tune of one historical reality and conscious of their own guilt, now see the Germans
in another light, namely as individual human beings. In the contemporary discussion nobody bothers to ask whether one should
remember, but rather how one should remember, how one's knowledge can be transmitted to future generations so that it does not
appear as a ballast, but as medication, as a signpost pointing the way
into the future. The Berlin Republic has liberated itself from the
German question that was still a burden on the Bonn Republic. As
a specific problem that harbored unrest and a threat to the international status quo in Europe, the German question is solved. Germany's division into two states, which had always officially been
declared to be a provisional arrangement, is over. For years it was
disputed whether Germany's unity as a state was compatible with
European integration. In the meantime, the Germans became the
motor of integration. This role emanated, on the one hand, from
an inner need on the part of the Germans, who were conscious of
how, as the largest and strongest state on the old continent, they
would only be accepted within the framework of a European structure. On the other hand, those states interested in joining the EU,
and for whom the Germans represent the natural advocate for Eastern European interests at the European forum, are pushing for
this role. Incidentally, in the eyes of Germany's traditional Western
allies, its newly won unification will not appear to be posing a danger to European security so long as the Germans remain interested
in the continued development and solidification of integration on
the European continent.

It seems to me that the gap between the role that Germany plays
internationally and the popular understanding of this role at home
has deepened over the last several years. Whether an attempt will
be made to harmonize the country's self-image with the changing
expectations that the outside world places on Germany remains to
be seen. It depends on domestic political developments in the Federal Republic and on international conditions. Each new outbreak
of extremism awakens new fears of the Germans.

Invoking history and morality does not always lead ahead. For
history does not, in all cases, supply unequivocal criteria for decisions that have to be made today. Thus, the discussion about the
crimes of the Wehrmacht in the former Yugoslavia during World
War II was used both for and against the Federal Republic's participation in NATO military deployments there.

When Germany's neighbors waver between fear of excessive German power and admiration for German accomplishments, this can trigger different reactions among the Germans. It can lead the German government to display a higher measure of responsibility for Europe's and the world's security; but the most natural reaction would certainly be indifference. Germany, unlike any other country, is burdened with both the East's and the West's problems and with the whole baggage of history and idealistic expectations. The Polish public now tends to be rather pragmatically inclined toward Germany; it would like to see the new Berlin Republic as a source of opportunity. But the future is full of difficulties and imponderables.

18. On Old and New Similarities: Italy and the Berlin Republic

Antonio Missiroli

An advertisement that appeared in the press in 2001 for the automobile giants FIAT and Ferrari portrayed Michael Schumacher, the Formula One world champion, celebrating victory under the heading "German fantasy–Italian technology." It was an excellent piece of advertising: it conveyed a clear commercial message by ironically epitomizing the quintessential mutual prejudices of the two peoples. Indeed, bilateral relations have long been strongly conditioned by cultural elements and historical experience: the commonplace idea whereby Italians admire Germans but do not like them, and Germans like Italians but do not admire them, is still widespread and impinges upon their respective mutual perceptions.[1]

This is all the more striking because, throughout the Cold War, the two countries actually displayed a number of similarities. Both had lost World War II (although Italy had been torn since 1943 by what was as much a civil war as a war of national liberation), and both had to come to terms with the legacy of fascism. Both were split along Cold War lines (Italy in terms of domestic politics, Germany in terms of national unity) and both struggled to regain some sovereignty and international rank. Both warmly supported European economic and political integration; both became convinced NATO members; both adopted a low international profile and a

---

1. For an overview and analysis of bilateral relations (and perceptions), see A. Missiroli, "Italia-Germania: le affinita' selettive," *Il Mulino/Europa* 2 (1995); idem, "Germania e Germanie nell'Italia del dopoguerra," *Europa Europe* 1 (1996). Cf. also A. Prosperi, "Typecasting Italy and Germany," *Italy Daily*, supplement to the *International Herald Tribune*, 2 December 1999.

markedly multilateralist approach. They also developed strong bilateral commercial ties—(West) Germany has been Italy's main trading partner since 1957—and societal links through religion (the first German visitors to Italy after the war came for the 1950 Jubilee, and Pope Pius XII and his entourage were notoriously Germanophile), through ideology (the main political parties in Bonn and Rome were both confession-based), through tourism (rather one-way, though), and through cultural exchanges. Especially the latter, however, never reached the size and density of those established by Germany with the United States or France.

Political leaderships in Italy and Germany found frequent occasions and motives for agreement and convergence. Former Italian Prime Minister Alcide de Gasperi and former German Chancellor Konrad Adenauer shared similar cultural roots and federalist ambitions, and the two Christian Democratic parties long dominated the Western European family (much as they eventually differed in their approach to former French President Charles de Gaulle and the Fifth Republic). After some tension in the mid-1970s—mostly linked to domestic instability in Italy and the resurgence of terrorism in both countries—the governments in Bonn and Rome were the driving forces behind most moves toward European integration as well as the establishment of European Political Cooperation (EPC), later turned into the European Union's Common Foreign and Security Policy (CFSP). They also spearheaded, though not without difficulty, the installation of NATO's "Euromissiles" in the early 1980s. They pushed for the enlargement of the Community to include Spain and Portugal, in the mid-1980s, and the creation of the Single Market, although they did not always see eye to eye on strictly financial and monetary matters (the "snake" and the Exchange Rate Mechanism [ERM]). Indeed, that was the policy field in which the cultures of the two elites differed most and in which the West German economic giant was definitely the bigger player. In addition, on issues related to European security and defense, Germany tended to reach out to France (the Franco-German Brigade, later the Eurocorps) and Italy to Great Britain: yet the common fundamental Atlanticist stance notwithstanding, this was rather a question of tactical nuances and moves.[2] Moreover, since the mid-1980s, the two political systems have come to look increasingly

2. On British-Italian relations in this field, see M. Dassù and A. Missiroli, "Becoming a Reliable Team Player," in *Britain and Europe: The Choices We Face*, ed. M. Rosenbaum (Oxford, 2001).

alike, so much so that the German electoral system—from the
Sperrklausel (exclusion clause) to the parliamentary election of the
chancellor—was considered in Italy to be a potential model for
much-needed reform. Even the two main left-wing parties (the
German Social Democratic Party (SPD) and the Italian Communist Party (PCI), both in the opposition) came closer to each
other, developed direct links, and fought similar battles in the
years that led to the fall of the Berlin Wall. Finally, Germany and
Italy clearly joined forces to isolate British Prime Minister Margaret Thatcher in the run-up to the 1990/91 Intergovernmental
Conference (IGC) and bring about the political union enshrined
in the Maastricht Treaty.

Nevertheless, there remained a lingering tension between Italy
and Germany that occasionally manifested itself. A case in point
was when the German newsweekly *Der Spiegel* printed a cover page
with spaghetti and a gun to portray 1977 Italy. Another such situation was when Italian Foreign Minister Giulio Andreotti declared in
1984 that there were two Germanys, and that this was a good thing
that should continue. It will come as no surprise, therefore, that
German unification temporarily reawakened some old (mis)per-
ceptions. On the one hand, the German government of the time
did not conceal its irritation with Italy's (vain) attempts to become
a player in the "2 + 4" negotiations by virtue of its presidency of the
European Community (EC). Furthermore, German politician Otto
Graf Lambsdorff first wondered whether the "new Bundesländer"
would become a sort of German "*Mezzogiorno*," that is, a permanent
burden for the whole nation; he then added that in no way could
the solid East German workers be compared with the "olive gath-
erers" from southern Italy:[3] needless to say, those remarks were not
well received in Rome. On the other hand, some segments of the
Italian elite and public opinion did not conceal their worry about
the pace and shape of the unification process: mention of a "Grande
Germania" or even a "Fourth Reich" was not infrequent, nor were
quotes from Thomas Mann's alternative between a "German Europe"
and a "European Germany." It must be stressed, however, that the
actual collapse of the Wall had an enormous emotional impact in
and on Italy.[4] The fall of the old Socialist Unity Party (SED) guard,

3. Cf. interview with Otto Graf Lambsdorff, "Ostdeutschland ist kein Mezzogiorno," *Süddeutsche Zeitung*, 15 December 1990.
4. Incidentally, it was an Italian journalist (the ANSA correspondent from East
Berlin) who triggered the whole dynamics of the evening of 9 November 1989 by
half naively asking a manifestly unprepared Günter Schabowski (of the Central

too, was very well received even on the left. Moreover, the fact that the president of the Soviet Union, Mikhail Gorbachev, ultimately supported the unification process and that it was soon embedded in a broader European framework dispelled most of the fears that the German *annus mirabilis* had ignited. In the end, both the wider public and the elites welcomed the outcome—including the decision taken in June 1991 on Berlin as the capital city—and focused rather on its implications and prospects.

Post-Unification Squabbles

One of the main implications of unification has certainly been a temporary parting of ways—or rather of short-term interests—between Germany and Italy. For a few years, in fact, the two countries would find themselves on different (if not entirely opposite) fronts on a number of issues. Take the crises in former Yugoslavia: the newly united Federal Republic of Germany (FRG) pushed hard for the early recognition of Croatia and Slovenia, whereas Italy gave priority to the preservation of the Yugoslavian Federation and tried above all not to antagonize Belgrade, following a long diplomatic tradition. Moreover, once the independence of Croatia and Slovenia was established, Italy got entangled in bitter bilateral disputes with both seceding republics on the rights and entitlements of the local Italian minorities.[5] A couple of years afterwards, Germany was included in the "contact group," while Italy, in spite of its similar historical record in and closer geographical proximity to the region, had to fight hard—and to put extra pressure on Washington—in order to be taken on board (which occurred only later, during Italy's EU presidency in 1996). Lastly, it was Germany (along with Great Britain) that in 1997 resisted the idea of making what would become "Operation Alba" in Albania a common European mission.[6] Similarly, in the case of NATO's expansion to Central Europe,

---

Committee of the East German Socialist Unity Party [SED]) when exactly the newly approved provisions on free circulation would enter into force.

5. See E. Greco, "Italy, the Yugoslav Crisis and the Osimo Agreements," *The International Spectator* 1 (1994). On the whole region, cf. V. Mastny, ed., *Italy and East Central Europe: Dimensions of the Regional Relationship* (Boulder, 1995).

6. As a result, the operation was run by a mixed "coalition of the willing"—all European, with Italy as a "lead nation"—with a UN/OSCE humanitarian mandate. See S. Silvestri, "The Albanian Test Case," *International Spectator* 3/4 (1997); E. Forster, "Ad Hoc in Albania: Did Europe Fail?" *Security Dialogue* 29 (1998). Shortly

Germany was the driving force from the outset (managing also to convince the Clinton administration), whereas Italy long resisted it or, in the end, supported rather a much broader enlargement than the one eventually agreed on.[7]

Finally, there is the highly controversial issue of reform of the UN Security Council: Germany long looked keenly on being promoted to some form of permanent membership—although no formal demand was ever formulated—whereas Italy tried long and tenaciously to block the so-called "quick fix" supported by the United States, whereby the Security Council would simply be enlarged to five new permanent members (among them Germany and Japan). Italy also proposed various alternative reform schemes that aimed at putting both Bonn and Rome in a sort of intermediate layer of semi-permanent members. Meanwhile, and quite inconsistently, German and Italian diplomats alike paid lip service to the prospect of a permanent seat for the EU as such. At stake there were rank and prestige on the international scene: German Foreign Minister Klaus Kinkel basically made the issue the defining battle of his tenure (1992–1998), while Italy's political leadership was increasingly sidetracked by the deep domestic crisis triggered by the Tangentopoli scandals—a series of bribes to procure public contracts. Weak and volatile governments in Rome, however, felt all the more compelled to fight for the country's rank: for his part, the Italian ambassador to the UN, Francesco Paolo Fulci, made it a point of national and personal honor to prevent a German success that would have made Italy the only big EU member excluded from the club. The issue, in fact, would long affect bilateral relations at the top diplomatic level.

Things went less smoothly than before also at the strictly European level. As could be expected, the traditional *entente cordiale* on Community matters did not evaporate overnight, but had to endure a series of trials and challenges. The most important one was, of course, the European Monetary Union (EMU). Germany and Italy had already been at odds over fiscal and monetary policy in the past, but the combination of the ERM disaster of September 1992 (when the lira was de facto ejected from the system and forced to float) and the crumbling of the Italian party system triggered a

---

after that, however, the situation changed, and the two countries began gradually to converge on a common approach to the Balkans.

7. Cf. M. Dassù and R. Menotti, "Italy and NATO Enlargement," *The International Spectator* 3/4 (1997); L. Ratti, "Italian Diplomacy in the NATO Enlargement Process," *Mediterranean Politics* 1 (2001).

serious crisis of mutual confidence. German officials seemed convinced that Italy would be a burden (or at best a problem child) within the EMU, and both the government in Bonn and the Bundesbank in Frankfurt reiterated their criticism and warnings to Rome. In addition, the famous paper drafted in 1994 by the parliamentary group of the Christian Democratic Union and the Christian Social Union (CDU/CSU) on a "core" Europe that would push integration forward in all policy areas happened to earmark all founding members of the EC bar Italy. Similarly, the fledgling Schengen agreement on cross-border regimes did not include Italy —at the outset, the Schengen agreement included only the governments of the Benelux countries, Germany, and France—whose frontiers were considered porous with insufficient police controls. Last but not least, Italian business groups were discovering how hard it was to try and penetrate the German corporate world, in the West (the Pirelli group bid for Continental) as much as in the East (the steel group Riva).

On the whole, in spite of the high popular ratings enjoyed by German Chancellor Helmut Kohl, the Italian public felt that "Grande Germania" was marginalizing Italy and resented it, as shown by most opinion polls.[8] In addition, occasional acts of violence by Nazi skinhead gangs in the former German Democratic Republic (GDR) were often overemphasized by the Italian press and found a disproportionate echo in the country, thus reinvigorating old prejudices. At the elite level, too, mutual confidence seemed slightly on the decline: in the negotiations that would lead to the Amsterdam Treaty, for instance, Italian diplomats felt at times sidelined or abandoned by their German colleagues. On the one hand, the whole issue of "enhanced cooperation," as raised by Kohl and French President Jacques Chirac in 1996, was largely interpreted in Rome as a legal device for a *directoire* excluding Italy and was therefore opposed.[9] On the other hand, the chancellor was criticized for giving in to the German Länder on "third pillar" issues, thus slowing down further integration. By contrast, the battles that were

8. For a comprehensive overview of the main trends over the entire decade, see the study "L'Europa degli italiani," conducted by *Il Sole-24 Ore* and RAI television and edited by the market research firm Pragma (Rome, I [1992]–VIII [1999]). For the domestic foreign policy debate, cf. R. Aliboni and E. Greco, "Foreign Policy Renationalization and Internationalism in the Italian Debate," *International Affairs* 1 (1996).

9. Cf. K. Junge, *Flexibility, Enhanced Cooperation and the Treaty of Amsterdam* (London, 1999); A. Missiroli, "CFSP, Defence, Flexibility," Chaillot Papers 38 (Paris, 2000).

fought in unison, for instance on the CFSP, bore modest fruits. Besides, while German pro-enlargement rhetoric was hardly shared by Italian officials, both the configuration of trade and economic interests and the orientation of domestic public opinion were much more convergent.[10]

As a result, Italy came to focus almost exclusively on the goal of meeting the Maastricht criteria for the EMU and thereby "staying in Europe," as it was presented at the time. The domestic political debate of the years 1996–1998 was entirely centered on that, and the majority that supported Romano Prodi as prime minister had that objective as its main (if not sole) unifying factor. Such concentration of political and administrative energy on a single overarching goal, however, paid off: in late 1996 the lira reentered the ERM, and, in spite of the lingering doubts voiced by Bundesbank officials and (decreasingly so) the German Finance Ministry, in May 1998 it became part and parcel of the first wave of the EMU.[11] A few months later, after meeting a series of increasingly sophisticated technical requirements, Italy was also admitted (in two steps) into "Schengenland."[12] The fact that the considerable efforts of the previous years were crowned by success, however, did not prevent the Prodi government from collapsing in Parliament. In October 1998 a vote of confidence failed to collect the necessary majority by one vote, and the team that had brought Italy "back" into Europe had to go. The new governments that followed—led by Massimo D'Alema (1998–2000) and Giuliano Amato (2000–2001), respectively—were supported by a marginally different coalition (the "Olive Tree" plus some splinter centrist parties) but would find it much more difficult to find and agree upon an equally all-encompassing and mobilizing raison d'être.

10. On all of these issues, see A. Missiroli, "Italiens Außenpolitik vor und nach Maastricht. Europa als Herausforderung und Reformzwang," *Aus Politik und Zeitgeschichte* 28 (1998).

11. It is extremely telling, however, that in order to motivate the Italian public in the final stages of the race to meet the Maastricht criteria, Prodi once declared that "the Germans know what Italy is capable of in overtime" (see *Corriere della Sera*, 25 April 1997). He was hinting, of course, at the famous football match between the two national teams in the 1970 World Cup semifinal that the Italians won 4–3, and that is still enormously popular on both sides as a showcase of their respective qualities and shortcomings.

12. Cf. F. Pastore, "L'expérience italienne dans la mise en oeuvre de Schengen," in *Von Schengen nach Amsterdam. Auf dem Weg zu einem europäischen Einwanderungs- und Asylrecht*, ed. K. Heilbronner and P. Weil (Bonn, 1999).

Back Together

In the meantime, however, the Kohl era had come to an end as well, and it is fair to say that the allegations of administrative irregularities and misuse of party funds that hit Kohl immediately afterwards have generated some Schadenfreude in scandals-ridden Italy. The new red-green coalition was still taking its first steps, of course, but the general impression was that it would be easier to work with a German government of similar political color. And since center-left majorities were in office at the time in a number of countries in the EU, including bigger ones such as Germany and France, the assumption was that things would go smoothly, both bilaterally and at the European level. At the outset the waters between Rome and (then still) Bonn were briefly troubled by the "Öçalan affair,"[13] that put to the test the credibility of EU-wide legal arrangements as much as the two countries' actual willingness to share risks and responsibilities. But the changed political climate in Europe certainly helped not only to sidestep that awkward episode but also put new common policies on the right track.

That was certainly the case with the European Security and Defense Policy (ESDP) formally launched at the Cologne European Council in June 1999. If it is true that the main impulse came from the Franco-British Declaration released at St. Malo in December 1998, the fact that Germany (in its capacity as EU president) and to a lesser extent Italy were soon taken on board helped multilateralize the initiative and make it more acceptable to other European partners. The traditional cleavage between the Franco-German and the British-Italian couples on European defense issues was over and done with, and there was an identifiable core of countries that were both politically willing and militarily able to support and sustain the new policy. In fact, a purely Franco-British push would not have convinced more restrained partners, while the very launch of ESDP, in turn, allowed both Italy and to a lesser extent Germany to set in motion a long-overdue process of reform of the military apparatus. Italians, in particular, tried to interpret and implement the new policy as a sort of EMU for defense, with necessary convergence criteria with which to comply.[14] Italy and

13. This refers to the arrest of the leader of the Kurdistan Workers' Party (PKK) (which had been instigating terrorist attacks in Germany), when the Italian court refused to extradite him to Turkey on account of that country's death penalty.

14. On that, cf. A. Missiroli, "European Security and Defence: The Case for Setting 'Convergence Criteria'," *European Foreign Affairs Review* 4 (1999). On ESDP and the

202 • *Antonio Missiroli*

Germany also concurred on keeping the new policy *within* the EU institutional framework, although outside of the area of competence of the Commission. Incidentally, after the sudden and shocking resignation of the team led by Jacques Santer, the extraordinary Council held in Berlin in late March 1999 appointed Romano Prodi as head of the European executive, thus giving also symbolic recognition to Italy's long march toward participation in the EMU and "back" into Europe.

The two years that followed would represent a neat return to political convergence at all levels. The new German foreign minister, Joschka Fischer, made it clear that permanent membership on the UN Security Council was no longer a top priority, thus setting aside a major source of bilateral tension. Both Germany and Italy supported, politically as well as militarily, Operation Allied Force in Kosovo, and managed to do so against important segments of their public opinions. Yet it is fair to say that opposition was stronger in Italy,[15] while in Germany "nie wieder Auschwitz" (Never again Auschwitz) largely prevailed over "nie wieder Krieg" (Never again war). Moreover, after the war, both countries engaged in postconflict reconstruction, through NATO's KFOR (the international force responsible for establishing a security presence in Kosovo) as much as through the EU's stability pact for the Balkans.

Most importantly, however, Germany and Italy converged once again on European issues, entering the 2000 IGC with similar positions on all the key institutional questions. These ranged from the need to further extend qualified majority voting (although some differences emerged over the preferred areas) to the demand for some reweighing of votes in the Council with a view to the forthcoming enlargement, up to the urgency of appropriately incorporating the decisions taken on ESDP into the Treaty. Yet the most significant point of convergence was, curiously enough, enhanced cooperation. Needless to say, the fact that Italy was also and felt returned to core Europe helped dispel previous fears of exclusion in Rome. The prospect of enlargement, too, made increasingly urgent the move toward more institutional flexibility. It was no surprise, therefore, that the speech on the future of Europe held by Fischer at Germany's Humboldt University in eastern Berlin in

---

reform of the Italian military, see A. Missiroli, "Italian Defence Policy: European Engagement and Domestic Reform," *The International Spectator* 2 (2001).

15. Cf. R. Balfour et al., "Italy's Crisis Diplomacy in Kosovo—March–June 1999," *The International Spectator* 3 (1999).

spring 2000 was very well received in Italy.[16] Consequently, in the following months, the two diplomacies worked side by side and, in October 2000, delivered a joint paper that set out possible new general conditions for triggering enhanced cooperation and included also ad hoc provisions for CFSP. The paper would represent the main basis for the final IGC negotiations, although the outcome of the European Council in Nice would not entirely meet the expectations of the promoters.[17]

In a way, therefore, the actual move of Germany's capital city to Berlin has coincided with a new golden age in bilateral relations with Italy. The squabbles of the mid-1990s seem to be forgotten, the old prejudice(s) to have stopped popping up again and again. Of course, new controversial issues—linked to differing interests, or just to rank and national pride—may reemerge and strain the relationship once again. In particular, it remains to be seen what impact the new coalition government led by Silvio Berlusconi since May 2001—let alone the composition of the Bundestag after the September 2002 elections—will have on the traditional *entente cordiale* regarding the shape of the EU institutions, especially as seen from the perspective of the Convention on the Future of Europe. Yet most of the (mis)perceptions of decades past appear to be losing their hold and resilience, the transition from (problematic) nation-states to (EU) member-states almost completed. In a European and—why not?—global framework, German fantasy and Italian technology are now, at last, equally conceivable.

16. See also G. Amato, "Un coeur fort pour l'Europe," *Le Monde*, 25 May 2000, reprinted in *The Future Shape of Europe*, ed. M. Leonard (London, 2000).

17. For an evaluation, cf. A. Missiroli, "Italy and Europe's Foreign Policy: Continuity, Change, and Adaptation," in *Europäische Außenpolitik*, ed. G. Müller-Brandeck-Boquet (Baden-Baden, 2002).

19. The Berlin Republic from the Austrian Perspective: Still Preoccupied with Itself or Tempted to Play Out Its Power?

Ewald König

Let us head out together on the hunt for the spirit of the Berlin Republic. As hunter's hideout, let us take the window of my office on the eleventh floor in Berlin-Mitte. Before us lies the Gendarmenmarkt with the German and the French cathedrals; behind that welcome the domes of the Catholic Hedwigs cathedral and the Jewish synagogue; to the left glimmer the Norman Foster dome of the Reichstag and the futuristic pavilion roof of the Sony Center at Potsdamer Platz. Everything presents itself very well. Hardly any other window in Berlin is more strategically situated than mine to track and to locate the spirit of the Berlin Republic.

The idea alone of deploying German soldiers in the conflict in the Middle East and of imposing Bundeswehr uniforms on the Israelis; the proposal to once again call Berlin and Brandenburg "Prussia"; the discussion about the assumption of new obligations and a new role for Germany as the largest, strongest, and richest member of the European Union; the reorientation following the end of the period in which Germany could claim a special role for itself due to the division into East and West; and last but not least the hypocritical sanctions against neighboring Austria: Are these already products of the spirit of a new Federal Republic?

To get to the point: Even the strategically well-placed location of our observation point does us no good. The spirit of the Berlin Republic does not reveal itself. The spirit that was so often summoned following reunification and upon the government's move from Bonn to Berlin remains in hiding.

It was clear from the beginning that the spirit of the Berlin Republic could only be solely a negative phenomenon. It has no chance of being unbiased. It will never be of equal status with the spirit of other capitals. The concept of the "Berlin Republic" will never be used free of value judgments but rather will automatically be put in relation to something else. It is compared to the idyllic Bonn Republic or is related to Berlin's inglorious past.

German illusions of grandeur also resonate with the idea of the Berlin Republic: economic power suppressing all others, an emotional nationalist outburst, a mental distancing of 80 million people of Europe, a paradigm change following the move from Bonn to Berlin.

If the spirit of the Berlin Republic had already established itself, it would have many prejudices against which to fight. The Prussian heritage, the leftover architecture of the Nazi insanity, the overly proportionate buildings of the past that consciously leave the individual standing next to them very, very small: all of this would be prematurely tied to the Berlin spirit. It is better for the spirit of the Berlin Republic that it is not yet there. It is still unfinished. It would be misused as a concept of battle because it would be connected with wars and dictatorships that originated in Berlin. The fact that the peaceful revolution of 1989 took place here is, as a rule, not suggested by "Berlin Republic."

If there had ever been a special spirit of the Bonn Republic, then it secretly also made the 410-mile move from the Rhine to the Spree River. That is already suggested by the conclusive fresh start, because in Bonn it can no longer be identified. Solely in the Haus der Geschichte der Bundesrepublik Deutschland (House of the History of the Federal Republic of Germany) that stands in Bonn can the spirit still be detected. Thus, it must have emigrated in the boxes and heads of the politicians and officials, the diplomats and editors.

What is evident in Berlin is still that spirit of the easily overlooked presence, the entity divided into small sections, the provincial sense of security. This is still the spirit of Bonn. It tries to continue playing its role in Berlin as if it were still in Bonn. We may not allow ourselves to be fooled by the too highly assessed Federal Chancellery.

But this spirit of Bonn that is used to reaching everything political in just a few minutes of walking and, among the population of 300,000, to always meeting the same people is finding it increasingly difficult to adjust in the 3.5 million Moloch. The Berlin Republic is faster, colder, more aggressive. The spirit of Bonn is chilly. It will gradually make itself scarce.

Its successor, the spirit of the Berlin Republic, will, however, not exist for a while. Germany still has problems with itself. It has overexerted itself somewhat with reunification. It is suffering from mistakes that were made at the time. The new political consciousness is lacking an economic basis. This is why Germany acts more like a brake rather than a motor among Europeans. It merely talks about its role.

Germany cannot so easily free itself from amazement at its own navel, from a fixation on its own problems.

Let us simply take the name. Foreign observers are already apt to be taken aback at this.

Bonn, the lasting provisional arrangement, was a "federal capital." Following the move of politics away from the city, the "federal" remained in Bonn. This is because as comfort for the loss of government and parliament, Bonn may now officially refer to itself as "federal city," whatever that may be. Federal establishments within markedly federalist Germany exist also in other cities; these may not, however, call themselves federal cities.

In contrast, Berlin will never be referred to as a "federal capital," although it is, of course, formally that. Berlin will always only be "the capital," which incites much mistrust. The one side sees in that an attack on German federalism and believes that the lack of "federal" is a political program and exposes Berlin's centralist claim. The other side sees in the label "capital" a catastrophe because during communist times Berlin's eastern section was named the "capital of the German Democratic Republic (GDR)," and they now see suspicious tendencies. The fact that the successor party to the former Socialist Unity Party of the GDR, the current Party of Democratic Socialism (PDS), since recently co-governs in the Berlin city government must appear to them as a logical consequence.

I recently had a conversation with the director of the Berlin tourist company, the Berlin-Tourismus-Marketinggesellschaft. As an aside he mentioned something that is presumably unique in the world because it could lead to problems in no other country: in foreign countries his marketing company can very successfully advertise Berlin's function as capital. The city is attractive and interesting as a constantly evolving, never finished capital, as shown by the numbers of overnight guests and the boom in new hotels. Yet in Germany itself, where he would like to guide domestic tourism, his company avoids mentioning that Berlin is the capital. This does not sit well with the Germans.

Similar signs mark the discussion about the name of parliament. The German Bundestag moved into the renovated building with Norman Foster's prominent dome, which is called the "Reichstag." Should the name "Reichstag" be used again for the parliament? Or should the building be renamed "Bundestag?" Now in linguistic usage it is referred to either as the "Bundestag in the Reichstag building" or in terms of the signs "Reichstag, Seat of the German Bundestag."

Furthermore, it is apparent that earlier mostly the term "Federal Republic" was used if it regarded Germany. Today it is increasingly only "Germany." It is also difficult with the designation of the area that from 1949 to 1990 was the GDR. The unspeakable term *Beitritts-gebiet* (region of accession) has fortunately disappeared over time.

One speaks of the "former GDR," whereby the additional "former" is never lacking. It would suffice to refer simply to the GDR because the GDR is, of course, well defined: there was only one GDR from 1949 to 1990. There is not anything like a successor GDR, which would make it necessary to differentiate from the "former" GDR. No one says "former Weimar Republic" or the "former Third Reich" because it is evident anyway from when to when this or that existed. "Former GDR" each time sounds to me as if one wanted consistently to verbally hold over the East Germans' heads that they are of a former status.

In contrast, one would, strictly speaking, have to say "former Federal Republic" if one were referring to West Germany up to 1990. This is because the country is, of course, now still referred to as "Federal Republic," but on 3 October 1990 grew by sixteen million people. And how should one promote the difference? But I hear no one saying "former Federal Republic." This would not be popular.

Already before reunification it was difficult to correctly express oneself. One had to count on great reservations if, instead of "Federal Republic," one said simply "FRG." This rang as provocative above all in conservative ears, however, presuming that one assumed the nomenclature of "GDR" and thereby made equal both Germanys. On the other hand, "FRG" was unbelievably practical if one were looking for a title for an article on Germany simply because it is so short. In contrast to the Germans themselves, the recipients of these articles certainly never presupposed anything bad with it.

Yet in the GDR, one consistently referred to the "FRG" and never the "Federal Republic (of Germany)." Chief of state and party leader Erich Honecker, in contrast, never referred to his own country as the "GDR," but rather as the "German Democratic Republic," whereby he accomplished the trick of slurring the monstrous wording into one syllable. In the West, in contrast, the media of the Springer Verlag put mention of the GDR—consistently until just before the fall of the Wall—to paper only with the use of quotation marks.

To be sure, the residents of the—sorry—"former GDR" occasionally themselves have problems with the designation. I remember an older Jazz musician from the GDR who always became confused whenever he spoke of the "new" and the "old" federal states. He also explained to me why he so often became confused: in the GDR heritage everything was old and rotten; nevertheless one still had to now say "new states." In contrast, the West has the image of the shining "new," but is called "old states." It is clear why they are easily mixed up.

A local politician from a little town in Brandenburg close to the border with Poland with whom I recently had a conversation stole the show. He was talking about the western federal states and said: "Well, you already know that I mean the right federal states...."

Why do I list all of this?

One reason is because just the complication of the categorizations alone already reflects a lot. It betrays how politically sensitive and laden with symbols the topic was earlier, and it betrays how a change in attitude is infiltrating. Young Germans are growing up with a linguistic usage of Berlin as capital and not as federal capital. They will also soon know the Bonn Republic only from the history books. Berlin will be for them a reality taken for granted. Hardly anyone will be able to comprehend the kind of bitter battles of belief that took place in Germany in regards to the question of the capital and the seat of government, how emotions boiled on the Rhine.

Austria is, like Germany, a federally constructed country but still has no problem being governed from a real capital such as Vienna. Hardly an Austrian can comprehend why the decades-long repeated sermons of German politicians about Berlin as capital of a once reunified country should no longer apply precisely when after the fall of the Wall the time was ripe. The anxiety about the costs was the one thing, the anxiety about the move of the government and parliament from the western border with France to the eastern border with Poland the other.

Perhaps the spirit of the Berlin Republic would gladly become tempted to play out its power. But it is not yet successful. Germany is by far still preoccupied with itself. It knows that it must take on more international responsibility. It is also working on it. To be sure, it was a cunning of history that of all things a red-green government coalition had to decide on military participation in Kosovo and in the international anti-terror coalition. If a conservative government had had to decide on this, there would have been weeks-long sit-ins and demonstrations.

How, then, should a spirit of a city develop for the entire republic if this city remains comprised of two souls a dozen years after the end of its division? And if the acting persons had still brought their Rhenish background, including Carnival? (Nowhere is the struggle for power of the old spirit of Bonn and the new of Berlin more apparent than with Carnival. Earlier there was no kind of Rhenish carnival in Berlin; recently the area of Berlin-Mitte had to be fenced in on a large scale due to 300,000 participants.)

Already a density and competitive struggle among the capital city media alone are taking care that the spirit does not become too swanky and cocky; this is broadened by approximately 500 foreign newspaper and radio correspondents who work in Berlin and whose main career it is to observe Germany critically with the eyes of their home country.

The view from the eleventh floor is thus of no further help. Let us divide the field of view systematically. We will begin directly in front of us in Berlin-Mitte. Even if the Gendarmenmarkt was called the Platz der Akademie during GDR times and the Academy of Sciences was located here, the spirit of the Republic does not exist here.

The fact that all around the Gendarmenmarkt in the central district almost up to 80 percent of the population has changed since the historical *Wende* rather says something about the spirit. It shows Berlin as the capital of well-earning singles who live and work with Germany's highest density of media centers and the highest density of luxury hotels and the highest density of offices—at the same time Berlin is through and through a proletarian city.

We expand the field of view. We take the entire city—and shudder in looking back, as if we had turned to the wrong page in the history books. But we have not. The island city of freedom that was defended for decades by Americans and the other Allies against the communist sea—this city will now be governed by the post-Communists. During GDR times, there was the forced union of the Social Democrats with the Communists into the Socialist Union Party of Germany (SED). And now of all parties both of these together govern Berlin. What a roiling hotbed for the spirit of the

Berlin Republic! It is no wonder if veterans of the Airlift find that hard to understand.

Let us expand the field of view one more time and take a look at Berlin and its surroundings, the new federal states. They are becoming run down. The former federal chancellor, Helmut Kohl, had based the rash introduction of the hard deutsche mark on the argument that "[i]f the deutsche mark does not come to the people, the people will come to the deutsche mark." The fact is that in spite of that the people are going west. More and more apartments stand empty; city districts decay; prefabricated buildings are torn down. Old buildings beautifully renovated with public funding and private enthusiasm find no renters. And one cannot begrudge the East Germans that they would rather move to the west to migrate to Baden-Württemberg or Bavaria, where workers are sought and where pay is good. The employment situation in the new federal states is rather wretched. Generations feel lost. In secret, politicians admit about the employment market that it should even be recommended to young people to leave their homeland and go west. In the East they have hardly a chance.

If the government had remained in Bonn, it would have seen the social problems at least from a distance and would not have been so affected. In Berlin, where day in day out numerous demonstrations take place, the hot issues make themselves known. In Berlin a government can better recognize the problems. Better solve them it certainly cannot. The expectations connected to the move to the capital —namely that in Berlin those governing would be closer to the harsh reality than in the "spaceship" Bonn and would act accordingly— have not been fulfilled.

It would be nice to throw out some questions at this point as a foreign observer. For decades there existed in Bonn an independent Bundesministerium für innerdeutsche Angelegenheiten (Federal Ministry for Internal German Affairs). It is puzzling as to what was actually done there, aside from payments for freeing people if GDR dissidents or those in jail from the GDR were traded, and aside from an inexhaustible font for the sermons for reunification, which apparently were not taken seriously by many.

The fact is that Bonn was utterly unprepared when the Wall fell in Berlin. In none of the many desks of the Federal Ministry for Internal German Affairs was there even just one drawer for this day X. People were completely surprised, and, despite the good secret service, no one knew the dismal truth about the weary condition of the worker and farmer country. This was a recognition that became very costly, paired with the very doubtful decision to introduce the principle of "return instead of compensation" regarding questions of real estate.

Instead of upgrading the Ministry at least at that hour to a key ministry of the Bonn government and tackling internal German affairs, the ministry was abolished. Unification became for Helmut Kohl a matter for the boss. The fate of such matters is well known to all.

It did not go any better under Social Democratic Chancellor Gerhard Schröder. He also made the "rebuilding of the East" a matter for himself as boss. There were many expectations when he built his government that he would make the East German deputy, Rolf Schwanitz, his most important minister, in order to show Kohl how the fabled "blühende Landschaften" (flourishing landscapes), which Kohl had promised in vain, could be produced by magic. However, Schwanitz remained a lesser deputy without any mentionable responsibilities. The public hardly knows him.

The pioneer spirit of working hard to make the worn out regions of the GDR into Germany's modern region and to surpass the satiated West failed to appear. There are many exceptions that unfortunately only confirm the rule. Billions of money transfers make their way from West to East following reunification. An end to the transfers is not in sight. Through the union with the Federal Republic the region of the GDR fell as a matter of course into the European Union and became a designated aid region of the highest priority. But the spirit, which perhaps would have moved Americans in this historical hour, failed to emerge in the Germans. One could even be tempted to say that the transfers of billions to East Germany did not produce only returns, if one compares the situation with the middle and eastern European countries that had to create the *Wende* on their own.

So also here a nil return: No spirit of the Berlin Republic.

We do not particularly want to credit a Berlin spirit especially with the wave of xenophobic offenses that took place in the years following reunification. Indeed, the probability of a foreign-looking citizen being vilified or persecuted is higher in one of the new federal states or the eastern section of Berlin than in the western section. Even the computer specialists coming to Germany from India or Russia would need to be given, besides their "green card," a "brown card": simultaneously with the work and residential permit a card from which they could ascertain which regions they should rather avoid and how they should make themselves inconspicuous so they do not have to reckon with xenophobic and racist attacks.

Nevertheless, the wave of xenophobia does not have a claim exclusively on the east, even if the fear of foreigners there (where, by the way, hardly any foreigners live) coexists subconsciously. Also in western federal states and in other European countries were foreigners' houses and homes of asylum seekers set on fire. This is not the outpouring of a new "spirit."

Let us widen the field of view once again. Let us look at the European Union and NATO, where Germany is nestled in and makes large financial contributions. Has the Federal Republic taken on the lead role there after it has by far become the largest and most important European country?

No, it has not. Not even the German language is becoming the official language in the EU, although it is the most frequently spoken European language. It cannot be found in the first place if the Americans are seeking support from those in the European Union and they find it primarily with the British. It cannot be found with the model countries, which are capable of fulfilling the stability criteria for the new euro currency (demanded by the Germans themselves). One finds Germany bringing up the rear in Europe.

Until reunification, German ground—in both West and East— was the most mounted with weapons and missiles worldwide. In the ensuing years the greatest military reform in German history took place. The number of soldiers, the tanks, the locations, the budget—everything was radically slashed. Germany became an example of conversion and disarmament.

The dismantling of everything military, the retreat of the Allies was so breathtaking that some of the smaller neighbors even turned to Washington and protested to the U.S. administration against pulling back American military presence even more—all under the motto: Do not leave us alone with the Germans!

But this dismantling also comprises no spirit of Berlin. This is because first, following the end of the Cold War, Germany had no other choice than this radical disarmament; and second, these were indeed decisions that were made in Bonn. No one will maintain that in Bonn a kind of "Berlin spirit" was already at play in anticipatory obedience.

Of course, Germany's small neighbors are watching exactly whether a spirit of the Berlin Republic threatens to make the neighborhood treacherous. Some things can be said about that from an Austrian point of view. Can the "sanctions" against Austria be attributed to such a spirit or was it an overeager, faulty political decision?

This all regards the first half of the year 2000. At that time the traditionally positive neighborly relationship between Germany and Austrian suffered greatly. The Austrian coalition of the conservative Austrian People's Party (ÖVP) and the right-wing populist Free People's Party of Austria (FPÖ) under the admiration-craving demagogue Jörg Haider, who had greatly damaged Austria's image with his domestic and foreign escapades, did indeed come about democratically, but it radically changed the bilateral relationship.

It was the red-green government that with enthusiasm pushed through the European Union sanctions against Austria. To be sure, it was alone in Germany. The German media, the public, the people, the opposition, the economy—they all failed to understand the punishing behavior toward Austria. The so-called sanctions of the EU partners against Austria were highly counterproductive and freely handed Haider ammunition.

Instead of having serious exchanges with the Austrian coalition, as would be normal in a family, instead of threatening immediate reactions and sanctions should Austria's government be guilty of even the slightest offense against basic rights, Austria was completely shelved.

Indeed, formally it was merely the representatives of the government who were boycotted. In actuality, however, the entire Austrian people suffered being handled as lepers of the EU. The measures were felt as "the highest punishment upon mere suspicion." When one of the "three wise men" of the panel established by the EU determined that there was then no basis for the sanctions, there was rather a shameful end for the Europeans, who later reacted completely differently to the Italian elections that produced the even more dangerous Silvio Berlusconi.

What was bitter for Austria was not so much the behavior of the other fourteen EU partners in general, but rather especially Germany's behavior. The German attitude weighed double the attitude of all other partners.

Even if the German government designated its actions with regard to the sanctions as being in the middle—it did not want to put on the brakes, yet did not want to apply force—it still was evident that Berlin, together with Paris and Brussels, had very strongly pushed the sanctions. They may have had thoroughly honorable motivations. This has to do with their own country, however. Chancellor Gerhard Schröder and Foreign Minister Joschka Fischer stressed continually at the time that Jörg Haider had very quickly become a German problem.

Besides that, no one wanted to give the French even the slightest cause for apprehension about the large German-speaking bloc.

It was the low point in the postwar relations, and it tarnished pretty badly the Austrian image of Germany. The neighborhood was disturbed. Even today it has normalized only superficially.

How come Berlin's stand weighed double for Vienna than that of the attitude of the other EU partners? Alone in their capacity as neighboring countries there was much to talk about between Germany and Austria—as is indeed necessary and usual between neighbors. The bilateral problems piled up.

This weighed double because Germany is not just *a* but *the* most important neighboring country. It weighed double because of all the EU partners, the German neighbors know the Austrians the best and know that everyone had not mutated into Nazi monsters overnight. And particularly the Germans themselves know the feeling of how it is to be repeatedly defamed and lumped together as Nazis around the world, whether it be while traveling in a foreign country or in the foreign media.

It weighed double because particularly Germany believed that with burning asylums, frightening neo-Nazi marches, and right-wing extremist violence it must influence Austria educationally.

It weighed double because in no other EU country was the discrepancy between government and the rest of the country as great as it was in Germany. The opinion of the red-green coalition was shared neither by the majority of the population nor by the greater part of the German media. In no other EU country were there such contradictions.

It weighed double because particularly the German government knew better than all others that the banishment of all of Austria would only benefit and aid Jörg Haider and his entourage.

It weighed double because according to the declaration of the "three wise men" under order of the EU, the sanctions were practically lifted, but no one said a word of any kind of explanation or even of regret.

It weighed double because the German handling of Italy following the victory of Silvio Berlusconi showed how differently things were measured. Everything that the German chancellor said after the Italian elections was precisely the opposite of how he had behaved in regards to Austria. He said that he would first have to read the party program; then he would have to analyze it; and only then could it be judged. Moreover, it had to do with the states and the population, not with people. And precisely Germany did not want to put on airs as a master of democracy. And so on and so on. Discussions and diplomacy between Germany and Italy take place with no troubles.

Was this the emphasis of a spirit of the newly powerful Berlin Republic? Or was it rather only a sign of German weaknesses in terms of the French, who could have been anxious about such a closely allied German-speaking bloc and whom one wanted to provide no pretext for mistrust.

Austria is European through and through, even if Haider's provocations convey another impression. No EU country voted with such a strong majority (almost 68 percent) for entry into the Union.

I dare say that this behavior of the German government toward the Austrians and the later differentiation with Italy, Denmark, France, and the Netherlands—where the right-wing populists have succeeded—is an uncomfortable topic of which one prefers not to be reminded even in Berlin. The physical reactions of the federal chancellor and the foreign minister when asked these kinds of questions spoke volumes. Both of them did not want to be reminded of it any more, even if they declare to have reacted properly at the time. The chancellor's former counselor on foreign affairs, Michael Steiner, had powered the boycott with fanaticism. If there had been a more discreet counselor on foreign affairs, it would have presumably not had to have gone so far.

What was the consequence of the German behavior toward its smaller neighbor? Other small EU countries as well as candidate countries drew their lessons from the matter and saw themselves as forewarned by the pressure. Not only does Germany act differently toward them; the smaller countries act more reservedly and superficially toward the Germans.

The chastisement of a country conveys the impression that Europe is only formally politically held together and that the dynamic of friendship is over. Egoism seems to be increasing. Bilateral relations seem to be cooling off, and the accession process of the Southern and Eastern Europeans seems to be abating.

There is probably no other city in the world that in history has already been capital as often as Berlin, and worldwide no city that following a division became half a capital and half not; and following the end of the division it was at first not a capital at all in order to first become one with the decision on a capital. Then it was indeed capital but for years the location of neither the government nor parliament.

Now Berlin is all of that but remains still other. This is because the government does not sit in historically significant architecture.

It sits behind completely new walls. This is as though the new beginning in Berlin should be poured in cement and made transparent with glass. The historical Berlin then serves only as a curtain for the new government district. The spirit of the Berlin Republic that will at some point originate from here will hopefully be a spirit of partnership. The small countries around the Federal Republic have every interest in Germany finding itself and things going well for it because then automatically things go well for them. Spirit of the Berlin Republic, please come.

20. From the Burden of the Past to the Promise of the Future: The Czech View of the German Neighbor

Vladimir Handl

> Germany has been our inspiration as well as our pain; a source of understandable traumas, of many prejudices and misconceptions, as well as of standards to which we turn; some regard Germany as our greatest hope, others as our greatest peril.[1]

The Czech view of the German neighbor has been characterized by two tendencies since 1989. First, there has been a disproportionate emphasis on the issues of the past that results in some cases in a simple projection of past experiences onto the present situation. More than Germany in Europe, it was the issue of Munich[2] and the issue of the Sudeten-Germans that came to dominate the Czech discourse.[3] Only the end of 1990s witnessed a certain change in the pattern of the Czech debate on Germany: the historical debate became predominantly sober and realistic, even if its polarization

This contribution is based on research undertaken by the author (in cooperation with Miroslav Kunstat, Charles University, Prague) as part of the Economic and Social Science Research Council (ESRC) Project "Germany and the Reshaping of Europe" (Award number L213252002). This project has been underway at the Institute for German Studies at the University of Birmingham since January 1998.

1. Vaclav Havel, "Czechs and Germans on the Way to a Good Neighbour Relationship," speech presented at the Charles University, Prague, 17 February 1995; see http://www.hrad.cz/president/Havel/speeches.
2. The Munich Agreement of 29 September 1938, signed by Germany, Italy, France, and Great Britain, resulted inevitably in the disruption of Czechoslovakia and became an "overture" of World War II in Europe.
3. See, for example, Olga Smidova, "Cesko-nemecke vztahy v zrcadle tisku" (Czech-German relations in printed media), in *Obraz Nemcu, Rakouska a Nemecka v*

increased. Second, where the historical issues have not been in the center of the debate, the primary focus has been directed toward multilateral institutions and processes (European integration and security), with Germany of secondary importance. The lack of focus solely on Germany, together with a tendency to focus on technical aspects of integration and security, means that the debate only partly influences the Czech perception of Germany.

The specific debate about Germany has developed therefore only very slowly and is not at the center of the attention of the Czech media and public. German policy has been debated mostly within the categories of the realist concepts: power, interests, and geopolitical and historical issues. A more complex and multifaceted approach has been only gradually gaining more ground.

A tentative attempt to differentiate the prevailing attitude toward Germany indicates four broad types of approaches:

- the negativist approach, extrapolating primarily from negative historical experiences and geopolitical and balance-of-power calculations;
- the critically skeptical approach, which prefers, roughly speaking, the Anglo-Saxon model of policy making at home and uses mostly the analytical tools of the neo-realist school while assessing international relations;
- the balanced, constructive approach, which struggles to take a multifaceted view of Germany; and
- the positivist approach, which accentuates reconciliation with Germany, is open to some positions of the Sudeten-German Landsmannschaft (Heritage Organization) and introduces some conservative German positions and concepts into the Czech debate.

The Czech debate on Germany developed in certain phases. The political context proved to be more important than the academic background. With considerable simplification these phases include:

- The short, initial, and euphoric postrevolutionary phase of optimism toward Germany (1989 to early 1990) was carried by a very wide and heterogeneous civic movement. Czech President Vaclav Havel visited both German states after his

---

ceske spolecnosti 19. a 20. stoleti (The image of Germans, Austria, and Germany in the Czech society in the nineteenth and twentieth century), ed. Jan Kren and Eva Broklova (Prague, 1998), 268–80.

election (2 January 1990) and issued his personal statement
of regret about both the expulsion and transfer of the Sudeten-Germans.[4]

- The latter was followed by a much more sober perception of
  coexistence with the unified Germany (1990–1992). Differentiation and polarization of the Czech political development
  increased and influenced the debate about its neighbor. The
  split of Czechoslovakia into the Czech Republic and Slovakia
  in 1992 resulted in a certain identity crisis, making the Czech
  national sense of self even less self-evident. Together with the
  intensifying Czech-German dispute over the past, the split
  burdened attitudes toward Germany.

- The apprehensions about Germany culminated during the
  negotiations and the ratification of the bilateral declaration
  (signed 1997). At the same time, the mostly positive experience of the Czech-German cooperation has strengthened a
  positive attitude toward Germany.

- Progressing political settlement of the conflicting issues after
  1997 improved the attitude toward Germany. The public debate about foreign policy became less "Germanocentric" but
  also less conclusive: the question about the nature of Germany and its policy has been tackled only on the margins.

The Debate on the Past

Vergangenheitsbewältigung, or the mastering of the past, was in a political sense a pragmatic task. Nonetheless, it touched upon the deep-
est levels of Czech political thinking and initiated the broadest
political debate after 1989, comparable with the debate on the
Czech national history as such.

The Munich experience remained the crucial historical event
influencing deeply ingrained Czech views about foreign and security policy. The refusal of German policy to proclaim the nullity of
the Munich Agreement *ab initio*, and to acknowledge the validity of
the Potsdam Agreement of August 1945 clashed with the Czech
rejection of the German demand that Prague abolish the Decrees
of President Eduard Benes. The vast majority of Czechs perceived
the Decrees as an integral part of the Czech legal system, though

4. Miroslav Kunstat, "Czech-German Relations after the Fall of the Iron Curtain,"
Czech Sociological Review 6, no. 2 (fall 1998): 153.

obsolete and a part of history. An abandoning of this position has been rejected because it might endanger—as it was perceived—the legal and political concept of the postwar settlement.

A historization of policy took place: the issues arising from the past dominated the general discourse on Germany. A discourse arose only after the two countries arrived at a general political understanding of the issues. The political settlement offered the major push to the ongoing, but less visible process of the constructive historization of the past: the historical research of the relevant issues using the contemporary methods of interdisciplinary and comparative historical science.[5]

The search for political understanding initiated political and societal contacts of unprecedented intensity. By the end of the 1990s, particularly intensive contacts developed between the Czech Social Democratic Party (CSSD) and Germany's Social Democratic Party (SPD). Also, the role of the German Green Party in the Czech-German dialogue was considerable. The conservative German parties were usually more distant from the prevailing Czech views or—in this mostly the Christian Social Union (CSU)—even opposed them, be it for genuine differences in approach to the past or for domestic, electoral reasons.

Two main streams of thought developed regarding the approach to the past in relations with Germany, which themselves were internally diversified: The mainstream Czech position emphasized the causality approach. It accentuated the principle of causality in the interpretation of the history of World War II and of the following transfer/expulsion of the Germans. It differed, however, as far as a moral assessment of the transfer/expulsion was concerned. A much smaller group emphasized primarily or exclusively a moral approach to the tragic past and regarded the historical context as secondary or even irrelevant. The general platform of this group has been called "Smireni '95" (Reconciliation '95), and its signatories called for direct talks between the Czech government and representatives of the Sudeten-Germans.[6]

---

5. Rudolf Vierhaus, "Historizacia" jako zvladnutie sucastnosti. Nemecko-cesky vztah 1918–1989" (Historization as mastering of the present: German-Czech Relation 1918–1989), in *Emancipacia Zidov – antisemitismus – prenasledovanie v Nemecku, Rakusku-Uhorsku, v českych zermich a na Slovensku* (Emancipation of Jews—anti-Semitism—persecution in Germany, Austro-Hungary, the Czech lands, and in Slovakia), ed. Jörg Hoensch, Stanislav Biman, and Lubomir Liptak (Bratislava, 1999), 10–11.

6. "Prohlaseni. Smireni 95 mezi Cechy a sudetskymi Nemci" (Declaration: Reconciliation 95 between Czechs and Sudeten Germans), *Lidové noviny*, 30 March 1995.

The debate on historical issues critically influenced the perception of Germany. A critical attitude toward the western neighbor seemed to prevail during the mid-1990s. A seriously distorted picture of German policy was no exception.[7] The most negative implication of the development was a growing distrust by the Czech public, including democratic circles, as regards the long-term intentions of German policy.[8] The way in which German policy dealt with some of the issues arising from the past was perceived as a reflection of ideological stereotypes, which the Sudeten-German Landsmannschaft has cultivated over many decades.[9] An ambiguous suspicion was shared rather widely that a certain German (Sudeten-German) interest was involved in the split of Czechoslovakia in 1992.

The attitude toward Germany became more relaxed after Germany confirmed the continuity of the Czechoslovakian state and its borders, endorsed the principle of historical causality, and showed readiness to approach the issue of compensation of victims of the Nazi regime.

The cool relations between the Czech and German governments (with German Chancellor Helmut Kohl and Prime Minister Vaclav Klaus at their heads) did not facilitate a mutual understanding. Nonetheless, Kohl and Klaus negotiated the bilateral declaration on a political understanding regarding the issues of the past (January 1997). A much better relationship between the governments of German Chancellor Gerhard Schröder and Foreign Minister Joschka Fischer and Czech Prime Minister Milos Zeman and Deputy Prime Minister for Foreign and Security Policy/Minister of Foreign Affairs Jan Kavan is perceived as important.[10] Even the conservative media acknowledged that the change of the party-political constellation did matter.[11]

---

7. According to some views, Germany rejects the Potsdam Agreement in order to put a revisionist cast on the outcome of the results of World War II in the case of the Czech Republic, the "weakest link in the chain." See Miloslav Bendar, "Evropský smysl cesko-nemeckeho sporu" (European meaning of the Czech-German dispute), *Lidové noviny*, 12 February 1996. This perception was shared by some historians as well.

8. Jan Pauer, "Moralisch-politischer Dissens in den deutsch-tschechischen Beziehungen," *WeltTrends*, no. 19 (1998): 69.

9. Alena Wagnerova, "Deklarace a studena valka" (Declaration and the Cold War), *Listy*, no. 3 (1997): 45.

10. Petr Zavadil, "Schröderova česko-německá revoluce má svá úskalí" (Schröder's revolution has drawbacks), *Lidové noviny*, 1 October 1999, 3.

11. Michal Musil, "Havel v Nemecku: ovace i ztracene iluze" (Havel in Germany: Ovations and lost illusions), *Lidové noviny*, 13 May 2000, 3.

In general, the mainstream academic debate about history—as well as its popular and political spillover—arrived at largely positive conclusions. As scholar and member of the Czechoslovak Society of Arts and Sciences Zdenek Suda argues, the "meaning of Czech history" as a zero-sum game between Czech and German ethnic and cultural forces has become no longer tenable.[12] It became increasingly obvious and widely acknowledged that Germany could no longer be perceived solely through the prism of the Sudeten-German issue and the past.[13]

Looking at Germany "an sich"

Other dimensions of the debate on Germany have been developing much more slowly, however. Beyond the historical/existential issues, Germany has not been the topic of priority of the Czech debate. The discourse has been diffused and considerably differentiated as far as perceptions of German EU policy and *Modell Deutschland* (Germany's institutional, normative, and political knowhow) are concerned.

A correlation developed between relations to Germany and some other major political issues: the most radical opponents of capitalist transformation of the Czech society took a mostly negativist position regarding relations with Germany. Also, the same political circles opposed accession of the Czech Republic to NATO. Regarding the accession to the EU the correlation has been less clearly defined, with only the Republicans opposing the EU enlargement in principle.

A strong conviction prevails that Germany represents a stable and prosperous democracy.[14] In detail, however, the Czech views have been divided. Some conservatives shared an apprehension of a revival of German nationalism and even reported about its

---

12. Zdenek Suda, *The Origins and the Development of the Czech National Consciousness and Germany* (Prague, 1995), 62.

13. Frantisek Svatek, "Vztahy Ceske republiky a Nemecka po roce 1945," in *Male zeme, velci sousede* (Small countries and big neighbors), ed. Miloslav Had and Vaclav Kotyk (Prague, 1998); Vaclav Belohradsky, "Dnesni Nemecko: vime-nevime" (Today's Germany: What we know and what we don't), *Lidové noviny*, 3 May 1999, 6.

14. Otto Pick, "Ceska republika ve svete" (The Czech Republic in the world), in *Ceska zahranicni politika. Uvahy o prioritach* (Czech foreign policy: Considerations about priorities), ed. Vaclav Kotyk (Prague, 1997), 13.

"wave."[15] Representatives of the negativist attitude toward Germany have maintained their skepticism regarding the postwar German democracy. Even some liberals, such as Miloslav Bendar, philosopher and prominent speaker of the Czech Democratic Party (ODS), argued that the Germans have remained in fact the same; it was argued that they merely changed their political language and instruments of their expansion.[16]

On particular occasions, such as the financial scandals surrounding the German party of the Christian Democratic Union (CDU), differing attitudes toward Germany come to the fore. Is there—in the longer run—a danger of "Haiderization" of German policy?[17] Speculations about the "unthinkable" revealed an inherent lack of confidence about the stability of German European policy: is Germany going to remain a part of Europe (the European Union)?[18] Such voices remained, however, rather isolated. As a whole, the debate on Chancellor Jörg Haider and the Free People's Party of Austria (FPÖ) showed a remarkable absence of references to Germany. The comparison with Austria has indirectly improved the image of Germany. German democracy has been perceived as more stable and predictable; the way in which it has dealt with its past has been seen as more self-critical and democratic.

At least two approaches to German power evolved: one developed within the realist school of thought and the other searched for a more comprehensive analytical method. The former has perceived Germany as the most important power in Central Europe. The limits of Czech relations with Germany are viewed as arising primarily from the vast asymmetry of potential of the two countries, the Czech Republic representing "a geopolitical minimum."[19] The more comprehensive approach does not follow one particular school of thought. The problem with this approach may be that it does not paint a picture of Germany as clearly and understandably

15. Miloslav Bednar, "Evropsky smysl cesko-nemeckeho sporu" (European meaning of the Czech-German dispute), *Lidové noviny*, 12 February 1996.

16. Dalibor Plichta, *Narod a narodnost v case globalizace* (Nation and nationality in the time of globalization) (Prague, 1999), 65.

17. The fear is that German policy will also come to reflect views of the extreme right such as that under Austrian Chancellor Jörg Haider, whose policies are deemed by many to be intolerant and nativist.

18. Daniel Kaiser, "Německá politická scéna v přímém přenosu: paralýza v přímém přenosu?" (German political stage: Paralysis broadcasted live?), *Lidové noviny*, 18 February 2000, 10.

19. Oskar Krejci, *Cesky narodni zajem a geopolitika* (Czech national interest and geopolitics) (Prague, 1993), 160–65.

as does the realist approach and that its conclusions remain often rather diffused.

Germany is widely perceived as the number one European power, and some experts argue that it has a tendency to seek the status of a great world power as well.[20] Minister Josef Zieleniec had once concluded that Germany has been returning to the logic of its history and becoming a great power, increasingly participating in developments in Eastern Europe.[21] On the tenth anniversary of the fall of the Berlin Wall, Germany was, indeed, referred to as a great power.[22] Generally, Germany is perceived as growing into a dominant position in Europe, and this renders highly relevant questions about its orientation. In the early 1990s, even some high-ranking officials evidently perceived unified Germany per se as a threat to Czech sovereignty.[23] Negativists present German policy as following a traditional strategic line characterized as a continuity of the "spirit and policy of Munich."[24] The much more probable "threat"—lack of German interest in and neglect of the region, enhanced also by the dissolution of Czechoslovakia—was largely ignored in the mid-1990s. The general conviction has been that a prosperous and dynamic small country, a member of the EU and NATO, has a good chance of playing a visible role on the international stage; this includes asymmetrical relationships such as the one between the Czech Republic and Germany.[25]

Such a view is only partly shared by Atlanticists, some of whom subscribe to elements of negativist perceptions of Germany. They argue that Germany followed a "megalomaniac vision of German Europe" and sought to create a "power center" by enlarging the EU;

20. Vaclav Kural, "Vnitropoliticky vývoj SRN a jeho dusledky" (Germany: Internal political developments and its implications), in *Nemecko ve volebnim roce 1994*. Studijni sesity (Germany in elections year 1994), ed. Vaclav Kural and Vladimir Handl (Prague, 1994), 3.

21. "Budoucnost cesko-nemeckych vztahu" (Future of Czech-German relations), interview with J. Zielneniec, *Cesky denik*, 29 September 1993, 1 and 3.

22. Lubos Palata, "Pad zdi byl pocatkem zmeny Nemecka ve velmoc" (Fall of the Wall triggered transformation of Germany into a great power, *Mlada Fronta Dnes*, 9 November 1999, 9.

23. Jaroslav Spurný, "Protinemecka ofenziva generala Prochazky" (Anti-German offensive of General Prochazka), *Respekt*, no. 9 (1999): 5; quoted from Wolfgang Oschliess, "Tschechen, Polen, Deutsche 1990–1996," *Berichte des BIOST* 22 (1996):15.

24. Dalibor Plichta, *Narod a narodnost v case globalizace* (Nation and nationality in the time of globalization) (Prague, 1999), 87.

25. See a number of contributions in Svatek, "Vztahy Ceske republiky a Nemecka po roce 1945"; Belohradsky, "Dnesni Nemecko: vime-nevime."

NATO was portrayed as the only obstacle to German-Russian hegemony in Europe.[26] Experts as well as representatives of the generally positivist attitude toward Germany vigorously opposed these views.[27] The economic aspect of the German role was discussed mainly in the early 1990s. While the influx of German capital into the Czech economy had raised apprehension at that time,[28] the situation changed considerably later. The Skoda/Volkswagen merger, having prompted massive criticism in the early 1990s, became widely acknowledged as being the most successful of industrial enterprises.[29] Even the radical critics of the government policy, who view the perspectives of the Czech industry in very dark colors, do not suggest a German "takeover" any more.[30] Acknowledging the positive role of German, American, and Dutch business activity in the country, Czech policy at the same time expressed regret concerning the low level of involvement of French business activity.[31] Critics expected the Germans to influence the Czech public opinion through the Czech press, which German firms for the most part dominated.

Some analysts focused rather on the positive aspects of German foreign and security policy.[32] Others maintained considerable skepticism regarding Germany's "Western nature."[33] Three cases illustrate the spectrum of differences: Czech liberals distance themselves

26. Miloslav Bendar, "Evropský smysl cesko-nemeckeho sporu" (European meaning of the Czech-German dispute), *Lidové noviny*, 12 February 1996.

27. Bohumil Dolezal, "Pohled na Nemce: prisne strezit, pozorovat" (General attitude toward Germans: Watch them closely!), *MF Dnes*, 12 September 1995,12.

28. In 1991, 73.1 percent of the FDI came from Germany. See Jiri Kosta, Judita Stouracova, and Michael Konstantinov, *Deutsche Direktinvestitionen in der Tschechischen Republik* (Bonn, 1993), 21. The German share was just above 30 percent at the end of the 1990s.

29. Lubomir Mlcoch, "Za kritikou EU je nedostatek sebeduvery" (Criticism of EU covers lack of confidence), *Lidové noviny*, 13 July 1999, 11

30. Vaclav Vertelar, "Soumrak nad existenci ceskeho prumyslu" (Decline of the Czech industry), *Halo noviny*, 16 March 2001, 5.

31. See, for example, press coverage of Prime Minister Milos Zeman's visit to France in February 2000. Katerina Safaríková, "Zeman: Mrzí me, ze Francouzi v CR investují méne nez Nemci a Americané" (Zeman: I regret that the French invest less than the Germans and Americans in the CR), *Lidové noviny*, 22 February 2000, 7.

32. Dagmar Moravcova, "Nemecka politika v kontextu mezinarodne politickych zmen po konci studene valky" (German policy in the context of international political changes after the Cold War), in Dagmar Moravcova, Bela Plechanovova, and Jan Kreidl, *Evropska politika sjednoceneho Nemecka 1990–1999* (German European policy 1990–1999) (Prague, 2000), 7–62.

33. See analysis written by Peter Bugge,"Czech Perceptions of the Perspective of EU Membership: Havel vs. Klaus," *EUI Working Paper*, RSC no. 2000/10 (Florence, 2000), 49.

from the German concept of integration. Also, there is a certain preference for Anglo-Saxon countries in the Czech security community. Regarding the moderate left, the social democratic leadership has been attracted by the French socialist rather than SPD/ Labour Party political concept.

Only a few analysts and commentators arrived at a largely negative assessment of German foreign policy.[34] As for the German role in the region, a re-emergence of Central Europe or even of a Mitteleuropa (in which Germany is considered the dominating center of Europe) as a political concept has scarcely been debated. While the radical left saw Germany as seeking dominance in the region, one of the few pleas for the establishment of Mitteleuropa accused Germany of a lack of interest in the region.[35] Prominent Czech historians perceived any returning to the Mitteleuropa of the past as ideological dead weight.[36]

With some exceptions, after 1989 Czech experts never really perceived Germany as a threat.[37] German military power has only scarcely been debated. If so, the topic was the lack of military potential rather than its build up. For the first time the two countries became allies, which has its political, psychological, as well as practical consequences. In the debate about the purchase of new fighter aircraft, some military experts considered a model of air defense that would rely on the Bundesluftwaffe for coverage of the Czech Republic's territory.[38]

German security interests were perceived as rational and legitimate—including German interest in East Central Europe (ECE) as an area "separating Germany from the unstable part of Europe (Ukraine, Russia)."[39] The use of German military force for purposes other than defense was met with understanding and relief in expert

34. One of the examples may be Miroslav Polreich, "Zahranicni politika Spolkove republiky—opet jina'" (German foreign policy—new approach once again), *Pravo*, 1 July 1996, 8.

35. Lubos Palata, "Verantwortung übernehmen—Deutschlands Rolle in Mitteleuropa," *Prager Zeitung*, 22 June 2000.

36. Miroslav Hroch, "'Central Europe': The Rise and Fall of a Historical Region," in *Central Europe: Core of Periphery?* ed. Christopher Lord (Copenhagen, 2000), 34.

37. Jaroslav Janda and Jan Eichler, eds., *Security Policy of the Czech Republic: Project Report* (Prague, 1996).

38. Kamil Houska, "Potrebuje Cesko stihacky za desitky miliard?" (Do Czech lands need interceptors for many billions?), *Pravo*, 12 May 2000, 3.

39. Antonin Sverak, "Germany's Military Policy vis-à-vis the Central and Eastern European Region," in Vladimir Handl, Jan Hon, and Otto Pick et al., *Germany and the East Central Europe Since 1990* (Prague, 1999), 133.

circles of mainstream political parties and the media.[40] The Czechs, however, intuitively still prefer a German "culture of reticence." Inevitably, this regards primarily the political left. A considerable similarity of views of Czech and German center-left parties surfaced after they had come into power in Prague and Bonn/Berlin in 1998. In contrast to the Polish rejection, Minister Kavan welcomed German Foreign Minister Fischer's proposal to open the debate on the first use of nuclear weapons in NATO.[41]

The proponents of Czech membership to NATO and the EU have acknowledged the German advocacy of the accession of the ECE countries to NATO and the EU/Western European Union (WEU). German self-interest and support has been, however, widely taken for granted.

The most striking feature of the Czech discussion on the German role in the Kosovo conflict is its absence. Also, there are similarities in the Czech and German debate about the use of force in Kosovo. Unlike 1991, Germany was only rarely suspected of having contributed to the unleashing of the conflict. German diplomacy during its EU presidency was perceived as deft, in particular as regards the Kosovo crisis.[42] German postconflict engagement was appreciated. The change in generations of German politicians was seen as a crucial factor in determining the involvement of German forces.[43]

Many critics of the EU integration process within the radical left and right perceive German European policy as a new version of traditional German expansionism.[44] The mainstream approach to German policy on integration is, however, grounded in the belief that integration is the best way to both the preservation of national identity and the transformation of the "secular rivalry

40. Moravcova, "Nemecka politika v kontextu mezinarodne politickych zmen po konci studene valky," 37. See also Michal Mocek, "Dlouha cesta Nemecka na Balkan" (Long journey of Germany to the Balkans), *MF Dnes*, 8 December 1995, 12.

41. "Protijaderná rezoluce nebyla dostatecne realisticka" (Anti-nuclear resolution was not realist enough), *Pravo*, 23 December 1998.

42. "S Nemci prosla Unie valkou na Balkane" (Germans led EU through Balkan war), *Mlada Fronta Dnes*, 1 July 1999, 8.

43. Petr Gregr, "Je Evropska unie schopna smysluplne politiky na Balkane?" (Is the EU capable of sound policy in Balkans?), *Mezinarodni politika* 8 (1999): 4.

44. For the radical left, see Josef Kuta, "Historicke souvislosti soucasnych cesko-nemeckych vztahu" (I) (Historical connotations of current Czech-German relations), *Halo noviny*, 1 September 1995, 4. Similarly, see Ludvik Tosenovsky, "Hrozi nam ponemceni?" (Does a Germanization threat exist?), in *K cesko-nemeckym vztahum, Sbornik ze seminare* (Brno, 1993).

between Czechs and Germans."[45] Neither Germany nor any other state could dominate Europe.[46] There has remained, however, a degree of uncertainty about Germany's continued commitment to integration.

The Czech debate acknowledged the prevalence of continuity in the German EU policy in principal political issues; Bonn's approach to the reform of the EU after the signing of the Maastricht Treaty, however, has been seen as less straightforward.[47] It was argued that the European Monetary Union (EMU) was created according to the "German way" ("Helmut Kohl boxed through the stability pact").[48] Unlike in Poland, Helmut Kohl's departure from office caused concern only as an exception: would Germany's pro-European stance survive, and how strong was the idea of European unification among the new coalition parties?[49] Some commentators criticized Germany for alleged use of the EU accession candidates as hostages, so that it might impose its concept of reform of the EU.[50] Others saw the German attitude as compatible with the interests of its small neighbors within the EU.[51] Czech comments on the German position on particularities of the accession talks—such as the German/Austrian request for the free movement of labor—generally lacked in emotion and bias. The same pertained to the German (and Austrian) critical attitude toward the Czech nuclear power plant in Temelin. The German position was simply noted without any anti-German sentiments. Only the direct memorandum of the German government (July 2001) echoed clearly negatively. Even Czech Minister of Foreign Affairs Kavan found the statement by the German government to

45. Lubomir Mlcoch, "Za kritikou EU je nedostatek sebeduvery" (Criticism of EU covers lack of confidence), *Lidové noviny*, 13 July 1999.

46. Petr Zavadil, "Nemecko ve sjednocene Evrope" (Germany in unified Europe), *Lidové noviny*, 8 July 1995, 5.

47. Kristina Larischova, "Flexibilita: kvalitativni zmena ve vzvoji evropske integrace (se zvlastnim zretelem na nemeckou politiku)" (Flexibility: A qualitative change in the development of Western European integration—with special attention to German policy), *Mezinarodni vztahy*, no. 11 (1997).

48. Daniel Kaiser, "Vznik Eura provazelo handrkovani a politicke boure" (Euro born in haggling and political storms), *Lidové noviny*, 4 January 1999, iv.

49. Author's interview with Michal Lobkowicz, Member of the Chamber of Deputies of the Czech Parliament (US), Committee for European Integration, May 1999.

50. Lubos Palata, "Rozsireni Evropske unie je v rukou Nemecka" (EU enlargement in German hands), *MF Dnes*, 6 January 1999, 10.

51. Dagmar Moravcova, "Mali sousede Nemecka ve sjednocujici se Evrope" (Small neighbors of Germany in uniting Europe), in Moravcova et al., *Evropska politika*, 87–131.

be arrogant.[52] However, the strict rejection of the memorandum and of a new dialogue on Temelin was criticized in the Czech liberal media as yet another example of the lack of political culture on the Czech side.[53] President Vaclav Havel, the Social Democrats and small conservative parties welcomed the general direction of the vision of Minister Fischer and German Federal President Johannes Rau regarding the finality of the EU. Minister Kavan perceived Fischer's suggestions as "not a classic federalist vision" and found it "a little bit provocative." Nonetheless, he expressed his "cautious support" to Fischer.[54] Liberals, such as Vaclav Klaus, predictably rejected it.[55]

The attitude toward Germany's institutional, normative, and political know-how has been influenced by a number of factors, including the particular political constellation. Many Czech conservatives find the federal and decentralized model of administration and power in Germany not very attractive. Also, an influential group of political scientists perceived the German (and Austrian) corporatist models as wrong for or not applicable to the Czech Republic.[56] A considerable diversity prevailed regarding different aspects of *Modell Deutschland,* and German experience does not dominate the Czech transformation strategy. The ODS and some other liberal center-right parties look in the Anglo-Saxon direction, and maintain their skepticism regarding the social-market economy. The left-wing CSSD looks with particular sympathy at the French socialist party. Its prior attention has focused on the differences between the concepts of British Prime Minister Tony Blair and French Prime Minister Lionel Jospin, much less on German Chancellor Gerhard Schröder. The impact of German know-how is pronounced in some specific policy sectors such as justice and domestic affairs—asylum and alien legislation; institutional framework of immigration policy, and border

52. "Kavan: Dopis ze SRN byl urážkou" (Kavan: German letter an offense), *Pravo,* 23 July 2001.
53. Lubos Palata, "Negramotný Zeman" (Illiterate Zeman), *Hospodarske noviny,* 20 July 2001.
54. "Kavan: Kato uz v cizine moc lidi nezajima" (Kavan: No interest in Kato abroad), *MF Dnes,* 8 July 2000, 6.
55. "Starkes Echo auf 'Europa-Visionen,'" *Die Welt,* 15 May 2000.
56. Lubomir Brokl, "Pluralitni demokracie nebo korporatismus?" (Pluralist democracy or corporatism?), in Lubomir Brokl et al., *Reprezentace zajmu v politickem systemu České republiky* (Representation of interests in political system of the Czech Republic) (Prague, 1997), 67–69.

policing.[57] On the other hand, Prague rejected the German model as irrelevant or not applicable in some other areas. The red-green government's decision to shut down all nuclear power plants by 2021 offers a good example. Prague showed no inclination to follow this example.

Conclusion

Czech public interest in Germany and the Germans is growing only slowly. A certain ambivalence developed after 1989: on the one hand, the Czechs perceived Germany as the closest and most obvious political and economic partner in Europe.[58] At the same time, Germany has the image of a "powerful ..., and not very considerate partner."[59] Evidently, Germany will be perceived in two separate ways in the future: on the one hand, as a challenge, or even a threat, and on the other, as an important link to Euro-Atlantic structures.[60]

The complexity of the attitude toward Germany and its implications for Czech policy making made the issue an object of major Czech-Czech dispute. A correlation developed between relations to Germany and other major political issues. Germany plays a central role in any foreign policy considerations in the Czech Republic. Only marginal, radical political groups and streams of thinking have arrived at a defensive concept of an *Abgrenzung* (disassociation) from both Germany and European multilateral institutions.

There is no unity in the question as to whether a special closeness between Germany and the Czech Republic will ever be achieved or, indeed, is needed. In any case, the image of Germany has been improving gradually. The public view of Germany will, however,

---

57. Author's interviews at the Ministry of Interior and Alien and Border Police, Prague, July 2001.

58. *Allensbacher Jahrbuch für Demoskopie 1993/1997*, 1120, quoted after Tilman Mayer, "Die Vertriebenen im heutigen Deutschland—Schrittmacher der Verständigung mit den östlichen Nachbarn?" in *Die Bundesrepublik Deutschland und die Vertriebenen*, ed. Christoph Dahm and Hans-Jakob Tebarth (Bonn, 2000), 193.

59. Jan Kren, "Deutschlandbilder bei den Tschechen," in *Deutschlandbilder*, ed. Süssmuth (n.p.d.), 224, 227, and 230. Kren came to the same conclusion in an updated version of the text in *Obraz Nemcu, Rakouska a Nemecka v ceske spolecnosti 19. a 20. stoleti* (The image of Germans, Austria, and Germany in the Czech society in the nineteenth and twentieth centuries), ed. Jan Kren and Eva Broklova (Prague, 1998).

60. Vaclav Houzvicka, "Die Haltung der tschechischen Bevölkerung gegenüber Deutschland," *Landes-Zeitung*, 15 February 2000, 2.

remain differentiated and partly ambivalent at least in the mid-term future. Given the considerable importance of political (ideological) preferences in mutual relations, a lot depends upon whether political party constellations in Prague and Berlin facilitate mutual trust and closeness. It is, however, most unlikely that any Czech political leadership, except a hypothetical government dominated by radical political parties, would perceive Germany as a threat. In the long run, the European context will have the most defining importance. It will influence both mutual relations and the perception of Germany in Czech society alike. At present, both countries have arrived at an asymmetrical partnership: the Czech partner, obviously, does not represent a long-term priority in German policy; Germany has the role of the most important and cooperative, however not exclusive partner of the Czech Republic.

Part III

CONCLUSION

21. Toward the Berlin Republic—Past, Present, and Future

Michael Naumann

The preoccupying question of recent years in Germany has lost none of its appeal: Just what is the "Berlin Republic"? With the move of the federal government from Bonn to Berlin, we have somewhat unwittingly arrived at it. The Berlin Republic? "The stupidest thing you can say," commented Heiner Geißler; Johannes Rau said it "didn't mean much" to him; and for Helmut Kohl it was "just talk." The Berlin Republic? Some politicians who are clearly afraid to enter treacherous semantic waters long refused to use the term before finally coming to accept this journalistic creation.

Johannes Gross, the alleged inventor of the term, said that the Berlin Republic meant a return to "European normality." For this clear-thinking journalist, normality signified the end of the intellectual and practical escape from politics: the end of the moratorium on shaping foreign policy, a farewell to "Kinkel-speak," and the rejection of the formula "growth plus redistribution equals domestic policy." The motto of the Bonn era was not "disillusionment with politics," but that strange attitude of passionate despondency that paralyzed the desire to shape policy in the face of the omnipotence of domestic constraints, the security environment, and the complexity of our many Alliance obligations. "Bonn" became the symbol of a political approach in which thousands of rustling pages on rules and regulations replaced a disputatious social debate. This debate about "government," i.e., justice, freedom, and all those universal virtues deemed "values," flared up again only briefly during the Kosovo conflict.

This essay is adapted from a speech given 19 April 2000 at Mount Holyoke College in Holyoke, Massachusetts, and at the Center for European Studies at Harvard University in Cambridge, Massachusetts.

In a word, the Bonn Republic was as comfortable as it was well balanced. It was also industrious. For more than forty years, all spheres of life were legalized to the point of intellectual impenetrability, in the name of state welfare provision, environmental protection, fair taxation, etc., etc. The juridification of the world was the revenge of the nineteenth-century German bourgeoisie for the failed revolution of 1848. By these means the middle class won the creative scope it had lost on the barricades of Berlin. This scope grows narrower from year to year.

So the idea of the Berlin Republic initially took form as a farewell to Bonn: a more or less wistful look back at what were probably the most civilized and prosperous years in our history, a question of how much of this we will be able to carry with us as we move toward the future. But my question is: Does the Berlin Republic still have the sense of joy and the readiness for a new start it did more than ten years ago, in those days and weeks of the fall of the Berlin Wall? The tenth anniversary was a melancholy party, more reminiscence than pride, more self-praise than an eye to the future.

A few days after the fall of the Wall, on 21 November 1989, the American singers Crosby, Stills & Nash were in Berlin. They performed a song they had done ten years previously at Madison Square Garden in New York City at the peak of the peace movement, and thirty years before at Woodstock. And there in Berlin, in front of the Brandenburg Gate, they sang it again: "Teach your children well/their father's hell/did slowly go by." The chromatic shifts transport the full self-doubt of the project.

Today, more than ten years later, we have long since forgotten the "old hell" of division, the Cold War, the fear of a nuclear showdown. But as a country, as a generation, as a leftover system, we have given ourselves no new code by which to live. Germany is living in a normative mist. It is as if the country were still searching for a really serious topic. It was not the supposed crisis of legitimacy of late capitalism, nor was it the historian's debate, nor was it the discussion about political asylum, and it is not the pension reform. And the attempt to turn Peter Sloterdijk's sociogenetic aphorisms into circulation-boosting sparks failed, too. The small town of Bonn can surely not be blamed entirely.

In 1989/90 there was no ceremonial founding act, no pay-out of the peace dividend pointing toward the future. Helmut Schmidt demanded a major address to the nation from the then-chancellor, calling for sacrifice, self-denial, and a contemporary, practical form of patriotism—but it was never delivered. Things were to proceed with Bonn pragmatism and silent state indebtedness. The call for a new constitution was restricted to a pleasant gathering in the historic St. Paulskirche in Frankfurt am Main. Konrad Adenauer's old promise, made long before the Wall—"We in the West may become rich now, but when we are together again, we will share"—came true, in a cool transfer of proven legal and economic structures financed neither by equalization of burdens nor by taxes, but by loans: a three-fold redistribution from West to East, from bottom to top, from the present to the next generation.

In German-German history there were few things left in common to provide the platform for an act of foundation based on equal rights. The indivisible responsibility for the historic break of 1933, the reason Germany was divided, had been obliterated by forty years of competing systems and Cold War. During that time, two different pasts had emerged, two Goethes, two Luthers, two Marxes, two Thomas Manns, two Brechts had been born—two different ways of looking at freedom, equality, solidarity. And most importantly, from the Eastern perspective, fascism was the historically notorious variant of capitalism.

Thus, it sometimes seems to me that the main theme of history over the last decade has been substitution. In the years since unification, we failed to create new symbols for the future, a new constitution, a large-scale project apart from the former chancellor's "flourishing landscapes." We sought a sustainable certainty in our different pasts. But it became apparent, not only in the debate about the Holocaust memorial in Berlin, that everyone mourns in his or her own way, and many seek to forget.

With a bit of historical mercy, however, this Holocaust memorial will not only keep alive the memory of the most monstrous genocide in the history of the world, but will also become a monument of the Republic, the symbolic pivot point between the past, the present, and the future, a painful document within the foundations of our democracy: only after the rupture of civilization that was Auschwitz were we able as a nation to develop a liberal political culture that could build on the, albeit scanty, traditional lines of German political history.

Our road to the modern age led us through the worst excesses of exclusion. Our return to the fold of civilized nations was choreographed in Bonn, with the help of our Western allies. We learned one thing above all: democracy and human rights essentially mean no one is excluded from the political community; everyone is respected in their differences. Appreciating the dignity of the individual means respecting and protecting them. The age of the religion of politics was behind us once and for all—together with its strident disclosures of racial purity, national community, orders from the Führer, and civil disobedience. So even if the practical politics of the Bonn Republic were despondent—sometimes too despondent—they were tolerant. Germany learned to listen. For my generation this remains the *raison d'état*, the code to live by, in Berlin as well as Bonn.

And so I have arrived at the present, a present in which both Social Democratic traditionalists and entrepreneurs accustomed to growth are—for different reasons—still seeking a return to the full-employment economy; but also a present in which doubts in the old faith are showing up everywhere. The young theorists of the self-dubbed "generation Berlin" sketch out with fresh realism the new three-class society spawned by globalization: in the words of Jan Ross, at the top a cosmopolitan "mobile elite keen for change," below that a "centre that has to flog its guts out," and at the bottom, of course, that "sediment of the excluded," a new "underclass of the overstretched." Against this background it is indeed true that new political formative tasks will emerge. A political culture other than that which held sway in Bonn is needed: the explosive social force inherent in such a diagnosis will not be defused through a uniform consensus of the forces of society. At any rate, such cool-headed visions of the future, in which "care" for the "sediment" is once again called "compassion," have the advantage of being clearer than those still-laudable commitments to the full-employment society that are, however, believed by fewer and fewer citizens (according to the Allensbach statistical institute, 75 percent of Germans no longer believe that the interests of business and society are identical).

It is my impression that, for fear of making the disheartened even more disheartened, we do not really want to look closely at the truth of the supposition that in future fewer and fewer people will necessarily produce more and more; that Peter Glotz's notion of "digital capitalism," of the "accelerated society," will exclude more and more people from the productive core of society; and that two-thirds of this productive core are ever less willing to integrate the unnecessary third, to finance equal opportunities for it—at least not voluntarily.

This is the key task of domestic policy in the Berlin Republic: to take seriously, and where possible to counter the little separatisms, the de-solidarizations, the withdrawals from collective agreements.

The proud regionalism of the richer regions that would prefer to terminate the financial equalization scheme between the federal government and the Länder does not suffice to make a republic. But surely a new republic cannot be had if more and more citizens are excluded from the economic process, dragged along, and supported. The findings of Saxony's Commission for the Future forecast that the lower third of society will descend into alcoholism, suburban poverty, and political apathy; at the top of society, the increasing distance between actual problems and politics will lead to cynical individualism and to non-participation in elections.

In his essay on "digital capitalism" Peter Glotz conjures up the cultural clash between accelerators and decelerators, technocratic heroes of innovation and conservative value-hugging ideologists of the excluded who defend the right not to have to be forever flexible, mobile, and adaptable. Notwithstanding skepticism about such attempts to turn marginal phenomena like "happy unemployment" into a cultural, not to say a new class, confrontation, I am convinced that in the republic into which we are now developing, this debate will have to take place. Up until the present, we have invariably simply adapted social policy; now, however, it is a matter of interpreting it in a new way.

Can we imagine a Europe whose citizens are largely excluded from influencing public life? Do we want a world in which the rich nations erect a new *limes*, a new border around themselves? If we do not want to imagine such a scenario, then we will have to face up to the re-politicization of those de-politicized by prosperity and globalization, to new questions of redistribution of wealth in the national and international spheres. This is presumably what Johannes Gross meant by a Berlin Republic that can no longer evade politics. And Berlin is unique in that all the issues raised here are very obvious, very real problem areas.

The Berlin Republic is no longer the land of the zero hour. In many respects, the twentieth century has been concluded; it has left us with problems that cannot be adequately solved by the old political tools.

The beginnings of the Berlin Republic are littered with questions, for example: What does it actually mean now, that word "republic"? What does it stand for at the demise of the nation-state? Who belongs to a republic when human rights are universally valid? Which social civil rights are still valid in a world in which there is no alternative to capitalism—following the end of the full-employment society, where inequalities of all kinds are increasing?

What does a republican public look like in the age of bread and games? What does a republic expect of its citizens and politicians in the age of limited growth?

The Berlin Republic will be the place where we decide whether we want to face up to such questions at all, or whether the continued expectation of prosperity cherished by the solidly well-off two-thirds can bring politics to a standstill. In other words, whether the West/the North still has a code to live by.

The Berlin Republic: the place for taking an active approach to these questions is not so bad. Berlin is a capital city—and a metropolis. All the mega-problems I have touched on are local politics, everyday commonplaces in a metropolis, be it Paris, London, New York, or São Paolo.

I have no intention of spreading the romance of the German metropolis—even that has become a common feature of the cultural pages:

• the fact that Berlin is about fifty miles from the Polish border;
• the fact that schools in our metropolis are seeing globalization of a kind far removed from the labor markets: classes where twenty-eight children from 6, 12, 16 nations receive their basic education in Grimm's fairy tales, Turkish gender relations, and American hip-hop;
• the fact that we must expect poverty-induced migrations to really make the so-called exile problem look trivial;
• the fact that the status of human rights in our metropolises is becoming part of domestic policy;
• the fact that every subway ride shows us that the division of society into full-fledged members and the socially excluded is not just a temporary phenomenon.

Metropolises depict all this. But unlike those writers in the newspapers' cultural sections who romanticize metropolises, I fear that an overly cool social policy will be untouched by this concentration of epochal problems in an area of only about 7,000 acres; that the problems of the twenty-first century and the institutions of the nineteenth century could exist independently alongside each other —just like in New York, São Paolo, Bangkok. Heimito von Doderer once gave the fundamental evil of our century a striking name: "perceptual refusal"—the refusal to look, to take note, to be open to reality, or the tendency, in the words of Stanley Kubrick, to keep one's "eyes wide shut."

First of all, therefore, we have to re-examine the term "republic," this German tradition that tended to reduce democracy to the rule of law that has characterized us since 1848 (in the better epochs of our history, I must say). Our best, yet ambivalent, benefit has been to juridify claims on the social state under the rule of law, which is manifest today in the transfer of large parts of our political scope to the constitutional courts.

More and more decisions—on media regulations, family policy, tax law—are being made if not in Brussels, then in Karlsruhe, the seat of the Federal Constitutional Court. But if there is no longer any debate in parliament, then there will not be any debate within the country: Do we still need a commerce and conglomerate-free sphere of public opinion and culture, and how much are we willing to pay for it? Do we really want childless singles to be the most privileged in society?

I am aware, even as something of a newcomer, that the Sisyphuses of parliamentary reform have already rolled plenty of stones up the hill, but I wish we would think again about how to create new empowerment in places where politics are threatening to disappear altogether.

I believe that if we curl up and ignore new realities, we will be gambling away the potential that lies in a Berlin Republic. Although it is difficult to be blind in Berlin, I can sense something there that is even stronger elsewhere: diminishing tolerance of foreignness, poverty, strangeness; the increasing battle for status and money—including between men and women; dwindling curiosity about the unfamiliar.

In my field of work I can see this in the falling demand for foreign films, in the political rhetoric. I see it in the economic chauvinism of the rich regions; in tourism, statistics reveal the lack of curiosity about the East, either of Germany or of Europe; in political journalism and election campaigns it is manifest in the weight given to a supposed debate on asylum in the second-richest trading nation in the world.

Worst of all—and this is the aspect that has the most political repercussions—there is a lack of enthusiasm for European unity, an opportunity we will be throwing away if we fail to endow this large economic area with a political and social constitution, a diverse cultural identity.

What can one do about this?

Everything remains to be done. We are free, at the beginning of this century, to let a new history begin, a history that looks to the future, no longer driven by old guilt but by a new and keen creativity. We could begin our talk with ourselves, about the code to live by, about how we can save the European republic, the European social state based on the rule of law, the tension between art and the world, by drawing them into digital capitalism.

I cannot entirely believe, as the young ideologists of the "generation Berlin" proclaim, that this will happen without state involvement with the single principle of, as Heinz Bude put it, the "entrepreneurial individual," with "transcendental sobriety allowing for no position outside the interplay of power, knowledge and money."

I would prefer someone whom I would like to appoint as spiritual godfather to this Berlin Republic—because he embodied the unity of intellect and industry and republican politics, because he knew what is meant by wealth of nations and public prosperity. He wrote into the charter founding the first Berlin Republic, which was subsequently to become the Weimar Republic, sentences such as these:

> One thing will benefit our petty bourgeois parliaments which … partly out of the restricted nature of the career, partly out of fear of the voter, would like to administer the state as a business with limited liability and limited resources: the rule of multiplication tables. May the resources of the individual diminish and the Thaler be recast as the Mark; all the more, then, must the billion replace the million as the state's unit of calculation. [Our polity] will acquire new energy only if we resolve to serve the commonwealth more charitably in times of restriction than in former times of surplus.… The economy is not a private matter, but a community matter, not an end in itself, but a means toward the absolute, not a right, but a responsibility.…
>
> We have no reason to replace competition with police-run bureaucracy in accordance with the quack formula for socialism; but once again we are being pointed in the direction of a reformation which will build a new realm of social freedom on the basis of fairer consumption, more equal distribution of wealth and greater prosperity of the state.

Walter Rathenau, a "plutocrat" (his own words), who was shot by right-wing radicals in the Grunewald in 1922, wrote the above words at the beginning of a century whose problems, catastrophes, "hells," grew in part from fights for justice and from excesses of exclusion. Do we actually have grounds to assume that in the coming century the Berlin Republic will face other, easier problems?

Epilogue

Most of the contributions to *The Spirit of the Berlin Republic* were written before September 11, 2001, the war in Afghanistan against international terrorism, and most recently the war in Iraq. September 11 created a unique global consensus with the United States and an almost universal opposition to this most destructive and catastrophic use of terrorism for political and ideological purposes. But in spite of its invocation of Article V immediately following September 11, 2001, the Atlantic Alliance did not play a significant role in the ensuing fight against international terrorism. The broad consensus between Europe and the United States with regard to fighting terrorism fell apart when the United States adopted a strategy of preemption, which also included the potential use of military force against Iraq as part of the fight against terrorism. Particularly, the Iraq issue produced considerable tensions between the governments of the United States and Germany. When President Bush, in his State of the Union Address on 29 January 2002, singled out Iran, Iraq, and North Korea as an "axis of evil," the concern emerged in Europe that after the peaceful end of the long East-West conflict about a decade earlier, the world might face a new, major long-term confrontation.

To what extent the new strategic doctrine of the United States will change existing Alliance structures is an open question. The doctrine enlarges the classical security policy of the Alliance from a concept of deterrence and defense to a new strategy of preemption. This new strategy has raised concerns about potential legal issues in view of Article 2 of the UN Charter, which outlaws the threat or the use of force in international relations. Efforts must be made, therefore, to begin a new strategic dialogue, particularly within NATO and between the United States and the European Union. The issue is whether current international law needs adjustment, so that the international community can be protected more effectively against catastrophic terrorism.

Germany and other UN Security Council members—in particular, the two veto-bearing powers France and Russia—refused to join the United States and Great Britain in their efforts to seek Security Council authorization for the use of military force to disarm Saddam Hussein of weapons of mass destruction. When a major humanitarian catastrophe as a result of "ethnic cleansing" by the Serb armed forces was in the making in Kosovo, Germany gave up its long-held and cherished civilian power paradigm and joined the United States in the use of force in order to prevent potential mass killings by Serb forces. Germany took this action even without a UN mandate, but rather on the basis of a NATO decision to use military force. In the fight against international terrorism, basic existential values were at stake, and Germany participated in military actions in Afghanistan on the side of the United States. The war in Afghanistan was a perfectly legal use of force by the United States as a matter of self-defense.

Germany's refusal to go along with the United States and Great Britain in the war in Iraq created the impression, particularly in the United States, that it was returning to a civilian power paradigm in its foreign and security policy conduct. If this is true also for future crises that might involve the use of military force, then some of the contributions to this volume on the spirit of the Berlin Republic might have been written differently.

We believe that the transatlantic tensions over the crisis in Iraq do not in any way render invalid these observations on the foreign policy conduct of the Berlin Republic. Hans-Ulrich Klose's analysis of German foreign policy interests and objectives as well as the views on German foreign policy from abroad included in this publication still hold. Germany's "No" to the war in Iraq is not a farewell to the Atlantic Alliance. Just as the United States, despite its overwhelming military power, will need partners in the future, Europe will need the United States for the fulfillment of its own objectives. Cooperation in the spirit of partnership is the safest way to guarantee common success.

Dieter Dettke
Washington, D.C.
April 2003

Notes on Contributors

Peter Conradi has served as president of the Federal Chamber of Architects since 1999. He was a member of the Bundestag from 1972 to 1998 where he was active in the areas of housing and urban development, parliamentary planning, and architectural engineering. A professional structural engineer, he studied architecture at the University of Stuttgart and is a professionally certified engineer. He served on the Control Commission of the Social Democratic Party and on the SPD Commission for Land Rights Reform. He has also been Director of the State Planning Department and Building Control Office of Stuttgart, and in the administration of the planning department for Baden-Württemberg. He has been a member of the SPD since 1959.

Philippe Moreau Defarges is Conseiller des Affaires Étrangères in France, senior research fellow at the French Institute of International Affairs, professor at the Institut d'Études Politiques de Paris (Sciences Po), and at the French Institute of Oriental Languages and Civilizations (Langues O). He is the author of numerous articles and books focusing on international issues, globalization, and European affairs. Philippe Moreau Defarges is a graduate of the École nationale d'administration.

Dieter Dettke has been executive director of the Washington Office of the Friedrich-Ebert-Stiftung since 1985. Prior to coming to Washington, D.C., he served as political counselor of the SPD Parliamentary Group of the German Bundestag (1974–1984) and was a research associate at the German Society for Foreign Affairs in Bonn from 1969 to 1974. He received his Ph.D. in political science from the Free University of Berlin. As a specialist in foreign and security policy, Dr. Dettke has published widely on security issues, East-West relations, and U.S. foreign and domestic policy. He is the author of *Allianz im Wandel,* a book about European-American relations in the Nixon-Kissinger era. Dieter Dettke is also general editor of *International Political Currents,* a Friedrich-Ebert-Stiftung series published by the Washington office.

Tobias Dürr is a political scientist working as editor-in-chief of the Berlin-based journal *Berliner Republik.* His publications include *Die CDU nach Kohl* (edited with Rüdiger Soldt) and *Die Heimatlosigkeit der Macht: Wie die Politik in Deutschland ihren Boden verlor* (coauthored with Franz Walter). Tobias Dürr also writes for the weekly *Die Zeit,* as well as for the dailies *Die Welt, die tageszeitung,* and *Frankfurter Rundschau.*

Bernd Faulenbach is professor of modern history at Ruhr University in Bochum, Germany, in the department of history and Institute for Labor, Education, and Participation. He was a member of the Enquête Commissions of the German Bundestag concerning the Socialist Unity Party's (SED) system in the German Democratic Republic from 1992 to 1998. He has served as president of the Historical Commission of Germany's Social Democratic Party since 1989, chairman of the Scientific Commission of the Stiftung Brandenburgische Gedenkstätten since 1991, and member of the Advisory Council of the Stiftung "Denkmal für die ermordeten Juden Europas" since 2000. He is the author of numerous books on German history in the nineteenth and twentieth centuries, historiography, and the politics of memory.

Peter Glotz is currently professor of communications management and director of the Institute for Media and Communications Management at the University of St. Gallen, Switzerland. There he is also the director of the Executive MBA program in New Media and Communication. Having received a doctorate in communication science from the University of Munich, he served there as vice chancellor. During his twenty-six-year political career in Germany, Professor Glotz has served as a member of the German Bundestag (1972–1977 and 1983–1996) and held the positions of Parliamentary Secretary of the Federal Ministry of Education and Research (1974–1977), senator for science and research of Berlin (West) (1977–1981), and as Secretary General of the Social Democratic

Party (1981–1987). He has authored numerous books and publications in the areas of communication management, education and politics, and political theory. He is a member of the German Writer's Guild and the German PEN (West) and most recently also served as a representative of the German government in the European Constitutional Assembly.

Daniel Hamilton is research professor and director of the Center for Transatlantic Relations at the Paul H. Nitze School of Advanced International Studies at Johns Hopkins University in Washington, D.C. He is also the executive director of the American Consortium on EU Studies (ACES); in 2001 he was the DaimlerChrysler fellow at the American Institute for Contemporary German Studies, where he produced the book *Fighting Terror: German and American Perspectives*. In the Clinton Administration he served as Deputy Assistant Secretary of State for European Affairs and as Director of the Policy Planning Staff for Secretary of State Madeleine Albright. Professor Hamilton coined the term "Berlin Republic" in his 1993 book *Beyond Bonn: America and the Berlin Republic*.

Vladimir Handl is a research fellow at the Institute of International Relations in Prague. He received a doctorate from the Moscow State Institute of International Relations and was a research fellow at the Institute for German Studies, University of Birmingham, from 1996 to 2000. His publications have regarded topics such as German-Czech relations, German unification, Germany and East Central Europe, and Germany and the Visegrad countries.

Richard Herzinger has been political editor of the weekly *Die Zeit*, based in Hamburg, since 1996. After receiving his Ph.D. in literature from the Free University of Berlin, he worked there as a research associate. He has written numerous essays and articles on topics ranging from literature, culture, and politics in Germany to the theory of liberalism and international human rights. He has conducted research for the daily *Tagesspiegel* and has written for the *Neue Zürcher Zeitung*, the *Süddeutsche Zeitung*, and the *Frankfurter Rundschau*. He has also written political cultural essays in *Lettre* and *Kursbuch*. His most recent book, *Republik ohne Mitte: Ein politischer Essay*, was published 2001 by Siedler Verlag in Berlin.

Hans-Ulrich Klose served as chairman of the Committee on Foreign Affairs of the German Bundestag from 1998 to 2002 and has been a member of the Bundestag since 1983. He was vice president of the Bundestag from 1994 to 1998, chairman of the Social Democratic Party's parliamentary group in the Bundestag from 1991 to 1994, and treasurer of the Social Democratic Party of Germany in 1987. Prior to entering the Bundestag he served as lord mayor of the Free and Hanseatic City of Hamburg, member of Hamburg's parliament, chairman of the SPD parliamentary group, and senator of the interior. Mr. Klose has been a member of the SPD since 1964. He studied law in Freiburg and Hamburg.

Ewald König is a journalist working since 1977 for the Austrian daily *Die Presse*. He has been its correspondent in Germany since 1985. From 1990 to 1994 he was chairman of the Society of Foreign Press in the Federal Republic of Germany.

Kerry Longhurst is a lecturer in German and European security (ESRC) at the University of Birmingham, England, and is currently finishing an ESRC research project entitled "Youth Perceptions of Citizenship and Security in Russia, Germany, and the UK," which is run jointly with the Centre for Russian and East European Studies. Dr. Longhurst is also director of the University of Birmingham's Master's program in European Studies. An expert in the areas of German security policy, the Bundeswehr, and youth perceptions of citizenship and security, she has published numerous works on these topics.

Antonio Missiroli is currently a research fellow at the EU Institute for Security Policy in Paris. He received a doctorate in contemporary history from the Scuola Normale Superiore in Pisa, Italy, and a master's degree in international public policy from Johns Hopkins University in Washington, D.C. From 1993 to 1996 he was a lecturer in Western European politics at Dickinson College in Carlisle, Pennsylvania, and Bologna, Italy, as well as head of European studies at Centro Studi di Politica Internazionale (CeSPI) in Rome. From 1996 to 1997 he was visiting fellow at the European Studies Centre at Antony's College in Oxford. He has authored numerous papers and books and edited works on CFSP, Scandinavia, political opposition, Central Europe, Italian foreign policy, and EU and security policy.

Andreas Nachama is a rabbi and historian and currently serves as director of the Topography of Terror, a center of learning located at the site of the former headquarters of the Gestapo, SS, and command center of the Third Reich's state security service. Rabbi Dr. Nachama was president of the Jewish Council of Berlin from 1997 to 2001. He is co-editor of the book *Jews in Berlin*, published in English by Henschel Verlag in 2002.

Michael Naumann is chief editor and publisher of the weekly *Die Zeit* in Hamburg, Germany. Having studied political science, history, and philosophy at the Queen's College in Oxford, Dr. Naumann was a professor at Humboldt University in Berlin. He first worked as an editor and foreign correspondent at *Die Zeit* from 1970 to 1983. He then served as senior foreign editor for the weekly magazine *Der Spiegel* until 1985 and publisher and chief executive officer of Rowohlt Verlag in Germany until 1995. Subsequently, he was chief executive officer of the publishing houses Metropolitan Books and Henry Holt, Inc., in New York until 1998. From 1998 until 2000 he served as the first German Minister of Culture in the cabinet of Chancellor Gerhard Schröder with the official title "Federal Commissioner of Cultural Affairs and the Media."

Julian Nida-Rümelin was Minister of Culture with the official title Federal Commissioner of Cultural Affairs and the Media from 2001 to September 2002. From 1998 to 2000 he was cultural commissioner of the city of Munich. He served as president of the Society for Analytical Philosophy from 1994 to 1997 and as member of the European Academy of Arts and Sciences. Having studied philosophy, physics, mathematics, and political science in Munich and Tübingen and receiving his doctorate, since 1993 he has been chair of the philosophy department at the University of Göttingen where his research concentrates on rationality, ethics, political philosophy, and epistemology. He has published widely on these topics. Following his political career, in October 2002 he resumed teaching philosophy at the University of Göttingen.

Gerhard Schröder has been Chancellor of the Federal Republic of Germany since 1998. He is also Chairman of the Social Democratic Party. He joined the Social Democratic Party in 1963. Educated as a lawyer at the University of Göttingen, he practiced law in Hanover for several years. Gerhard Schröder started his political career in Lower Saxony, where he served as Prime Minister from 1990 until he was elected Chancellor of the Federal Republic of Germany in 1998. Gerhard Schröder held numerous public offices, for example, Chairman of the Young Socialists of the SPD (1978–1980), Member of the German Bundestag from 1980–1983, Chairman of the SPD District of Hanover (1983–1993), and Chairman of the SPD in Lower Saxony (1994–1998). Reelected in 2002, Gerhard Schröder leads a coalition of the SPD and the Green Party as Germany's head of government, the most powerful elected office under the German constitution.

Faruk Şen has been a professor at the Essen University and Polytechnical School since 1990 and director of the Center for Turkish Studies in Bonn since 1985. From 1983 to 1985 he served as director of a model experiment carried out at Duisburg University, "Advanced Education for Teachers in Transition from School to Work of Foreign and German Students." As manager of the "Maßnahmen zur Berufsvorbereitung und soziale Eingliederung junger Ausländer" (MBSE) for the city of Duisburg from 1980 to 1983, he worked to support young foreigners in their preparation for working life and social integration. Professor Şen studied business and received a doctorate in economics at Münster University and has held teaching positions at universities in Essen, Bonn, and Duisburg. He has published numerous works on Turkey and migration.

Ditmar Staffelt currently serves as Parliamentary State Secretary in the Federal Ministry of Economics and Labor (formerly Ministry of Economics and Technology). Before taking up his post in the Ministry in March 2002, he was the SPD spokesperson on economic policy. He has been a member of the German Bundestag representing Berlin since 1998. Prior to his election to the Bundestag, Ditmar Staffelt had been a long-standing member of the Berlin House of Representatives. From 1980 to 1994 he served on the SPD Executive Committee for Berlin and in 1992 took on the Chairmanship of the SPD Berlin Parliamentary Group. At the same time, he became a member of the SPD Executive Committee at the national level. He is Executive Director of VEBA Kommunalpartner GmbH and a member of the Board of Directors of the Hölter Industrie AG and of the Advisory Board of the Landesbank Berlin. He holds a degree in history and political science as well as geography and received his doctorate in 1986 from the University of Göttingen. He is a member of the European Academy Berlin.

Jochen Thies has been special correspondent for DeutschlandRadio in Berlin since 2000 and was previously head of its political department. He has been an active journalist in various media for almost twenty-five years. He was director of the English program for Deutsche Welle Hörfunk in Cologne and departmental head for foreign policy at the weekly *Die Welt* in Berlin. Previously located in Bonn, he was editor-in-chief of EUROPA-ARCHIV at the Deutsche Gesellschaft für Auswärtige Politik, e.V., for six years and parliamentary correspondent for radio and television for two years. Working for then Chancellor Helmut Schmidt, Mr.Thies was deputy director of his speechwriting team from 1980 to 1982. He has also been an editor at Bayerischer Rundfunk. He studied history, political science, and Romance languages and literature in Kiel, Freiburg, and Cologne. From 1972 to 1975 he received training as an educator in Baden-Baden, Lahr/Schw., and Hamburg. He received his doctorate in 1975.

Garrick Utley was named Chairman of the American Council on Germany in 1998. He is a senior correspondent for CNN based in the network's New York bureau. Before joining CNN in 1997, Mr. Utley served as ABC New chief foreign correspondent for three years. Educated in political science and Eastern European affairs, he spent 30 years with NBC News covering international affairs and reported from more than 70 countries. While at NBC, he moderated *Meet the Press* in Washington, D.C., anchored *Sunday Today* from 1987 to 1992, hosted the monthly magazine *First Tuesday*, and anchored *NBC Magazine*. He also covered the 1972, 1980, and 1988 presidential conventions and elections. From 1982 to 1987 he served as NBC's chief foreign correspondent and during this time received several of journalism's most distinguished honors, including the Overseas Press Club's Edward R. Murrow Award and the George Foster Peabody Award.

Anna Wolff-Powęska received a master's degree and doctoral degree in history and pedagogy from Poznań University and received professorial certification in 1986. From 1964 to 1969 she taught at an elementary school in Poznań, after which she joined the Instytut Zachodni (Western Institute) there as a research fellow. Having received a grant from the Alexander von Humboldt Foundation, she spent several months in research at Bonn University. After the political change in Poland, she was elected director of the Institut

Zachodni in 1990 for a first term and has been since reelected. From 1994 to 1999 she co-chaired (for the Polish side) the Polish-German forum. Dr. Wolff-Powęska has authored and edited several books on the history of philosophical and political thinking in Germany, on the democratization process in East Central Europe, on Polish-German relations, the Polish minority in Germany, and on problems of European integration.

Andrei Zagorski is currently a professor at the Geneva Center for Security Policy and since 2001 has been director of the project Networking of the Early Warning Systems of the EastWest Institute (EWI) and has also served as a senior vice president at EWI, located in Prague. After receiving a Masters and Ph.D. in international relations from the Moscow State Institute of International Relations (MGIMO-University), he served there as a full-time researcher at its Center of International Studies from 1981 to 1992 and as Vice Rector from 1992 to 1999. Professor Zagorski's research and teaching focuses on European Security, particularly relations between Russia and European institutions such as OSCE and NATO, on the Commonwealth of Independent States, and on negotiation studies. He has guest lectured at, among other institutes, the Vienna Diplomatic Academy, the George C. Marshall European Center for Security Studies in Garmish, Germany, the Geneva Center for Security Policy, and at the East-West College in Brühl, Germany. He has published close to fifty works on his specialty topics.

About the Friedrich-Ebert-Stiftung

The Friedrich-Ebert-Stiftung, founded in 1925, is Germany's oldest political foundation. Named after Friedrich Ebert, one of the founding fathers of Germany's first democracy after World War I and president from 1919 to 1925, it is today a nonprofit, private educational institution committed to the advancement of public policy issues in the spirit of social democracy. The work and programs of the foundation focus on the promotion of democratic values and political education on the basis of pluralistic principles, research, and publications on public policy issues, development cooperation, and international dialogue. The foundation also offers scholarships for gifted students and young scholars.

Headquartered in Bonn and Berlin, the Friedrich-Ebert-Stiftung maintains four educational centers and thirteen regional offices in Germany. With ninety offices in Europe, Africa, Asia, Latin America, and North America, the Friedrich-Ebert-Stiftung is a major contributor to international cooperation, particularly in the fields of economic and social development, research, and education, as well as political, economic, and trade union cooperation. Two hundred fifty projects in over one hundred countries worldwide receive support from the Friedrich-Ebert-Stiftung.

The Mission of the Washington Office of the Friedrich-Ebert-Stiftung

The mission of the Washington Office of the Friedrich-Ebert-Stiftung is to contribute to a comprehensive transatlantic dialogue by offering public programs (such as seminars, workshops, and conferences) as well as publications on the following issues:

- Overall political developments in Germany and Europe, including domestic policy issues and attitudes, as well as public policy programs
- General social topics, including migration, minorities, multiculturalism, education, and gender issues
- Economic developments in Germany, Europe, and the United States, including labor market and trade union issues, as well as problems of economic and political transformation in Eastern Europe
- Foreign policy and security issues such as NATO and European Union enlargement, ethnic conflicts, as well as arms control and disarmament
- Political and economic consequences of German unification
- Historical and cultural issues

Programs of the Washington Office of the Friedrich-Ebert-Stiftung are based on partnership and cooperation with American universities, research institutions, think tanks, and the media. The Washington Office also offers visitor programs in Germany and the United States for high-level representatives and experts.

Index

Neiße River, 188
neoclassicism, 117
neofascism, neofascist, 185
neo-Nazism, neo-Nazis, 121, 214
neo-realist school, 218
Netherlands, the, 64, 88, 113, 130,
    134, 215
Neue Mitte, 15, 175
New York (city), 108, 236, 240
New World, 123
Nice Summit, 61, 203
Nobel Prize, 103
Nofretiti, 126
North Korea, 243
North-Rhine Westphalia, 13
North Sea, 90
nuclear deterrence, 163, 166–67;
    installations, 65; weapons, 56, 63
Number 10 Downing Street, 172

Öcalan affair, 201
Oder River, 180, 188
ODS. See Czech Democratic Party
Ollenhauer, Erich, 41
open society, 28–30, 36
Organization for Economic Coop-
    eration and Development
    (OECD), 80, 160
Organization for Security and
    Cooperation in Europe
    (OSCE), 50, 55
Osnabrück, University of, 106
Ostpolitik, 15, 58, 163, 166
ÖVP. See Austrian People's Party

Pakistan, 63, 160, 167
Palace of the Republic, 119–20
Palestinian, 40
Pallenberg, Max, 125
Paris, 61–62, 100, 119, 162–63, 185,
    213, 240; Book Fair of 2001, 104
Paris Bar, 108

Pariser Platz, 127
Parliamentary Council, 12
Partnership and Cooperation
    Agreement, 157
Party of Democratic Socialism (PDS),
    15–16, 46–47, 128, 146, 206
Paterson, William E., 171, 176
patriotism, constitutional, 18, 191;
    German, 4, 190, 236
Patten, Christopher, 64
Pau, Petra, 128
Paul-Löbe-Haus, 116
Pax Americana, 30
PCI. See Communist Party of Italy
pension system, German, 83
Petersberg Tasks, 54
Pierer, Heinrich von, 108
Pirelli group, 199
PKK. See Kurdistan Workers Party
Platz der Republik, 115
Playmobil, 42
pluralism, pluralistic, 24, 28–29,
    49; cultural, 96
Poland, 11, 76, 180–93, 208, 228
Pompidou, Georges, 163, 166
Pope Pius XII, 195
populism, right-wing, 47, 215
Portugal, 131, 195
Potsdam, 98; Agreement, 219
Potsdam University, 126
Potsdamer Platz, 118, 120, 204
Prague, 227, 230–31
preemption, 243
procreation, 25
Prodi, Romano, 66, 200, 202
protectionist policy, 78
Protestant work ethic, 87
Protestant Church, 128
Protestantism, 126
Prussia, 3, 93, 120, 126, 145,
    204–5; Cabinet, 126; Christian,
    124; Upper Chamber, 126

Related Titles from Berghahn Books

BEYOND 1989

Re-reading German Literature since 1945

Edited by **Keith Bullivant**

"This volume makes abundantly clear the fact that the cultural unification of Germany ... is as arduous and painful as the political/economic merger... An excellent collection, well-conceived and highly informative." —**Choice**

1997, 224 pp., 1-57181-037-4 hardback, 1-57181-038-2 paperback
Modern German Studies, Vol. 3

AFTER UNITY

Reconfiguring German Identities

Edited by **Konrad H. Jarausch**

Contributors: K. H. Jarausch, D. Conradt, H. C. Seeba, M. Ash, C. Lemke, J. Peck, A. Pickel, D. Rosenberg, H. Welsh, G. Giles, S. Lennox, J. Mushaben, V. R. Berghahn, G. Flynn, P. M. Lützeler, C. Lemke

1997, 224 pp., 1-57181-040-4 hardback 1-57181-041-2 paperback
Modern German Studies, Vol. 2

GERMANY'S NEW POLITICS

Parties and Issues in the 1990s

Edited by **David Conradt, Gerald R. Kleinfeld, George K. Romoser,** and **Christian Søe**

1995, 336 pp., 1-57181-032-3 hardback 1-57181-033-1 paperback
Modern German Studies, Vol. 1